Classical and Modern Thought on International Relations

The Palgrave Macmillan History of International Thought Series seeks to publish the best work in this growing and increasingly important field of academic inquiry. Its scholarly monographs cover three types of work: (i) exploration of the intellectual impact of individual thinkers, from key disciplinary figures to neglected ones; (ii) examination of the origin, evolution, and contemporary relevance of specific schools or traditions of international thought; and (iii) analysis of the evolution of particular ideas and concepts in the field. Both classical (pre-1919) and modern (post-1919) thought are covered. Its books are written to be accessible to audiences in International Relations, International History, Political Theory, and Sociology.

Series Editor
Peter Wilson, London School of Economics and Political Science

Advisory Board
Jack Donnelly, Duke University
Fred Halliday, London School of Economics and Political Science
David Long, Carleton University
Hidemi Suganami, University of Keele

Also in the Series

Internationalism and Nationalism in European Political Thought
  by Carsten Holbraad

The International Theory of Leonard Woolf: A Study in Twentieth-Century Idealism
  by Peter Wilson

Tocqueville, Lieber, and Bagehot: Liberalism Confronts the World
  by David Clinton

Harold Laski: Problems of Democracy, the Sovereign State, and International Society
  by Peter Lamb

Liberal Internationalism and the Decline of the State: The Thought of Richard Cobden, David Mitrany, and Kenichi Ohmae
  by Per Hammarlund

The War Over Perpetual Peace: An Exploration into the History of a Foundational International Relations Text
  by Eric S. Easley

Classical and Modern Thought on International Relations

From Anarchy to Cosmopolis

Robert Jackson

CLASSICAL AND MODERN THOUGHT ON INTERNATIONAL RELATIONS

First published in 2005 by
PALGRAVE MACMILLAN™
175 Fifth Avenue, New York, N.Y. 10010 and
Houndmills, Basingstoke, Hampshire, England RG21 6XS
Companies and representatives throughout the world.

PALGRAVE MACMILLAN is the global academic imprint of the Palgrave Macmillan division of St. Martin's Press, LLC and of Palgrave Macmillan Ltd. Macmillan® is a registered trademark in the United States, United Kingdom and other countries. Palgrave is a registered trademark in the European Union and other countries.

Library of Congress Cataloging-in-Publication Data

Jackson, Robert H.
　　Classical and modern thought on international relations : from anarchy to cosmopolis / Robert Jackson.
　　　　p. cm.—(Palgrave Macmillan series on the history of international thought)
　　Includes bibliographical references and index.
　　ISBN 1–4039–6856–X — ISBN 1–4039–6858–6 (pbk.)
　　　1. International relations. I. Title. II. Series.

JZ1305.J319 2005
327.1′01—dc22　　　　　　　　　　　　　　　　　　　　　　2004057316

A catalogue record for this book is available from the British Library.

Design by Newgen Imaging Systems (P) Ltd., Chennai, India.

First edition: April 2005

10　9　8　7　6　5　4　3　2　1

Printed in the United States of America.

For Steven
Kindred Spirit and Fellow Traveler

Contents

Preface

This is a study of political thought on international relations, or international thought. For many years I was involved in teaching Canadian undergraduates the history of modern political theory, from Nicollò Machiavelli to John Rawls. I always wanted to write a book on the subject. I made an attempt twenty years ago, but abandoned the project when I became caught up in the study of international relations. Questions of international thought—fundamentally although not exclusively normative questions—have been at the back of my mind in everything I have written since that time. They are brought forward and addressed explicitly in this volume.

International thought calls to mind images and conceptions of the political world as a discernible and distinctive sphere of human activity, of which a foundation element is ideas, beliefs, and values. Isaiah Berlin summarizes, with characteristic eloquence, what such an approach involves:

> Ethical thought consists of the systematic examination of the relations of human beings to each other, the conceptions, interests and ideals from which human ways of treating one another spring, and the systems of value on which such ends of life are based. These beliefs . . . are objects of moral inquiry; and when applied to groups and nations, and, indeed, mankind as a whole, are called political philosophy, which is but ethics applied to society.[1]

Berlin is emphasizing the normative presuppositions, and one is tempted to say foundations, that all human relations involve, and that international relations cannot completely escape. What ideas and what sort of thinking are at the back of world affairs? Every chapter is occupied, in one way or another, with this question. My concern is not only with concepts and categories: such notions as anarchy, war, sovereignty, security, national interest, diplomacy, international law, human rights, among many others. My concern is also with the preconditions of thinking in terms of these fundamental ideas. What are the preconceptions and presuppositions of an anarchical system? What are the preconditions of sovereignty, diplomacy, or human rights? To raise such questions is to get involved in international thought, which tries to look behind or beneath the surface activities and happenings of world affairs.

World affairs compose the most diverse and far-flung sphere of human relations. Yet in spite of its global range and its encapsulation of numerous, assorted countries, it nevertheless has a certain discernible coherence. The international world is one world in some basic ways. It is embodied by the global system or society of states that is comprised of territorially separate political systems. This worldwide political arrangement is thus holistic and pluralistic at one and the same time. Any attempt to reflect on it in fitting theoretical terms also must be pluralist, if its diversity is to be comprehended. By "pluralist" in this latter sense, I am referring to the various political and moral doctrines at the back of world affairs, the different traditions of reflecting on international relations over the centuries, which have to be taken into account in the study of international thought.

The leading traditions range from realism, at one extreme, which focuses narrowly on the nation-state, to cosmopolitanism, at the other extreme, which envisages a worldwide community of humankind. The narrative in the following chapters proceeds from an initial examination of a body of thought, identified with Thrasymachus, which denies there is anything of substance in political life—either domestic or international—that could be characterized as genuinely ethical. It moves on to a closely related body of thought, identified with Thomas Hobbes, which acknowledges the reality of political ethics but sees that as confined within the domestic sphere of the sovereign state. The international sphere is anarchy. From that classical realist tradition, the narrative proceeds to a body of thought, identified with Hugo Grotius, which locates international ethics in the pluralist society of states. International society, in that way of thinking, is a historical arrangement of political life, with distinctive institutions and practices—international law, diplomacy, and so forth—and corresponding ideas, beliefs, and values. Finally, it examines a body of thought, identified with Immanuel Kant, which envisages a world that is progressing some distance beyond a society of states, and is becoming a solidarist community or *cosmopolis* of humankind, where ethics are truly universal, in the sense of applying to every man and woman on earth.

In writing this book, I have incurred debts to institutions and individuals whom I wish to acknowledge. Preliminary versions of several chapters were published previously. They have been revised for this study. Chapters 3 and 4 on Martin Wight's international thought appeared in *Millennium* (1990) and *Diplomacy and Statecraft* (2002). Chapter 5, on the idea of sovereignty, was published in *Political Studies* (1999). Chapter 7, on Richard Falk's "Grotian moment," appeared in *International Insights* (1997). I am grateful for permission to publish them here. For financial support for researching and writing some of the chapters I would like to express my gratitude to the Social Science and Humanities Research Council of Canada, the Danish Social Science Research Council, and the Department of International Relations at Boston University.

I also wish to thank friends and colleagues scattered across the United States, Canada, Britain, Denmark, Australia, and Israel who in various ways, either directly or indirectly, helped me reach closure in this lingering and occasionally languishing project. Some provided comments on earlier drafts of individual essays. Others influenced or provoked my thinking by their own work on questions addressed in this study. They are: Barry Buzan, Tonny Brems, Chris Brown, David Clinton, Claire Cutler, Michael Donelan, Roger Epp, Mikulus Fabry, Mervyn Frost, Martin Griffiths, David Hendrickson, Andrew Hurrell, Alan James, David Long, James Mayall, Terry Nardin, Cornelia Navari, Nicholas Rengger, Adam Roberts, Joel Rosenthal, Paul Sharp, Sasson Sofer, Hidemi Suganami, Georg Sørensen, Nicholas Wheeler, and especially Peter Wilson, the editor of this series.

I owe a particular debt of gratitude to several friends and colleagues at Boston University. Erik Goldstein and David Mayers opened the doors wide on my arrival at the Department of International Relations and the Department of Political Science in 2001. Cathal Nolan was instrumental in my move to Boston and made me feel at home from the start. Michael Field enlightened me on pacifist thought and introduced me to the Boston Red Sox Nation, the most militant form of nationalism I have witnessed at close hand.

My greatest intellectual and personal debts are owed to Will Bain, who engaged me in stimulating dialogue on these topics for half a decade, during which time my thinking evolved and hopefully matured, to my daughter, Jennifer Jackson Preece, who cheerfully kept me on my academic toes the whole way while providing perceptive critiques essential to the improvement of the argument, and to my wife Margaret, who kept our household in good running order while providing the love and encouragement that was absolutely necessary to sustain my enthusiasm for this project during some trying moments in our late-career trek from the Pacific coast of Canada to the Atlantic coast of the United States. This relocation fortified my conviction that moving across international borders—even the most tranquil border in the world—is not as smooth or as swift as our globalization theorists make it out to be. Nation-states still have a lot to say about human mobility across the planet. I have dedicated this book to my son-in-law, Steven Preece, who came to my rescue—when my analytical skill seemed at the point of deserting me—with his incisive legal mind, lively conversation, good humor, and excellent wine and spirits.

R.J.
Boston
June 2004

CHAPTER 1

International Thought

It is unbelievable how many systems of morals and politics have
been successively found, forgotten, rediscovered, forgotten again, to
reappear a little later, always charming and surprising the world as
if they were new, and bearing witness, not to the fecundity of the
human spirit, but to the ignorance of men.

Alexis de Tocqueville

International thought is an inquiry into the fundamental ideas and
beliefs involved in the arrangement and conduct of world affairs over
time: international anarchy, the society of states, the cosmopolis of
humankind, hegemony, empire, confederation, the practice of diplomacy,
international law, war, espionage, world commerce, international organization, global civil society—to mention some of the most prominent. It is also
an inquiry into the values at stake: peace, security, independence, order,
justice, human rights, prosperity, and progress, among others. Most of these
ideas, beliefs, and values occupy center stage in the following chapters.
International thought is an inquiry, as well, into the language and discourse
of world affairs. Furthermore, any study of international thought calls for
attention to leading thinkers, past and present, whose accumulated writings
constitute the most important body of knowledge on the subject. The work
of several such thinkers is examined over the course of this study.

A suitable starting point for such an inquiry is to conceive of world affairs
as Shakespeare portrayed the human scene: namely, as a great stage on which
the dramas of life are played out. To contemplate world affairs in terms of
drama, which is an ancient image at least as old as Sophocles's play *Antigone*,

written in the late fifth century B.C., is to be drawn into a profoundly human world: a scene of various players engaged in activities of seeking security from others or advantage over them or benefits from collaborating with them or conspiring against them. It is, thus, a world of self-regarding, self-interested, and self-seeking behavior, an instrumental world. Instrumental behavior should be understood as activity, of either individuals or groups, that "seeks the satisfaction of their wants" and is conducive to their goals and interests.[1] No perceptive observer could fail to notice that much, perhaps most, human activity is instrumental in character. The activities of government are notably instrumental. This is evident in political discourse, particularly concerning foreign policy and international relations.

However, the human drama is also a scene of players engaged in activities of claiming or disputing rights and privileges, of calling for justice and condemning injustice, of demanding security, of seeking peace, of justifying war or intervention, of condemning terrorism, of condemning or justifying weapons of mass destruction, and so forth. It is, thus, also a normative world in which other people are recognized or engaged—not out of fear, desire, or utility but out of regard for standards that prescribe proper, moral, or lawful conduct.[2] Instrumental activities need not go against normative standards. Often they do not, but there is always a possibility that they will. If this happens, it may provoke a concern or even a demand that the transgression be addressed, perhaps corrected, compensated for, or punished, so that the standard is upheld and enforced. If this fails to happen, we are given reason to think that the normative standards of a society are undemanding, irrelevant, lax, or incapable of being enforced. This is often the case in international relations. Nations and states are self-interested human organizations: they have goals they strive to achieve and interests to defend. Instrumental behavior is a powerful part of human relations generally and especially of international relations. But it is not the whole.

By definition, human relations involve people other than ourselves, who are never anything less than human and must always be treated accordingly. These others may be individuals or they may be groups, perhaps organized as independent nations or states, which have long been the preeminent political formations of world affairs. The humanity of all people, all human beings, demands certain standards of conduct in dealing with them. One fundamental standard is recognition of their entitlement to our regard and respect, which is the rule or practice of acknowledging the existence, status, and independence of people. Recognition is one of the oldest and one of the most fundamental norms of international relations. The *Oxford English Dictionary* defines the word as follows: "The action of acknowledging as true, valid, or entitled to consideration; formal acknowledgement as conveying approval or sanction of something; hence, notice or attention accorded to a thing or person."[3] We recognize people as having a standing in our eyes and a claim on our activities toward them or involving them.

Recognition as an individual, however, is not the same as recognition as a state: international recognition. The difference is crucial. It reflects the parallel distinction between human rights (or natural rights) and sovereign rights (or civil rights) that lies at the heart of international ethics and international law. A right is the basis of a claim of what is properly, morally, or lawfully our own. A human right is an inherent right of a person: we have them by virtue solely of being human, that is, by being differentiated from lower animals, from Gods or other supernatural agents, and from merely mechanical or physical objects.[4] A sovereign right is categorically different: it is a right of a corporate political body, a nation or state that is formed or constructed around a particular territorial group of people who are its citizens or subjects. We have civil rights by virtue of being members of political communities, such as states, that make them available to us. How this distinction is handled—where the emphasis is placed, whether on the human individual or the sovereign state—will say a great deal about the international thought of any thinker. Immanuel Kant is inclined to place it on the human individual and the cosmopolis of humankind. Thomas Hobbes is inclined to place it on the sovereign state and the anarchical system of states. These are two important traditions of international thought— usually labeled as idealism and realism—that are examined, along with others, in the chapters that follow.

Unlike so many of the realist thinkers of our era, Hobbes does not confine his thought merely to the instrumental world of self-seeking behavior, for he considers that people have liberties and rights, including a natural right to live.[5] Hobbes's *Civitas* or Commonwealth is constructed not only with an acute awareness of the "Natural Condition" of human beings but also with a high regard for the "Laws of Nature." A natural rights doctrine exists in his political thought alongside a hardheaded analysis of the instrumental character of much human activity. The natural condition of humanity is one of vulnerability, fear, rivalry, and war. Natural law demands respect for the inherent rights of human beings. The confrontation between the naturally self-seeking behavior of people and the normative claims of natural law, the encounter of human desire and striving for power and gain with human forbearance and restraint out of regard for others, presents a conflict or dilemma of human relations that he attempts to resolve. This is one of the inherent dilemmas of human relations and it is conspicuous in international relations. For Hobbes, the "science" of natural law is "moral philosophy," which is "but the science of what is good, and evil, in the conversation, and society of mankind."[6] Many great thinkers on the subject, including Kant, have said more or less the same thing, even if their approaches differ in important ways. This well known conception will serve as a point of departure for this book.

Most classical and modern thinkers on international relations have understood politics in the context of ethics. The guiding image is of a fully human world. This image (or something like it) is what any study of international relations must have in mind if it is to be true to its subject. Politics and ethics are inseparable in practice, and if they are divorced in theory something of fundamental importance retreats or even disappears.[7] The normative reality of international relations is lost to view. It is perhaps surprising that one should have to make this point explicitly. But its expression is made necessary by the fact that many contemporary studies ignore the point. Such a divorce was attempted in twentieth-century social science theories of international relations, and as a consequence a misleading and unfortunate impression was left that world affairs is a sphere devoid of ethical questions, and that it can be studied using models and methods derived from the natural sciences. We can, of course, attempt to study normative questions by translating them into empirical questions that postulate international relations as a naturalistic system or structure in which norms are defined as given or existential patterns of behavior—rather than historical standards that prescribe proper, moral, or lawful conduct. But such research strategies rule out ethics and they consequently fail even to discern, much less to come to grips with, the dilemma that Hobbes and other classical thinkers explored, usually at length and often with piercing insight.

The international system is not a physical cosmos like the solar system, or even a sociobiological world such as a pack of wolves, each of which displays permanent and unchanging characteristics that are open to inquiries modeled on the natural sciences. International relations is a historical world. What exists today is not exactly the same as what existed yesterday or will exist tomorrow. People change their minds and also their ideas and beliefs about how they wish to organize and carry on their lives. They change their values. They not only discover or invent ways to enhance their power, but they also craft standards of conduct and other norms according to which they decide to live. Even when they think and speak of natural rights as God-given or permanently fixed in the nature of things, they are expressing an ethical idea they have come up with. This idea, like any other political or ethical idea, can be acknowledged, affirmed, adopted, disseminated, reformed, disputed, contested, condemned, prohibited, abandoned, and so forth. Unlike wolves, which are destined to forever repeat themselves, people are historical agents: they make, unmake, and remake the worlds in which they live. This has happened time and again over the course of history. At one time it was generally held, by secular rulers and clerics alike, that the pope was the sovereign ruler of the Latin Christian world. At a later time European kings invoked a divine right to rule. Later still, sovereignty was claimed to reside in the people. Each one of these arrangements was understood to be proper, legitimate, and lawful during its particular time. The international system or society is, in itself, historical: it has existed only for the past three or four centuries. The medieval world that existed previously—Latin Christendom or *respublica Christiana*—was markedly different: it did not recognize locally sovereign authorities; kingdoms, republics, and principalities were not independent as we understand the term. On the contrary, they were part of *respublica Christiana*, and subordinate to it. Bernard of Clairvaux puts it thus: "The Kings of Germany, England, France, Spain and Jerusalem, with all their clergy and people, cleave and adhere to the lord Pope, as sons to their fathers, as members to the head."[8] Latin Christendom was, in turn, a significant change from the more substantial and centralized Roman Empire that had gone before. The latter was markedly different from *Hellas*, the loose constellation of Greek city-states that existed previously. One could keep on going farther back in time. But that would only repeat the point, which is that historical change is a characteristic of international relations brought about by the people involved and the ideas, beliefs, and values they conceive, avow, and pursue. "Everything is temporary."[9] We are temporary. The political worlds that we construct are temporary too. That makes change inevitable, in both the shorter and the longer term.

The people involved in world affairs at different periods of history have decided and determined, for example, that the state should have authority over the church (rather than the other way around, as in the medieval era), that religion should not be a *causus belli* (as it was during the Reformation and perhaps still is for some people in the Middle East and elsewhere), that foreign conquest and colonization should be prohibited rather than allowed (as they were during the era of Western imperialism), that self-determination should be a universal right of all peoples (rather than a right only of European or Western peoples), that wars of aggression should be unlawful (rather than lawful), that wars of national liberation should be lawful (rather than unlawful), that the great powers should have a collective responsibility to uphold international peace and security (rather than merely a national interest in sustaining the balance of power), that weapons of mass destruction should be subject to international inspection and control (rather than be left to the sovereign decisions of statesmen), and so on. These are but a few examples of noteworthy changes in international standards in recent centuries.

Practices of international recognition also change over time. What they happen to be will say much about the international system or society and the conduct of its members at any particular period of history. During the later Middle Ages it was the practice to recognize only Christian rulers or *regna*, a practice that was necessary to uphold Latin Christendom. Following the religious wars of the sixteenth and seventeenth centuries it became the practice to recognize Protestant as well as Catholic rulers and regimes. Still later, in the seventeenth century, Russia, an Orthodox Christian Kingdom, began to be widely recognized by the states of Western Europe.[10] At a later period the practice of recognition was secularized and changed to one of recognizing only European states, then only Western states. In the mid-nineteenth century the practice of recognizing non-Christian and non-Western states was initiated, tentatively, for the Ottoman Empire and Japan. It was not until the twentieth century that non-Western states began to be widely recognized, starting with British and French mandates in the Middle East—Iraq (1930), Syria (1944), and Lebanon (1944)—and accelerating with the independence of India and Pakistan in 1947. Before that time European Empires existed in most non-Western parts of the world. Those empires recognized each other and refused to recognize the indigenous political systems they ruled. Decolonization turned that upside down by acknowledging that non-Western peoples had rights of self-determination and self-government, and that Western imperial powers had no right to refuse or resist their demand for independence. All of this taken together obviously adds up to very significant and rather sweeping historical change. It cannot be adequately understood without grasping the fuller meaning of international recognition as a normative idea.

The history of international thought, in significant part, consists of reflection on episodes such as these. It, too, is a story of change. But it is also a story of continuity. Many questions of world affairs are anything but new, and many good answers to them have been given before. These questions involve, for example, the justification of war, the rights and responsibilities of sovereign states, the rights and roles of individuals, and the laws and practices regulating world commerce. The history of international thought, in some fundamental respects, is a history of questions and answers in regard to persisting issues of world affairs, one of the most important of which—arguably the most important—is war. It has been justified by self-defense, by necessity, by the balance of power, by the goal of restoring peace, and even by the goal of permanent peace: war to end all war. State sovereignty has been justified by the occupation of uninhabited territory (*terra nullius*), by conquest, by cession, by religion or civilization, by imperialism, by nationalism, by popular government, and by democracy, among other things. Human rights (variously conceptualized) have been justified on the grounds of natural law and universal human community, liberalism, and socialism.

Good answers to important questions tend to be repeated over time. Some answers stand the test of time. But good answers are not final answers. In the study of any historical subject, there cannot be any final answers because the unfolding of human history never stops. New questions are asked. Old questions are also asked, although not usually in exactly the same way. Answers are given that are similar, but not identical, to those we already have. Many questions Kant asked in the eighteenth century about the cosmopolis of humankind are being asked again today, but in a somewhat different form influenced, if not dictated, by the considerably changed international conditions and circumstances of our time as compared with his time. He saw duties in the cosmopolis of humankind. We see rights. But the fundamental moral idea that he came up with has scarcely changed over the past two centuries: the assertion that humans are ends, and should not be treated as means to other ends.[11]

People involved in international relations pose normative questions, and it has always been that way because people cannot be involved in relations with other people, including people in other countries, without being obliged morally to confront their humanity. It would be intolerable if some people, including foreign people, were treated merely as things or objects. This does of course happen in international relations, as in other branches of human relations. There have been great theological and philosophical debates over this issue, one of the most famous being the Spanish encounter with the Indians of the Americas during the age of discovery in the sixteenth century, which provoked ground breaking international thought, by the Spanish theologians Bartolome de Bas Casas and Francisco de Vitoria, on what it is to be human and what obligations are owed to people of distant and alien civilizations.[12] Their thought—which is rooted in traditional Christian ethics of universal mission and recalls ancient stoic conceptions of human community—gives intimations of twentieth-century thinking on human rights. People ought to be treated as human beings. The Spaniards ought to treat the Indians as fellow creatures. Of course, there can be no guarantee they will be treated that way. Even in the event of contemptuous, callous, or abusive treatment, however, we are equipped with ideas and language for condemning such misconduct. People have moral faculties that they can abandon only if they are prepared to repudiate their humanity. Even when that happens other people can stand in judgment of their conduct.

Indifference to the consequences of human actions (or omissions) is also intolerable. This happens when we fail to notice that other people are present and are affected, adversely, by our own activities or failures of activity. The phenomenon is particularly evident during war. When aircrews of World War II bombers explained that they were not thinking of the people on the ground in the target city, whom they could not see when they dropped their bombs from four or five miles above, they disclosed a breakdown of morality that is surely understandable in the context of impersonal, high-technology warfare but cannot pass without being noticed and questioned. That is because cities are not merely physical objects composed of buildings, streets, harbors, and the like. Cities are human habitats, places where people live, work, and play. They may contain soldiers and other military targets, but they are populated disproportionately by civilians. In the ethics of war there is an important distinction between combatants and noncombatants. The latter have rights and immunities that the former do not possess. One of the most important is the right not to be targeted and attacked, which is why intentionally bombing cities raises serious moral questions. This is not to imply that cities should never be bombed—although that argument can be made. It is to say that such a policy must be justified, or else it must be condemned. Indifference is not an option.

Normative issues do not disappear when moral neglect or moral callousness take control of human affairs. If anything, they make an appearance on such occasions, because it is only by reference to a normative standard of some sort that human activity and human relations can be recognized for what they truly are, and not merely seen as a physical fact or an instrumental calculus. The policies and activities of statesmen, both men and women, are not exempt from normative inquiry either, and these include their foreign policies and their international activities. International relations is not a field of conflict or combat in which the principal players can do anything they wish and escape moral judgment. If it were such a world we would be studying monsters or brutes rather than men and women—which is not to deny that some people involved in international relations have been capable of extreme cruelty and brutality. Adolf Hitler, Joseph Stalin, Pol Pot, and Saddam Hussein come immediately to mind. The worst human catastrophes are precipitated by willful and powerful leaders, people who frequently are driven by their own megalomania and are prepared to trample on the legitimate affairs and concerns of others in their unrestrained striving for domination. Keeping such people in check, if they cannot be put out of business, is one of the long-standing concerns of international society. At base it is a moral concern and not only a self-interest. It recognizes the existence of malevolent and lawless people by the human suffering and destruction they cause without any valid justification for doing so. And it refuses to tolerate that.

Not all anguish and devastation is open to moral condemnation, however. Not all suffering can be laid at the feet of others. Some people bring disaster down upon themselves owing to their neglect of, or disregard for, their own affairs, their fatalism, their failure of judgment, or their exaggerated sense of honor or pride. Some people are capable of self-harm and even self-destruction. Some people are accidents waiting to happen. They are a danger to themselves. That might also be said of some nations. Were the king and government of Denmark suffering from some kind of self-delusion or misconceived honor or hubris when in 1864 they elected to fight a war they could never hope to win, against Chancellor Bismarck's vastly more powerful German–Austrian alliance, over the possession of Schleswig-Holstein, a small bordering territory between the two countries that was under Danish sovereignty? Looking back we may be tempted to say so. And we may be reminded of Thucydides' memorable dialogues on similar episodes between the great and the small, for example, the Melian Dialogue during the Peloponnesian War more than two millennia ago. There is folly in world affairs, as in all human affairs—so much so that one historian was moved to write of history as "the march of folly."[13]

There is also misfortune and tragedy, the unforeseen or unpreventable adverse consequences of human actions. The power involved in world politics is sometimes so enormous and unwieldy, and the uncertainty so pervasive and widespread, that events are difficult to guide and control. Foreign policy, particularly war, can be and often is a leap in the dark. Machiavelli, in his theorizing on politics and war, placed great emphasis on the unpredictable and dangerous role of *fortuna*.[14] British and American soldiers in combat make reference to "Murphy's Law," namely that if something can go wrong, it will. Politics and war are entirely human activities but they are not entirely subject to rational control. Even with the best information and the best efforts the unintended or unexpected may happen. The tragic dimension of international relations is particularly evident and has been remarked upon by leading commentators.[15]

Some academic accounts of world affairs are flawed by the extent to which they are inclined to exaggerate the significance of rational and controllable human activity. In the human drama that is international relations the people involved are often called upon to carry out their responsibilities under conditions of imperfect knowledge and considerable uncertainty regarding the circumstances, the intentions and the actions of others. International relations are more prone to uncertainty than domestic relations. Perhaps this is because foreign policy is conducted at greater distances and with fewer authoritative and reliable means than domestic policy. We plan for the worst, in both politics and war, but we do so knowing full well that there can be no plan for every contingency. There may be danger lurking around the next corner. Often we cannot know what this danger will be in advance. Unforeseen and uncontrollable circumstances are a reality of world affairs that must be recognized and cannot be ignored, downplayed, or dismissed by our inquiries. Otherwise we distort reality. If there is international ethics for such an uncertain and dangerous world it must include norms of caution, circumspection, and foresight—the ethics of prudence. That is a world in which conservatives and realists are more at home than are progressives and idealists.[16]

World affairs is an ethical sphere, but one whose norms and standards are not exactly or entirely those of common morality, which may be defined as the obligations we owe to other humans and they owe to us. International relations involve common morality in part, a point captured by Socrates, Athenian citizen and moral philosopher: "to suffer wrong oneself is always better than to wrong others"—the "sovereignty of virtue."[17] This is also the moral teaching of Jesus Christ. But there is another morality to which statesmen in particular are subject: their responsibility to safeguard and defend the interests of their people, the morality of statehood and the ethics of statecraft. Hobbes based his thought on this proposition: "The safety of the people is the supreme law."[18] Political leaders are subject to common morality just like everybody else. But no statesman could responsibly follow the ethics of Socrates or Jesus to the exclusion of all other normative considerations. There is something we refer to as political ethics: the moral life of nations or states, the ethics of Pericles, Athenian citizen and leader in war and peace.[19] Political ethics tolerates, and sometimes justifies what common morality would condemn, such as intentional killing, for example, during war. The norms and standards of international society are not, and cannot be, the same as those of domestic society, which forbid intentional killing almost without exception, one of the few exceptions being capital punishment in some countries. War is tolerable and for many it is a necessity. Peace is desirable but pacifism is a liability and for many it is an absurdity. If we wish to understand international relations in fitting and proportionate terms we have to come to grips with this important normative distinction.

Some vital matters of international concern surfaced after the demolition of the Berlin Wall in 1989. They echo many similar issues from previous eras: war, genocide, forced population transfer or "ethnic cleansing," refugee crises, failed states, state partition, military intervention and occupation, trusteeship and reconstruction of occupied territories, terrorism, weapons of mass destruction—to mention some of the most important. What is different, of course, is the particular historical manifestation: the Gulf War to liberate Kuwait, the violent partition of Yugoslavia, the genocide in Rwanda, the flight of refugees from more than a few failed states or states in the throes of war, the interventions in Somalia and Bosnia, the war over Kosovo, the terrorist attacks on New York and Washington, the antiterrorist military campaign in Afghanistan, the preemptive war against Iraq and the postwar search for weapons of mass destruction, the heightened fear of nuclear proliferation and war provoked by North Korea—these episodes, among others, gave the post-1989 and post-2001 eras of world affairs their distinctive historical coloring. But as important as these events may have been, they did not mark a complete break with the past. Our links with the past are rarely completely broken.

These episodes will keep journalists and historians busy for years to come. Yet none of them suggests to anyone familiar with international history, that anything like a brave new world has come into existence—a world that is changed in ways that fundamentally alter our thinking. The international changes of the late twentieth and early twenty-first centuries were dramatic and widely felt. But they were not more significant or more consequential than those marked by World War I and its outcome, or by World War II and its aftermath, or by the Cold War, or by the end of the era of the European Empires and the emergence of a postcolonial world of new states in Asia, Africa, and elsewhere. All those episodes involved alterations in the distribution and alignments of power in world affairs. They also involved efforts to reform international relations by changing, or attempting to change, some of the rules of the game: the League of Nations, the United Nations, various conventions on human rights, and so on. But none of them repudiated or abandoned the most basic norms and arrangements of world politics, including those of state sovereignty.

What was expected of states and tolerated by states, however, changed in significant ways after the Cold War, and changed again after September 11, 2001. The responsibilities of states to each other were raised several notches; their international society was deepened. States were expected to conform to more elaborate and more demanding standards of human rights. They were expected to police their sovereign jurisdictions and exercise their sovereign powers in ways that upheld more intrusive and more exacting norms of international society. It was no longer tolerable that states should turn a blind eye to acts of genocide, harbor or support international terrorists, or use or dispose of any nuclear, chemical, or biological weapons they might possess without regard for international norms. These are examples of a shift in the international rights and responsibilities of state sovereignty in the direction of more restriction and less freedom. Yet in spite of such changes, which are undoubtedly important, world politics was still, recognizably, a world of states. The war on terrorism was arranged and conducted by states and the national and international organizations controlled by states.

None of these episodes foretells the approaching demise, transformation, or transcendence of the states system. What they indicate is the system's continuing, sometimes surprising, evolution. Since it came into existence in the sixteenth and seventeenth centuries, the postmedieval system or society of states has witnessed many noteworthy changes marking "new" periods that at the time were viewed as surprising, perhaps even shocking: the scientific revolution of the seventeenth century, the European Enlightenment of the eighteenth century, the French Revolution and the rise of nation-states, the Industrial Revolution, the mass migrations from rural areas to urban areas and the consequent explosion and multiplication of cities, the revolution of mass mobilized and mechanized warfare, the rise and spread of democracy, the antislavery and anticolonial movements, the antiapartheid and antiracism campaigns, the communications and transportation revolution, the nuclear revolution, the electronic revolution, the computer revolution, and so on. The system or society of states adapted to all those challenges, and others as well. We should be mindful of that historical evolution before we pronounce on the system's decline or demise.

Important continuities between the present and the past are evident in world affairs beneath or beyond these evolutionary episodes. The most important are revealed in the continuity of the basic ways we continue to think and talk. We still reflect and discourse on international relations using the concepts and vocabulary of statehood and statecraft that were fashioned three or four centuries ago, and there seems to be a compulsion in doing so, for it is very difficult to do otherwise.[20] Kant was in some respects a revolutionary thinker of the European Enlightenment. His thought anticipated a future cosmopolitan world of liberalism: his language, however, is almost entirely traditional, and even his ideas draw heavily on those of other thinkers of his time and earlier times, which is hardly surprising given that he was a creature of his time just as we are creatures of our time. Even for a revolutionary thinker it is difficult to escape from time-honored conceptual and linguistic categories.

This brings us back to an important point about the history of international thought: most of the big questions of international relations are well known and have been known for a long time. Leading thinkers of the past have dealt with them, often at great length and usually in great depth, as in the example of Grotius's thought on the laws of war or Hobbes's thought on state sovereignty and the international state of nature or Kant's thought on the cosmopolis of humankind.[21] From reading the writings of Grotius, Hobbes, Kant, or any other leading thinker of the past we discover that the contemporary world is neither as new, nor as exceptional, as we might believe. The most outstanding and enduring international thought proceeds in studied awareness of what has been said before and seeks to add something to it and hopefully to improve upon it. But it always remains in considerable debt to it—even when a thinker is striving to be original, as with Thomas Hobbes's thought on war, which is heavily indebted to that of Thucydides and Hugo Grotius.

International thought involves reflection on world affairs seen as a part of the overall sphere of human relations but with its own distinctive characteristics and modus operandi. Anyone who reflects gets absorbed in contemplating, pondering, considering, weighing, or in other words exercising his or her mind on something. Reflection is thought that tries to grasp the significance of something, to think it through to some conclusions, to understand it as fully as possible.[22] Reflecting on something is trying to reach a point where there are no more questions, at least for the time being. Reflecting on world affairs does not aim to prescribe a solution to an immediate international problem—that is what policymakers and practitioners do. Nor is its aim to get to the bottom of an event or episode in factual terms by reporting on it or telling its fuller story—that is what journalists and historians do. Rather, its aim is contemplating a problem's meaning, specifying its place and role, and ascertaining its significance in the human drama that is world affairs.

International thought cannot be divorced from the actuality of world affairs. International events and issues cannot be ignored. Reflection is always on something and cannot take place without something. Making sense of the international drama is the point. International thought is empirical in that indirect way. It is preoccupied with the concepts and language by which world affairs are understood and carried on. It is concerned with the suppositions and implications of world affairs: interpretation. What is the meaning and significance of war, international law, diplomacy, or espionage? How does this war, that legal controversy, this diplomatic dialogue, or that case of spying fit into our received understanding of these subjects? What is their place in the cosmology of world affairs?

Leading international thinkers reflect on the most important issues of their time and that is no less the case today than it was in the past. Whatever time our time happens to be, it is always the period that matters most to us, because we witness it and experience it: our lives are involved with it, entangled in it, and even trapped within it. We cannot escape from our time. We are held hostage by our era. The issues of the world in which a thinker lives consequently are what usually drive his or her thought. Machiavelli studied and wrote extensively on the ancient Romans. But he witnessed and experienced the shrewd, nimble, and ruthless statecraft of the Italian Renaissance and that registers in his thought. Hobbes translated Thucydides's history into English, but he lived during the European Thirty Years War (1618–48) and the English Civil War (1642–49), and that registers in his thought. Hannah Arendt, a mid-twentieth-century American political thinker, wrote with enormous insight on the human condition generally and the life of the ancient Greeks in particular.[23] But her thought was provoked to remarkable depths of perception by the origins and nature of totalitarianism.[24]

What sets leading international thinkers apart, however, is the fact that their thought retains its intellectual force long after it was written down and the events that provoked it have faded into history. We turn to outstanding thinkers of past eras and find in their writings something that uncannily speaks to our time and perhaps to all time. We can read Hobbes or Kant with fascination and considerable benefit even though we know little of their historical world and the events that provoked their thought. That is because they are tapping into enduring characteristics of the human condition when they address issues of their day. How they manage that is impossible to say. That they have managed it is obvious to anyone who reads Thucydides on the ethics of power, Machiavelli on the virtues of statecraft, Hobbes on sovereignty and the state of nature, Kant on perpetual peace, J.S. Mill on nationhood and nonintervention, Hannah Arendt on totalitarianism, E.H. Carr on power and morality, Raymond Aron on political community, Hedley Bull on international order, or John Rawls on justice and fairness. The greatness of a text on human affairs is marked by its capacity to outlive, and often far outlive, the life of its author. The leading classical and modern thinkers are those who have thought most profoundly and written most powerfully on world affairs and whose thought consequently has a long shelf life.

As indicated at the start of this chapter, most leading international thinkers, classical and modern, reflect on world affairs in terms of international anarchy, the society of states, the cosmopolis of humankind, hegemony, empire, confederation, the practice of diplomacy, international law, the activity of war, espionage, world commerce, international organization, global civil society, and so on. Many of these important ideas are at the center of attention in this study. It bears repeating that they exist for a reason: it is difficult to think acutely on world affairs without them. And it is worth remembering that most of them are centuries old. Their historicity is deep. When we employ them to reflect on world affairs, we are made aware of something fundamental: the long-standing conceptual and linguistic elements of international life.

Since fundamental ideas and language usually change rather slowly, it is convenient, and instructive, to portray international thought in terms of traditions.[25] Traditional knowledge has remarkable staying power, as compared with technical or scientific knowledge, which places emphasis on innovation and is always under threat of becoming obsolete.[26] Computer hardware and software exemplify innovation as perfectly as anything could. Word processing software is a good example: it is continually changing and, supposedly, improving, but it is very short-lived. Computer hardware is not much better: laptop computers are replaced every two years in my university department, for reasons of obsolescence. So-called cutting edge technology usually loses its edge rather quickly. That is the way of much technology, especially nowadays, when the speed of innovation is greater than ever.

By comparison, the English vocabulary and syntax I am using to word process these sentences and paragraphs is very long lasting. Although contemporary English is different in many superficial details, it is still fundamentally the same language, the same grammar, the same syntax, and even much of the same core vocabulary, as Hobbes employed in the seventeenth century. A shared language connects us to his thought in spite of the centuries that separate his time from our time. Traditions of thought are distinctive, long-standing, and evolving ways of reflecting on human activity. They are currents of thought that connect the texts of different thinkers—despite the fact that they may have been written at widely separated times or in widely separated places. Traditions are adaptable and durable. They are the opposite of innovations. They are both old and new rather than merely being new and entirely up to date or else out of date. They are survivors. Survival is a mark of success. They are an inheritance of deeply insightful and wide-ranging thought that our intellectual ancestors have handed down to us. The traditions discussed in this book are modes of thinking on international affairs that refuse to die.

Classical and modern thought is called for nowadays, not least to counter fashionable studies that make the bold claim that the world has recently changed out of all recognition, and that international studies must change along with it by abandoning "old-fashioned" and presumably outmoded approaches. The chapters in this book were written, in part, as a rejoinder to such arguments, which often disclose a startling lack of knowledge of the history of international relations—including the history of international thought. As noted by Tocqueville, and quoted at the beginning of this chapter, anybody who is ignorant of the past is likely to see important changes as surprising, even as brand new.[27] A comment by Martin Wight on this point is especially apposite at the present time of proliferating academic fads and fashions:

> One of the main purposes of university education is to escape from the *Zeitgeist*, from the mean, narrow, provincial spirit which is constantly assuring us that we are at the peak of human achievement, that we stand on the edge of unprecedented prosperity or unparalleled catastrophe . . . It is a liberation of the spirit to acquire perspective . . . to learn that the same moral predicaments and the same ideas have been explored before.[28]

These chapters are written in support of the anti-provincial claim, made by Hedley Bull in the 1960s, that most of our inherited thought on international relations, what he labeled as classical or traditional thought, is intellectually superior to other approaches on offer.[29] The thinkers he was recommending, many of them identified in this book, were prepared to take on board larger and more perplexing questions of world affairs and were able to furnish compelling answers to them. Although some international relations theories that Bull vigorously repudiated at that time later suffered the fate of becoming unfashionable—which can happen to academic work that is preoccupied with being innovative and up-to-date—the approach he recommended continues to thrive among circles of scholars in America, Europe, and elsewhere. This study is intended as a contribution to that literature.

CHAPTER 2

Conversing with Thrasymachus: Voices of Realism

> Human life is dialectic, that is dramatic, since it is active in an incoherent world, is committed despite duration, and seeks a fleeting truth, with no certainty but a fragmentary science and a formal reflection.
>
> Raymond Aron

Classical political thought, in one of its unmistakable modes of expression, is a dialogue, discourse, or conversation. Politics, too, is dialogical; it is "three-quarters talk."[1] In contemporary idiom, politics is an exchange—of thoughts, ideas, points-of-view, opinions, observations, judgments, communiqués, diplomatic notes, and so on—on issues of mutual interest or common concern. International politics, perhaps even more than other politics, lends itself to dialogue because of the horizontal character of international relations, particularly evident in diplomacy, which is characterized as a dialogue of states.[2] One of the oldest dialogues in political science is a conversation between Socrates and Thrasymachus in Plato's *The Republic*. Another is between the Athenians and the Melians in Thucydides's *History of the Peloponnesian War*. These ancient discourses capture the *persona* of realism. This *persona* reappears, forcefully, in the writings of Machiavelli and Hobbes, from whom, along with Thucydides, modern realists derive their leading ideas. These ideas are not entirely instrumental. They disclose a normative discourse, but one that is reticent and fenced in.

Two Archetypal Ancient Realists

In Book I of *The Republic*, Plato rehearses a conversation between Socrates and Thrasymachus, the archetypal realist in the history of political thought.[3] Socrates is expounding on justice as a political virtue that seeks the good of all: crafts exist not to enrich the craftsman but to bring their goods to others, which it is in the nature of vocations to do; the vocation of statecraft is for the good of the city and its citizens, and not merely the rulers. Having listened, with growing irritation and impatience, Thrasymachus blurts out that Socrates' argument is nonsense: it fails to capture the world as it really is. He counters with the claim "justice is the advantage of the stronger." Those who have power determine what justice is. When they decide, they have their own interests foremost in mind. Contrary to Socrates' view, that justice is disclosed by showing consideration for others which is their due, Thrasymachus sees it as self-regarding and self-interested: a political tool employed to perpetuate the rule of an individual, a class or—by implication—a state.

With prompting from Socrates, Thrasymachus spells out his argument which, briefly summarized, runs along the following lines: those who rule in any state naturally desire to hold on to power and its privileges, so they establish and enforce laws that perpetuate their rule. Thus tyrants make tyrannical laws, oligarchs make oligarchical laws, democrats make democratic laws, and so forth; in every state the rulers—whether one, few, or many—punish those who go against their laws, claiming that the punishment of lawlessness is justified. The craft of ruling is an activity by which the rulers oblige their subjects to do what they want them to do, and to desist from doing what they do not want; subjects who disobey the rulers or do not respond in the required way can be condemned and punished as outlaws. And such a punishment would be an example of justice, because it upholds the laws of the state. According to Thrasymachus, this is the way of the world and anyone who denies it is blind or naive. Socrates' argument is nonsensical and useless. It is also dangerous, for anyone who claimed justice on his exalted basis would bring the ship of state to grief on the rocks and shoals of political reality. Socrates' doctrine could only lead to anarchy, disorder, and chaos—in which circumstances the good life would be impossible. Order is better than chaos. This should be obvious to anyone with experience and common sense.

We can readily translate this ancient but immediately recognizable argument into a political theory of the modern state. It might go something like this: whatever is instrumental to the interests of the state is deemed to be just, because the good life is obtainable only within the orbit of the state.

Whatever is good for the rulers of a state is also good for the citizens. Undermining the laws is bad—not only for rulers but also for citizens who depend upon the state for security and order. If citizens carry on in ways that are contrary to the laws and requirements of the state, any state, the chances are they will learn the errors of their ways by coming up against the state's law enforcement agencies. And that would be justified. If some lawless citizens succeeded in putting an end to that particular government by overthrowing it and replacing it with their own, as rulers they could not escape from the discipline of the state now that they are in power. For if some, who previously were citizens, became rulers by means of revolution they would have to secure obedience to the new state and its laws, which they obviously would have to regard, and arguably would regard, as necessary and inviolable. They, too, would then have to punish disobedience and lawlessness, no doubt claiming that their laws are just, and that rebellion against such laws cannot be tolerated. In short, if we want to enjoy the advantages of life under the protection of the state we must do our part in bringing it about by submitting to the state authority, by obeying the laws, and by supporting the governments who enact them—even if they are not to our liking or offend our sense of right and wrong.

The voice of Thrasymachus has echoed in international thought across the centuries. The classical realist argument might be stated as follows: states exist in a circumstance of international anarchy, which is a world without an overarching authority, and thus without law. The word derives from ancient Greek, signifying without a chief or head. The modern meaning in English is the absence of an overarching government authority or the condition of lawlessness.[4] States cannot command other states, for they lack the authority to do so. They cannot deal with each other in terms of law. They can only do that in terms of power, guided by their interests, which is their compass, seeking to gain advantages or at least not to suffer disadvantages from their foreign relations, whether these relations are peaceful or combative. States can only influence other states, either by persuasion and inducement or by intimidation, coercion, and force. Necessity is a defining characteristic of international relations, and recognizing and doing what is necessary, or opportune, in the circumstances is a political virtue. Statecraft involves mastering the instrumental art of dealing effectively with other states, whether by negotiations or by threats, by diplomacy or by warfare, or by any other efficacious means. This logic is inescapable as long as anarchy exists and states are politically and legally independent of one another.

Another Athenian, the historian Thucydides, presents the most famous argument from classical realism in one of his dialogues on the Peloponnesian

War. In relations between unequal powers, such as between the powerful state of Athens and the powerless state of Melos, the demands of the stronger party and the rights of the weaker party can never be at issue: "the strong do what they have the power to do and the weak accept what they have to accept," which is a reality defined by the political situation.[5] Confronted by the hard choice of either capitulation (and subjugation) or war (and destruction), the rulers of Melos—perhaps understandably—hope for an escape from their political dilemma by trying to engage the Athenians in a dialogue of reasonableness. They call upon the Athenians to defend the principle of fair play, claiming that someday when they find themselves up against a mightier power they, too, would benefit from general respect for that principle. The Athenians dismiss this talk of hope and fair play and remind the Melians of their perilous circumstances, in which they could easily be destroyed by vastly superior force. They should therefore confine themselves to pursuing their own best interests, because they are in no position to demand justice or anything else:

> You seem to forget that if one follows one's self-interest one wants to be safe, whereas the path of justice and honor involves one in danger . . . This is no fair fight, with honor on one side and shame on the other. It is rather a question of saving your lives and not resisting those who are far too strong for you.[6]

This is the ethics of statecraft according to classical realism. The Melians cannot reasonably hope that the Athenians will acknowledge and respect their rights out of a sense of honor or justice. Discussion of rights and wrongs, of honor and justice, is only possible between equal powers. The Athenians call attention to what they consider to be the fundamental truth of their argument: "This is the safe rule—to stand up to one's equals, to behave with deference toward one's superiors, and to treat one's inferiors with moderation."[7] The Melians nevertheless persist in standing on their rights and refuse to submit to the Athenians' ultimatum. The latter make good on their threat by proceeding to launch a war against them, eventually obtaining an unconditional surrender from them. Afterward they put to death all the males of military age and enslave the women and children.

Thucydides's message is certainly plain enough: international relations involve inescapable questions of power and necessity that can only be astutely recognized and prudently responded to. Any talk of justice in such circumstances is to commit an error in political analysis; to persist in such talk in the face of danger is to act recklessly in disregard for common sense.

The hard facts of international anarchy leave no room for questions of rights and duties, or of rights and wrongs, because that would require substantial equality between states, which is usually absent. The Athenians were obviously reluctant to employ armed force against the Melians. They would rather persuade them to see their dire situation in a clear and unsentimental light, which called for them to bow down to their superiors. This is the justice of the powerful, as Thucydides defines it, and it is the only justice available under the circumstances. If small or weak states wish to survive they must be prepared to do the bidding of their powerful neighbors when demanded of them; even then they may not survive, for these neighbors may not be prepared to tolerate their independence—if necessity or opportunity tells them otherwise. This is the reality of political life in the anarchical world of states in which there is no superior law enforcement body, and power is always unequal to a greater or lesser extent. As long as these stark conditions exist, relations between states cannot be subject to norms and requirements of civilization.

Two Realists of the Early Modern State

Thrasymachus and Thucydides have successors, and the most outstanding are Machiavelli and Hobbes whose political thought, taken together, captures the modern *persona* of classical realism. The goal of foreign and military policy, according to the famous (or infamous) Florentine with the worldly wise Mona Lisa smile, is security and survival, and also success.[8] Statesmen are, and they must be, out for themselves; otherwise, they risk being overcome and perhaps destroyed by their rivals, who exhibit the same self-regarding devotion. Our leaders must always be on their toes to seize the advantage in their endless rivalries with other leaders who will destroy us if it is to their advantage and we let them get away with it. In an uncertain world, where we cannot have complete confidence in anyone else, we are driven to pursue our political goals through force (*forza*) and deception (*fraude*), we must be both a lion and a fox, and being the latter is even more important than the former. Secrecy and conspiracy and, if necessary, betrayal are the ways of political survival and success. "Open covenants openly arrived at," as recommended by U.S. President Woodrow Wilson at the end of World War I, is a recipe for disaster.[9]

For a statesman to expect straight dealing and fair play from political rivals is to grossly misconceive the nature of international politics, which leaves precious little room for morality. This is only conceivable among private individuals, and even in private life it is a hostage to fair-mindedness and compassion, which could never be automatically forthcoming. Machiavelli is referring to Christian love and charity, *caritas*, recognizing and assisting others out of kindness. There is no room for Christian ethics in politics and anyone who tries to make room is surrendering to self-delusion and wishful thinking. If our leaders acted as though there really was justice in politics, they would be sowing the seeds of their own destruction—and what is worse, the destruction of the states they rule and the people who depend upon them. "In politics the Christian ethic was worse than valueless, it was positively harmful."[10] The people cannot and should not expect their political leaders to conduct themselves in accordance with private morality; they must expect them to divorce themselves from such morality, and to seek after the survival and security of the state by whatever means, fair or foul. If rulers are successful in that self-interested and sometimes necessarily ruthless and unforgiving endeavor, it will rebound to the advantage of every citizen.

For the ethics of the church, Machiavelli substitutes the ethics of the state (*stato*). He turns Christian virtues on their head, when he characterizes virtue (*virtù*) as a desirable and indeed necessary trait of effective leadership, both in politics and in war.[11] The virtues of statecraft are whatever is conducive to survival and success, and the vices are of course anything that leads to defeat and failure. Political and military leaders should resort to whatever promotes their goals, and should not worry unduly about the morality or legality of the means. Having too many scruples is opening a path to defeat and destruction. War is about victory and defeat; it is not about justice and fairness. Survival and success are far more important than compassion and fair play. What is the use of being in the right if one is robbed or destroyed in the process?

Political and military virtue, for Machiavelli, is rooted in the attributes of masculinity, that is, soul (*animo*), ambition (*ambiozione*), ingenuity (*ingegno*), intelligence (*prudenza*), cunning (*ingagnno*), and closely related dispositions and capacities that are required to respond successfully to difficult, dangerous, or dire circumstances under which political and military leaders must expect to find themselves from time to time. Of all the political and military virtues, the most important for Machiavelli is *prudenza*. This is not the Christian virtue of prudence, which is synonymous with good judgment, care, and concern, not only for us but also for others who are counting on us. *Prudenza* is clear-headed thinking, calm and detached calculation, put to the service of political ambition or political necessity. Thus the art of politics and the art of war are—and for Machiavelli they must be— instrumental rather than moral in the usual meaning of that term. These arts consist of precepts and stratagems designed to promote victory and with it greatness and glory, and to avert defeat and with that disgrace and the loss of one's position, one's wealth, one's freedom, and everything else that makes life enjoyable, including most devastating of all, life itself.

On a reading of Machiavelli's *The Prince*, realism is a pragmatic political art intended to uphold the ruler and defeat his rivals, adversaries, or enemies. The state is identified with the ruler and his principality. What is good for the ruler is good for the state: here is a clear echo of Thrasymachus. But on a reading of *The Discourses*, statecraft is a political skill and responsibility to defend the city understood as a republic, that is, a polity that involves the people.[12] Here Machiavelli is writing in the republican tradition, and his realism can be construed as a civic ethic of statecraft, that is, concerned with civic life (*vivere civile*) and with the good of the people (*popolo*).[13] At this point one can no longer say that Machiavelli's realism is entirely instrumental, for it is in fact civic minded and public spirited: he endorses patriotism and civic duty. Realism is now disclosed as genuine political ethics and not merely a recipe for achieving political success or avoiding political disaster narrowly defined. Niccolo Machiavelli is rubbing shoulders with Thomas Hobbes, as will be evident.

Thrasymachus, Thucydides, and Machiavelli speak to us across vast stretches of time. That we still listen to their voices indicates that their realist arguments contain a fundamental truth about the human condition. We might try to summarize it as follows. Human beings are in the first place living, thinking, and acting creatures dwelling among their own kind whom they must deal with and some of whom—not all, but more than a few—will, at one time or another, present a threat to them or seek to take advantage of them in some way. This is a central and persistent predicament and not merely an ephemeral or transient problem of human affairs. We cannot reasonably expect that predicament to go away. Realist doctrine is rooted in basic facts of human nature and human existence, which are not subject to historical change or political manipulation. We cannot rise above our nature. We are not Gods. Nor can we permanently escape from danger. We might get away from one threat or menace, only to find ourselves exposed to another. The world has danger built into it. History cannot change that. We are imprisoned in our mortality from which the only escape is death:

> For in that sleep of death what dreams may come
> When we have shuffled off this mortal coil.[14]

We might put Shakespeare's sobering point about the human condition, what realists see as a plain truth, in slightly different terms, by recalling the political thought of Thomas Hobbes. Hobbes translated Thucydides's history into English, and he was undoubtedly aware of Machiavelli, as evident by the emphasis he gives to the passions of human beings, and to force and fraud in international affairs. For Hobbes, men and women are, first of all, "natural machines" seeking felicity, and wanting peace and security in order to live as long as possible and to enjoy life with as much certainty and confidence as possible.[15] This life quest of every man, woman, and child, which only ends at their death, is rooted in the nature of human beings and the circumstances of human relations. The natural condition of humans is a state of war "of every man, against every man."[16] This is the original, or primordial, state of nature. Part of human nature is a driving passion to live a long and enjoyable life. But another part is reason, or intelligence, which helps men and women to correctly grasp their security predicament, and deal with it by fitting collective means. By these means they can be "drawn to agreement." People recognize they must come together and contract to build "cities" or "commonwealths," that is, sovereign states, to avoid war among themselves and thereby facilitate the good life for all. The overriding goal of making covenants is to obtain peace, which can only be secured and enjoyed within the framework and under the legal authority and power of the sovereign state. The state is "that *mortal god*, to which we owe under the *immortal God*, our peace and defence."[17]

Peace cannot be obtained between sovereign states. For at the same time that particular collections of men and women make peace pacts among themselves, a second condition of war, potential or actual, is created—somewhat inadvertently—between the "artificial machines," the particular states, established in that way. This is the secondary, or political, state of nature. States, in their most significant aspect, are machines of war. What was previously a quest for security from other human beings, an endeavor to escape from the natural condition of humankind, is now a search for security from other states. But a further covenant between sovereign states, comparable to that between the individuals who set them up in the first place, is impossible and unnecessary so long as sovereignty is retained—which is likely so long as states are able to generate the domestic peace that makes the good life obtainable by peace-loving and law-abiding citizens living within their jurisdiction. Citizens who are not inclined to obey the law, and there are always some, will be kept in awe and held in check by the credible power of the government, the sovereign ruler. But sovereigns cannot be under any higher law without ceasing to be sovereigns. This anarchical condition means, according to Hobbes, that there can be neither law nor justice in international relations: "The notions of right and wrong, justice and injustice have there no place.

Where there is no common power, there is no law: where no law, no injustice. Force, and fraud, are in war the two cardinal virtues."[18] Here is a loud and clear echo of Machiavelli.

Statesmen—sovereigns in Hobbes's terminology—are responsible, following from the social contract, for providing security for their citizens. In one of his books Hobbes makes this point by borrowing a memorable phrase from Cicero: *salus populi suprema lex est*, the safety of the people is the supreme law.[19] Here Hobbes is expressing the fundamental realist justification of law and the state. The people are legally bound by their covenant to obey the sovereign's commands, which is the constitutional and legal means by which security is arranged. If sovereigns will not or cannot command, or if people will not and do not obey, or both, security will not be forthcoming, the commonwealth will collapse, and everybody will find themselves back in the primordial state of nature with all its uncertainties and dangers and privations. Nobody wants that, neither rulers nor ruled. Statesmen thus must protect citizens from any individuals who might be disposed to threaten or harm them, and they must punish anyone who breaks the law, which forbids such hostile actions. People must obey the law.

Statesmen must also protect the citizens from threats emanating from other states: the state must be a war machine built for defense from predatory foreign governments. Here the state is a city (*civitas*) that is fortified, equipped, and prepared in all ways and means for war.[20] The relations of these literally or metaphorically walled cities, the condition that exists in the space between them, is that of war:

> . . . in all times, kings, and persons of sovereign authority, because of their independency, are in continual jealousies, and in the state and posture of gladiators, having their weapons pointing, and their eyes fixed on one another; that is their forts, garrisons, and guns upon the frontiers of their kingdoms; and continual spies upon their neighbours, which is a posture of war.[21]

Statecraft—what we would call foreign policy—involves doing whatever is necessary to provide external security, and to counter or avoid whatever is likely to undermine that security. Here we begin to move away from Hobbes's text, which has practically nothing to say about international relations. States may covenant with each other, as when they sign treaties. But security from foreign attack and conquest can never rest on international covenants alone, for they can be broken at will: "a commonwealth, without sovereign power, is but a word without substance, and cannot stand."[22]

Treaties between sovereigns can never be as solid as constitutions between governments and their citizens. National security can only rest, in the final analysis, on military power, if necessary the state's own military power, if possible the joint military power of our state and other states in alliance with us, to deter or defend against external menaces. But the latter arrangement is a poor second best compared with the former, which relies on nobody except oneself.

Although composed in different languages at different historical periods in different geographical locations, the basic message of these classical realists run along the same tracks and are expressed in the same basic discourse. They all begin with the proposition that human beings live in a dangerous world and must look after themselves, and look out for themselves, before they can do almost anything else. This requires a lively sense of their own vulnerability and a sharp awareness of the designs and actions of others who must be assumed to be looking out for themselves. In the realist world, everybody is poised to act. This instrumental perceptiveness applies even more to sovereign states in the anarchical system than it does to individuals in the original state of nature: international relations is a sphere in which self-regarding inclinations and self-interested actions have their most complete expression. But the shift, from a narrower desire to defend the self-interest of the rulers—most clearly expressed by Thrasymachus—to a broader concern to protect the people—most explicit in Hobbes—marks the emergence of realism as a bona fide political ethics, focused on the well-being of the state and its people, which are seen to be one in matters of security and survival. This is the ethical shape that realism has taken in classical thought since the seventeenth century.

There is thus a weighty political literature that reaches back to the ancient world, which rests on the proposition that international relations is an anarchical world of more or less powerful states. Because ethics and law are seen to have at best a marginal place in that world, the subject must be approached and explained in terms of raison d'état, realpolitik, power politics, the "security dilemma," and similar ideas that capture the rights and interests of the sovereign state and the ethics of statecraft.

A Twentieth-Century Scientific Realist

Realist thought flourished in the latter half of the twentieth century, most of it prompted by the failure of the League of Nations, by World War II, and by the Cold War.[23] I must be selective, however, so I shall confine myself to a summary analysis of an outstanding and distinctive voice, the argument of

Thomas Schelling in *The Strategy of Conflict*.[24] The modalities of Schelling's analysis are rational behavior, communication, bargaining, decision, strategy, strategic moves, reaction, retaliation, promise, threat, fear, apprehension, warning, alarm, and similar essentially instrumental and dispositional subjects, that is, subjects which postulate human volition and human choice. Realism for Schelling, as for Machiavelli, is a heightened perception and an acute grasp of the instrumental opportunities and stratagems of international relations. On the surface, his argument has very little ethical content. He is mainly concerned to lay out in some detail a strategic doctrine, based on game theory, which could be applied to manage the nuclear rivalry between the United States and the Soviet Union.[25] Ethical questions exist, however, between the lines of Schelling's text, for the basic point of managing that rivalry is to prevent disaster in the form of nuclear war. This is a heavy responsibility of statesmen. Responsibility, like duty, is a fundamental ethical idea.[26]

Schelling's general argument proceeds as follows. Foreign policy choices—such as the ones involved in nuclear deterrence or nuclear arms control—are never wholly independent or context free because they are made by agents who always face each other: each player is trying to prompt action or respond to action from the other. Players have their eye and their mind on each other; they are looking to see what the others are doing, or wondering what they might do, how it might affect them, and how to respond to it in successful ways. Foreign policy decisions are thus social and interactive—between agents. International decisions, and the games of strategy they invoke, are in Schelling's terminology "interdependent" decisions: wars, threats of war, deterrence, warnings, retaliations, negotiations, blackmail, and the like, are nonzero-sum games that involve not only conflict, as in zero-sum games, but also mutual dependence, mutual accommodation, joint expectations, communications, coordination, and so forth. International relations is rarely a game of pure conflict; it almost always involves the parties in a more elaborate, a more artful, and a more collaborative contest which comprises distinctive stratagems and moves of a social kind. Strategic statecraft is a sort of wary, yet compelling dance between statesmen.

This does not mean, however, that international negotiations or other foreign policy transactions between adversaries involve social obligations. They do not. The dancers are not married. They are joined only by their desire or willingness to dance with each other. The strategies of conflict that Schelling investigates are substitutes for social obligations in situations—of which international relations is the paradigmatic expression—where such bonds cannot be relied upon. In that regard, the instrumental theory of Schelling, and even more the clear-eyed vision, cool calculation, and lack of sentimentalism that underlies it, is reminiscent of Machiavelli and Hobbes—and by implication the ancient Greeks and Romans to whom, along with the ancient Chinese, he makes brief, laudatory reference.[27] These realists of long ago recognized the limits of trust and good faith in international relations, and in so doing they clarified compensatory political arrangements—such as drinking from the same cup to prove the absence of poison.

My aim in this brief discussion is not to summarize Schelling's book. It is merely to convey the gist of his argument as an expression of late-twentieth-century realism. This argument, as I have indicated, is recognizably Machiavellian. Just as Machiavelli had in view a prince who could, by following certain political and military maxims, be successful in rivalries with other statesmen who present a threat or an opportunity, Schelling, too, has in mind someone in a similar situation, perhaps the President of the United States in the nuclear age, who by employing certain stratagems could be successful in negotiations with the Soviet Union—and by extension other nuclear powers who are in conflict with the United States and present a danger to the American people. The purpose of both theories is to equip decision-makers with the mental outlook, the diagnostic skills and disciplines, and the designs, stratagems, and moves that are essential if one is to have any reasonable hope of avoiding or averting disaster in a dangerous world.

Apart from the artistic/literary style of Machiavelli's writing and the analytical/mathematical style of Schelling's, there is only one fundamental difference between them that demands our attention. Machiavelli views the Renaissance Prince in isolation from his enemies, actual or potential, who are lurking in the shadows or offstage as sources of threat or opportunity. They are not dancing with each other. They are portrayed as rivals: either prey to be defeated and subjugated, or predators to be deterred and discouraged. This might be achieved by war or by subterfuge, or by a combination of the two, and the Prince at any rate should always be both a lion and a fox, if he wishes to succeed. Both writers make allowance for chance or luck—*fortuna*—and they share the belief that it can be managed through the application of reason even if it cannot be eliminated. But Machiavelli's political maxims do not extend to socially engaging one's adversaries, involving them in a communicative and collaborative enterprise—except to deceive or dominate. Foxes and lions do not dance. Thus, Machiavelli is writing about political struggle that ends in victory or success for one side and defeat or failure for the other side. In logical terms, his theory is zero-sum. However, Schelling's theory is nonzero-sum: both sides can gain, and they can lose from the same transaction at the same time. There is a discernible and telling social element in his argument. The adversary can become a dancing partner if approached in the correct way.

Schelling has the nuclear statesman's opposite number clearly in view, at center stage, and in close contact and communication at all times. The underlying methodology is diagnostic: how to gauge, correctly, the power, interests, and dispositions of one's adversary *and* the relationship one could have with him or her, in seeking to avoid dangerous or high-risk outcomes, especially inadvertent ones. There is no prospect, or thought, of total victory or complete defeat of one side by the other. In the nuclear age that is out of the question. There is only apprehension and fear of the disaster that will befall everybody if something goes wrong. Schelling's argument is about how to engage an adversary, how to involve that adversary in a mutually expedient relationship, how to communicate intelligently, how to establish reciprocal expectations and transactions that foster desirable outcomes, how to collaborate with the adversary to find rules of the game that can avert disaster, and so on.

Behind the many fascinating games that are analyzed at length there is one clear vision, a national leader—such as a democratically elected American president—should avoid driving an adversary to extreme or desperate measures. Rather, the adversary should be engaged in such a way as to share as fully as possible the interest of averting disaster in a dangerous nuclear age. The circumstance of nuclear weapons experienced by both sides is the almost determining consideration for each player. Schelling's American president is not a misty-eyed altruist. He is a clear-eyed realist. His Soviet counterpart is assumed to be the same. The recipes for understanding and managing conflict contained in Schelling's book, which in many ways is a handbook on sagacious nuclear statecraft, are viewed as a practicable substitute for disarmament or nonproliferation treaties, diplomatic agreements, international declarations, and similar norms, which could never generate sufficient confidence to regulate and manage weapons of mass destruction.

Schelling not only recognizes but also builds into his argument "the problem of two or more partners who lack confidence in each other," who reciprocally fear that the other will, for example, carry out a surprise attack or bring about some other catastrophe. This shared mental condition of heightened anxiety might generate a "multiplier" effect of cascading mutual alarm, which may get dangerously out of hand.[28] In an age of nuclear weapons, the portentous nature of the problem requires no further comment. But even this acknowledgment of the real dangers of human emotions and the definite limits of human rationality in international relations is itself presented as a rational problem that must be understood in order to be avoided or at least reduced. This pursuit of—even faith in—human rationality, it seems to me, is

Schelling's underlying message. In some respects it discloses a moral perspective.

Schelling's theory of international strategy presupposes values and carries normative implications. For example, a "threat," which he discusses at length, has a definite normative drift, namely the value at risk.[29] What is that value? If it is a personal threat, the value at stake is the security of the person at risk. Personal security is a generally recognized value of fundamental importance. If it is an international threat, the value at stake is the security of the state or nation at risk. National security is also a generally recognized value of fundamental importance. But the value in this case is not narrowly self-regarding and self-interested which is so when we worry only about our own personal security. On the contrary, it is other-regarding, publicly interested and indeed publicly spirited for it involves the security and well-being of many other people besides ourselves, our relatives, friends, colleagues, or acquaintances: usually large populations organized as nation-states and consisting almost entirely of people unknown to us. In short, national security is a political and social good and not merely a personal or private value.

For Schelling, as for Machiavelli, the activity of statecraft is exclusively and unsentimentally instrumental, although in the case of Schelling, as I have tried to indicate, it involves a diagnosis of one's rival not as somebody to be bested but, rather, as someone to be involved with so as to reduce the chances and risks of war and other dangerous outcomes. The nuclear-armed superpowers should learn to dance with each other. But even though Schelling assiduously identifies and dissects a variety of moves and steps that could generate collaboration and avoid disaster, his analysis does not probe the ethics of statecraft that are involved in such a laudable endeavor; it merely presupposes them without comment. The normative aspects of foreign and military policy are intimated by his argument but hidden between the lines of his text.

To bring them into view we can ask a couple of questions. Why should foreign policymakers behave in the sophisticated and enlightened way that Schelling, in effect, recommends? What is the point of knowing and mastering the stratagems he sets forth? The only reason, it seems to me, is because they carry very heavy responsibilities; namely, the security and well-being of the nations on whose behalf they are working, and that of innocent third parties who could be caught in their cross fire. But these responsibilities are nowhere discussed explicitly and thus the reader could think, and most readers of Schelling's book perhaps do think, that the subject about which they are reading is a technical–instrumental subject, a scientific subject, and not an ethical subject, which at base it is. What Schelling does not furnish is the underlying ethics of statecraft, which would make his analysis of strategy ultimately intelligible in terms of fundamental human values and concerns, such as the values of security and peace which in a nuclear age are simultaneously personal, national, and global concerns.

Behind and beyond the many perceptive stratagems and astute moves that Schelling brings to light is an unacknowledged political norm, namely, that nation-states, for him the United States, are repositories of a way of life cherished by millions of citizens and as such are worthy of the greatest concern and care in the conduct of foreign and military policy. Although Schelling is furnishing a scientific analysis of foreign and military policy based on game-theoretic reasoning, whether he realizes it or not, his important book is intimating a sophisticated international ethics. It is, first, an ethic of the nation-state and is recognizable as a classical realist doctrine. But Schelling takes that doctrine further by showing how the national interests of states are entangled, and how that demands a social, that is, collaborative, response. It is, second, an ethic of statecraft, which rests on prudence as a cardinal political virtue but takes the technical aspects of the logic of prudence farther than any previous writer on the subject. The national interest and political prudence are inherently normative categories: standards of conduct for preserving and promoting what is of value and indeed of extreme importance not only for ourselves but also for others besides ourselves who might be affected, one way or the other, by whatever we do or fail to do.

What Schelling is indirectly probing is nothing less than the heart of international ethics, which is lurking behind his entire analysis. But owing to his desire to be "scientific" in the natural science meaning of the term his book, unfortunately, provides hardly more than a tantalizing glimpse of that vital underlying subject. Despite the sophistication of his book, this is a major shortcoming of his contribution and the contributions of most other late-twentieth-century realists, as compared with the traditional contributions of Thucydides, Machiavelli, and Hobbes.

Might without Right and Wrong

In the later part of the twentieth-century international relations came to be portrayed, especially by leading American thinkers, as devoid of ethics, as amoral. Realism became a scientific explanation of how the international system was supposed to work. It ceased to be a humanistic interpretation of how the people involved in the tough game of foreign policy were supposed to carry on responsibly. This American doctrine, commonly termed neorealism, was widespread among scholars who adopted a social science view of international relations, that is, as a structural and instrumental world devoid of ethical considerations and concerns. The neorealist concept of realism was even taken up by some idealists and self-proclaimed antirealists. According to John Rawls, realism is what neorealists say it is, that is, it has no ethical theory and can therefore be dismissed as irrelevant for studying normative issues of international relations, such as justice.[30] I address his view of realism in chapter 9.

As compared with traditional realists who pay great attention to the limits and circumstances of power under the condition of anarchy, neorealists employ a naturalist concept of structural constraint: something confining or compelling that exists in the nature of things, like gravity or genetic inheritance: physical or biological constraint. This should not be equated with the notion of human nature that traditional realists employ, such as Hobbes's notion of natural rights. Kenneth Waltz, the leading neorealist, compares a "political structure" to "a field of forces in physics."[31] The reader is left with the definite impression that the structure of international relations is nonvolitional, amoral, and thus amenable to scientific analysis in the natural science meaning of the term. If we employ Waltz's concept of political structure there is not much point in studying the inclinations and choices of statesmen and other international actors. All of that—as the expression has it—is a dependent variable. Statecraft—what he refers to as "the management of international affairs"—comes into his study only as a final chapter in which the main points to note are its limited scope in the face of compelling and profoundly unequal power, and its totally instrumental nature.[32]

In our conventional human understanding, however, constraint and closely related notions such as coercion, compulsion, necessity, pressure, and so on are volitional concepts. They are not something external to human will. Necessity is what we must accept and compulsion is what we must do in our dealings with others under certain circumstances. This is conveyed by expressions such as Hobson's choice, last resort, force of circumstance, no alternative, blackmail, and so forth that points to the confinements that human activity is often subject to. They are something we recognize and have to deal with. Facing a "Hobson's choice," for example, is not only having no real choice in the matter but also knowing that the choice is being made by somebody else, in this case by Hobson, who rented out horses "and is said to have compelled customers to take the horse which happened to be next [to] the stable-door, or go without."[33] Somebody wanting a horse could accept Hobson's choice or go somewhere else to hire a horse. This is what compulsion often comes down to in human relations.

The international world contains many Hobsons. When Thucydides noted the dire position of the Melians in their relations with the Athenians, he was pointing to their extremely limited choice under the circumstances they were in. They could either submit to the Athenian ultimatum or be destroyed by the army of Athens. Either way, it was up to them; they had a choice, albeit an extremely difficult one. When in April 1940 the Danish government claimed they had no choice except to submit to military occupation by vastly superior German forces, we are catching another glimpse of confining volition in world affairs. The Danes could have decided to resist the Nazis by military means—as the Norwegians did—but it would have been crazy to do so because they could not count on the British, the French, or any other great power coming to their aid and they lacked the remote and mountainous vastness of Norway. When in September 1992 the British government claimed they had no choice except to leave the European Exchange Rate Mechanism and devalue Sterling in the face of a run on that currency by the international money markets, we are catching yet another glimpse of confining volition in world affairs. The British could have decided to remain within the mechanism but it would have been crazy to do so without the full support of the German Bundesbank, which was not forthcoming. Each of these important decisions are part of a backward-and-forward chain of related decisions of greater or lesser compulsion: the Athenians decided to impose their political and military will on the Melians in their war against Sparta; the German High Command decided to occupy Denmark for strategic reasons related to that stage of World War II; money market managers decided to target Sterling for reasons related to the European currency markets at that time.

Necessity and compulsion are not something external to human affairs; they are not physical or biological constraints. On the contrary, they are something some people sometimes do to other people whether intentionally or not; they are occasions when human relations take a certain distinctive turn—namely one party is boxed in by another party. Exactly the same can be said of international relations: necessity and compulsion arise on certain occasions. Some countries experience it more regularly than others: the Poles more than the Russians and the Germans, the Koreans more than the Japanese and the Chinese, the Canadians and the Mexicans more than the Americans, Third World states more than anybody. Being wholly internal to human relations, including international relations, necessity and compulsion are fundamentally historical—as the above examples indicate.

To sum up thus far, one unfortunate result of this marginalization of ethical subjects by social science realists has been a tunnel vision of international relations theory that fails to address, often even to discern, important normative issues beyond its narrow field of vision. It is as if sociological theorists employed a definition of marriage based exclusively on individual desire, such as a desire for sex and children, and excluded all other facets of marriage and family life, such as marriage customs, family law, religious teachings, cultural practices, linguistic usages, and so forth—on the grounds that it would be unscientific to take such normative elements into account. Or it would be as though political theorists employed a definition of the state as a wholly instrumental device and excluded any and all conceptions of it as a sphere of political obligation, responsibility, rights, duties, law, equality, liberty, justice, and the rest. Yet neorealists are inclined to operate with a definition of the international system that is no less narrow and unrealistic.

Neorealists ignore the form of ethical argument, outlined earlier, that classical realists are making. They stand outside the realist tradition of international thought. Even Machiavelli—who of all the traditional realists is perhaps the nearest to being a purely instrumental thinker—makes room for the ethics of statecraft, when he identifies the heavy responsibility involved in the art of protecting the state and its citizens, especially during times of war. Much the same can be said of the international thought of Thucydides and Hobbes and other thinkers in that tradition. Traditional realism is normative thought of a restrictive and special kind, but it is normative thought nonetheless.

Realist Ethics

We live in a world in which it is safe to assume that all people some of the time, and perhaps some people all of the time, are out for themselves and will put themselves before others when the opportunity or necessity arises. This must be obvious to everyone: we not only recognize that in our theories but, what is far more significant, we take it more or less for granted in the practical conduct of our everyday lives. If we did not take it for granted we would surely have difficulty carrying on. And if our theories denied that traditional realist assumption about human behavior they would surely, and correctly, be dismissed as not only naive but ignorant also. They would fail to recognize and account for a universal spring of human activity.

Power is inherent in human relations because humans are power agents in themselves, possessing not only muscle power but, far more importantly, brain power for making intelligent (or foolish) choices: the seat of humankind's dominion over all other living things. As Hobbes argued so well, humankind's natural power, in the form of brain power, has led to the invention of all sorts of instruments that are used both for success and survival in human affairs and for mastery over nature, artificial power or what we refer to nowadays as technology. A fundamentally important part of that artificial power—arguably the most important part—is the organization of corporate agencies by which humans greatly enhance their individual powers—such as gangs, clans, tribes, companies, unions, churches, or states. The state undoubtedly is the most powerful and one of the most noteworthy of all the social technologies that human beings have come up with to date.

One can agree with twentieth-century realists that power is fundamental in world affairs without having to deny that other things are also important, such as a lively sense of good and bad, wisdom and folly, and the like. The reality of power always raises questions of how it shall be addressed, employed, and controlled. Of course, these include questions of expediency: prudence in the narrow, self-regarding sense; instrumental questions. But they also include questions of prudence in the social meaning: prudence as a virtue, as the required conduct of somebody who has power, particularly military power, and is expected to exercise it with due care and attention for the well-being of others who might be affected one way or another. Such an expectation is inherently normative. More than that, they include questions of moral and legal obligation: of what we owe to others, of their legitimate interests, of their rights and duties, of responsibility, recognition, consideration, toleration, and much else.

Statecraft cannot be divorced from such questions. Practitioners speak the language of threat and inducement or adjustment and negotiation in Thomas Schelling's instrumental meaning; but practitioners also speak the language of recognition and consultation and cooperation in the normative meaning of these words, that is, communication and transaction between formally equal and legally independent states parties. If we can assume, as seems plausible, that each of these linguistic toolkits, the instrumental and the normative, have important practical uses it would be reasonable to expect practitioners to avail themselves of both. And practitioners do put them both to use. What is strange is that some contemporary realist thinkers do not. In their curious reluctance to face that reality they separate themselves not only from practitioners, who have little choice in the matter, but also from traditional realist thinkers.

This criticism cannot be leveled against all twentieth-century realists. A concern about morality is clearly evident in the international thought of E.H. Carr—a leading British realist of mid-century. His thought is driven by a determination to repudiate the avowed erroneous intellectual doctrine of "idealism"—as exemplified by the public statements of Woodrow Wilson—and to launch an authentic political science of international relations—what he conceives as realism. Unlike American neorealists, Carr does not question the existence of morality in international relations. He questions erroneous conceptions and misleading judgments of it, particularly the confusion of international ethics with private morality.[34]

Carr is concerned with the foundations and limits of bona fide international ethics, which he sees as deriving from concrete practice and not from abstract principles, and from the experience of states and not that of individuals. States do not and should not observe the same morality as individuals. Individuals can be altruistic, can make sacrifices for other individuals, and can perhaps even be expected to do so—at least up to a point. But states cannot do the same for other states: it would patently be wrong for statesmen to sacrifice their own country to save other countries. Statesmen can follow Socrates' or Jesus' teachings without regard for themselves. They cannot do that without regard for the many others who depend upon their statecraft. Statesmen may have to authorize morally dubious acts, for the good of their state and of its people, such as lying or killing. Individuals must not do the same for the sake of themselves, without special extenuating circumstances to justify it. "The state thus comes to be regarded as having a right of self-preservation which overrides [individual] moral obligation."[35] Carr elaborates on his conception of political morality: "Any international moral order must rest on some hegemony of power. But this hegemony . . . must, if it is to survive, contain an element of give-and-take . . . It is through this process of give-and-take . . . that morality finds its surest foothold in international . . . politics."[36] Morality therefore has a place within the structures and instruments of international power. But it is definitely a limited place, a foothold, and power is fundamental. Hans Morgenthau, the leading American realist thinker of the twentieth century, makes an argument that runs along similar lines.[37]

For traditional realists, international relations has an ethical dimension: it is a sphere of human conduct in which normative judgments can be and have to be made, for example, about war and peace, poverty and prosperity, foreign policy and military policy, diplomatic relations and commercial relations, and much else besides. On almost any view of politics as a human activity, it would be inconceivable if it were otherwise. Human beings are not mechanical or functional things. They are social creatures and agents. When Thucydides implicitly chides the leaders and citizens of Melos for refusing to accept the terms of the Athenians, he is pointing to an international ethic that he believes is correct in the context, namely that there cannot be any justice or fairness between unequal states. When Machiavelli dismisses

Christian virtue for encouraging foolhardiness and irresponsibility that could lead to disaster, he is identifying an ethic of statecraft, namely political prudence based on a lively sense of one's situation, one's strengths and weaknesses, and one's interests. When Hobbes claims there is no justice in the anarchical relations of states, he is noticing the difficulties of establishing and enforcing the rule of law when an overarching sovereign is not present.

The foregoing observations are no more than glosses on some outstanding realist texts, classical and modern. I have rehearsed them to emphasize that traditional realists advance normative arguments—or rather a family of arguments—about the nature of political life whose importance to the study of international relations it would be difficult to exaggerate. The arguments of Thrasymachus, and his predecessors and successors, concern the limits of ethical conduct in politics generally and international politics specifically. They register a particular ethical outlook, namely one that is skeptical of private morality in politics and also one that recognizes that political life has a distinctive ethics all its own. Realist political ethics is marked by reticence in going beyond instrumental considerations, it is fenced in by qualifications that have the effect of restricting the scope of moral considerations, and it pays great heed to the force of circumstances. In the chapters that follow, I shall nevertheless maintain that traditional realist commentators give an account of international ethics that is one-sided and incomplete and, if accepted on its own terms, misleading as well. But when times are difficult and demanding, when the hazards and dangers of world affairs close in on us, as when economic depression or war threaten our welfare and security, it must be admitted that the ethics of realism are what we often fall back upon.

CHAPTER 3

Martin Wight, Realism, and the Good Life

All states and nations, even welfare states, have been built by struggle and war.

Martin Wight

Political Theory and International Theory

Martin Wight argues, in a celebrated essay, that political theory is a fully developed "theory of the good life," whereas international theory is merely a residual "theory of survival."[1] Wight's simplifying distinction may be inviting because it eliminates thorny normative issues and it confines theoretical reflection on international relations to instrumental questions. I shall argue, however, that it cannot be sustained and should be rejected.[2] Furthermore, he fails to observe the distinction in his own writings on states systems, which disclose the unity of political theory and international theory.[3] International theory and political theory diverge at certain points but they are branches of one overall theory of the modern state and states system. States are *janus*-faced: they simultaneously look inward at their subjects and outward at other states. Although each facet can of course be distinguished analytically and theorized separately, neither is ontologically independent of the other. There is not on the one hand "the state" and on the other hand "the states system"; there are only "states" whose actions, arrangements, and entanglements can be studied from either the internal or the external angle, or both. Survival may be threatened by internal war. The good life may be fostered by external aid. International theory, understood in Wight's own terms of "realism," "rationalism," and "revolutionism," proves on examination to be a theory of the good life and therefore a branch of political theory in its own right.

By "political theory" he is, of course, referring to classical political thought and not to contemporary endeavors to establish a "scientific" theory of politics, which he considers to be a misguided enterprise. Political thought is conventionally conceived as the systematic reflection on the relations between the state and the citizen. Classical political theorists seek to apprehend the conditions and arrangements required for a life of order, justice, liberty, fraternity, equality, prosperity, or whatever values they consider important. And without forgetting for a moment all the controversies in the long history of reflection on values such as these, about this most classical and modern thinkers agree: if the good life is to be obtained in this mortal world it can only be within the framework of the state.[4] The theory of the state and the theory of the good life are entangled to the point where it is almost impossible to separate them. What the best state is, how it ought to operate, what its institutions should be, how they could best be arranged, what is required of statesmanship and citizenship for such a state to exist— these are perennial questions of political thought. The debate is about the conceptions and priorities of different political goods and about the institutions and conduct deemed most likely to foster them. Political theory is therefore a "tradition of speculation about the state."[5]

The contrast with international theory, according to Wight, could not be sharper: here there is not to be found a preoccupation with the good life and a corresponding literature whose great works purport to disclose the way to it. There are of course the classical legal texts of Hugo Grotius, Samuel Pufendorf, Emerich de Vattel, and others. But the international lawyers do not provide the same service as the political philosophers. Although of unquestioned importance, their works are not read in the same way as Plato's *Republic*, Hobbes's *Leviathan*, or Mill's *On Liberty*. Similarly, the classical political thinkers who have reflected on international relations are not remembered primarily for that part of their contribution. There is no classical text in international thought except, perhaps, Thucydides' study of the Peloponnesian War. International theory is a "tradition of speculation about the society of states" and is often handled best by historians, which in the main Wight himself was.[6]

This traditional neglect of international theory by political theorists calls for explanation. Should they not be as curious about the international aspect of the modern state as the internal aspect? Should not the theory of the modern state therefore be an international theory in significant part? Indeed, could it not be argued that international relations are more provoking and challenging because their normative puzzles are more baffling: they involve not only the obligations of the citizen and the state but also those of states to each other and of humankind at large. Should not the political theorists be fascinated by that? Of course some were: Kant responded with a deservedly well-known philosophy on "universal history" and "perpetual peace," and Edmund Burke with memorable commentaries on international subjects, including British imperialism in America and India as well as the French revolution. Yet they are exceptions. "Few political thinkers have made it their business to study the states system, the diplomatic community itself."[7] International theory is "at the margin of their activities."[8]

Wight explains the meager fare of classical international theory by reference to its subject: it is a theory not of the good life but merely of survival. "International politics is the realm of recurrence and repetition."[9] There cannot be a political theory of international relations because "there is no *respublica* there."[10] At least there has not been since the end of late medieval *respublica Christiana*. Because the good life can only be lived within the state, it is a domestic and not an international issue. Nobody lives in the states system as such—except a few stateless persons shunting back and forth from one airport transit lounge to the next desperately seeking domicile. Their bad life is owing to their statelessness. The population of the world is merely the aggregate of the populations of the states of the world. There are no citizens of the world in any intelligible meaning of the word. Political goods are therefore a given for international theory, whereas they are an end for political theory. The problem of international theory is reduced to that of survival, which is a question of means and expedients and not one of ends. The theory is conservative rather than progressive. It is usually labeled as realism.

Perhaps it can suffice for the moment to say, pursuing this line of argument in Wight, that international theory ignores the good of the people living inside states because states are assumed to be "perfect associations": that is, the good life can be pursued and realized entirely within state frameworks, making it unnecessary to look any farther afield. It is worth remembering that this idea of state perfection originated as a radical response of political thinkers (such as Hobbes) to the contrary claims of the Christian fathers and the classical natural lawyers, who held that the state (the city of man) was necessarily imperfect because the only perfect world was the city of God. State "perfection" in modern political thought, it must be emphasized, signifies political completeness and legal validity—sovereignty—rather than excellence or flawlessness as such. But behind that assumption is the conception of the sovereign state as a sphere in which the good life can be not only pursued but also realized and enjoyed. This clearly is the view of Hobbes where he writes in *Leviathan* of the "incommodities" of life in the state of nature (discussed below) as compared with the "felicity" of civil life in the sovereign state.[11]

This has always been a crucial step in the justification of modern statehood rather than an actual fact about modern states, which of course vary considerably in their provision of political goods. Today, it is certainly the case that many states cannot or will not provide their populations with anything resembling the good life, as a glance at the living conditions in many quasi-states or failed states. However, if states cannot be justified in terms of the good life, the classical norms of state sovereignty will be undermined because their point will be lost. What is the point of nonintervention, for example, if the population of a state is suffering at the hands of a repressive dictatorship? What is the point of independence if a population is suffering from starvation or Civil War or both? To address such questions, modern thinking frequently reverts to the position of the natural lawyers by invoking human rights violations as a ground for intervention.

International theory also ignores the good life because diplomacy and international law, by and large, ignore it. Not only does diplomacy ignore it, but arguably diplomacy could not exist without ignoring it because statesmen would not be inclined to engage in dialogue if they were not treated with more or less equal dignity and respect regardless of the conditions of their countries and the domestic policies of the governments they represent. For diplomatic dialogue to occur, the internal practices of statesmen that do not adversely affect other states would have to be off limits. If the internal were probed rather than ignored, disorder, instability, and similar international evils would be provoked including, in the extreme case, war. If diplomacy exists to prevent anything, surely it is that. There consequently is a characteristic agnosticism in traditional diplomacy when it comes to domestic politics. This is also a feature of positive international law. It is expressed by the fundamental principle of international toleration (often at the expense of domestic intolerance): *cujus regio, ejus religio*. Initially, this principle operated only within Christian Europe and later the West. With the ending of Western Empires it was established worldwide. The more universal the states system and divergent its membership, the more necessary is this basic norm.

International Theory and the Good Life

Wight might not agree with the foregoing remarks because he sees a "tension between international theory and diplomatic practice," the origins of which he attributes to Hobbes's "identification of international politics with the pre-contractual state of nature."[12] There can be insecurity and fear among states in an international state of nature as there can also be among individuals in a domestic state of nature. But insecurity leads to very different actions in each sphere: the social contract in the second, but only state protective measures such as defense or deterrence in the first. "International anarchy is the one manifestation of the state of nature that is not intolerable." It is evident in Hobbes's remark, noted by Wight, that the international state of nature is not a circumstance of misery like the domestic state of nature: "because they [sovereigns] uphold thereby [i.e. by their 'posture of war'] the industry of their subjects; there does not follow from it that misery, which accompanies the liberty of particular men."[13] Wight sees this as "an inconsistency" in Hobbes's concept of the state of nature. He quotes Pufendorf who remarks in the same vein that the co-existence of states "lacks those inconveniences which are attendant upon a pure state of nature." Wight comments that this "is empirically true" but "theoretically odd."

I believe that is theoretically odd only if one accepts states as analogous to real persons questing for survival, in which case they might be driven to abandon sovereignty and unite to form a universal polity of some kind. Yet they are not driven to it because they are far from being persons in reality. On the contrary, they are political organizations (notional persons) that are justified by providing political goods to those real persons who populate them. They are postulated communities in themselves, which pursue foreign policies and international arrangements (national defense, military alliances, diplomacy, commercial agreements, etc.) calculated to preserve their independence and ensure their survival and success. International anarchy is therefore tolerable. Indeed, it is desirable because it is a condition of liberty that supports and helps make possible the good life of people within their domestic jurisdictions. Political independence enables populations to define and to shape their good life according to their own ideas, beliefs, and values.

Survival, as Arnold Wolfers points out, presupposes the value of independence: "It would make no sense to say or assume that nations must seek power adequate for survival if high value were not placed on the existence of independent nations."[14] Wolfers does not specify what this high value consists of. The point, however, is the survival not merely of sovereigns but also the "commodious living" of their subjects (as Hobbes puts it), by which he means the civil and material conditions necessary for their well-being.[15] In other words, the state, when it is doing its job properly, is providing for the good life of its population. There would be no point in external security if Leviathan afforded little or nothing of domestic value. Here is the underlying morality of realism. An international state of nature is consequently more tolerable than a domestic state of nature and probably more desirable than a far-flung world polity, such as Kant's *Cosmopolis*—even if such a political arrangement were possible.

The limited attention given to international theory by Hobbes and most other classical political theorists is consistent with this point. Leviathan's arms and fortifications are necessary means of ensuring the good life of the subject, of providing security of person and property against the conceivable threat posed by other Leviathans in the neighborhood. International theory, being about these provisions and that security, is necessarily a part of Hobbes's "theory of the state." However, international theory is secondary in Hobbes's text because most of the arrangements for the good life are between the state and the citizen and do not involve other states. The international aspect of statehood is merely the consequence of the domestic aspect. Although that is changing, as international relations becomes more important to the preservation and welfare of states, it still remains true of states today. Hence, international theory traditionally takes second place to political theory. But as even Wight points out, the theory of survival is anything but unimportant because it "involves the ultimate experience of life and death, national existence and national extinction."[16]

Consequently, although international theory in the first instance is indeed a theory of survival, in the second instance it is a theory of the good life. There is an immediate but not an ultimate distinction between international theory and political theory, for the point of the balance of power and similar arrangements among a plurality of Leviathans is to safeguard the civil and socioeconomic goods of people organized into states. There is a Latin expression: *ubi bene, ibi patria*: where it is good for me that is my country. If there were no basis for the good life in states, there would be no point in their survival. In other words, international theory is part of the theory of the state and not separate from it, just as, for example, diplomacy, international law, and military alliances are part of the means of good government. They can only be justified in terms of the good they provide: for example, national security. Their *justification* is part of the justification of the state. I believe this turn, which is pursued in the remainder, renders a more satisfactory answer to Wight's question concerning international theory.

There is no tension, at least in this respect, between international theory and diplomatic practice: the theory of survival is a branch of political theory, just as diplomacy is an activity of good government. The tension arises rather from the obvious fact that the political interest or good of one state may be discordant with that of another, leading to the possibility and even likelihood of conflict and the urgency, if not the necessity, of defense, diplomacy, espionage, and other external policies and arrangements. But this does not alter the fundamental connection between political theory and international theory. Nor does it raise any tension between international theory and diplomatic practice. It only brings to the surface the difficulties, dilemmas, and paradoxes that both diplomatists and international theorists must wrestle with. Although there is no single *respublica* in the international realm this should not be taken to imply that it is a jurisdictional vacuum, which it is not. For in the states system there are many coexisting *respublicas*. World jurisdiction is pluralist rather than monist.

Realism, Rationalism, and the Good Life

The theory of survival discloses itself as a branch of the theory of the good life in the international traditions labeled by Wight as "realism" (or "Machiavellianism") and "rationalism" (or "Grotianism").[17] Realist theory is the conception of international relations as shaped predominantly, if not exclusively, by national self-interest or <u>raison d'état</u>. The latter is traditionally defined as "the rule of conduct for a state"[18] and the former as that which is to the advantage, benefit, or good of the state and, by implication, its inhabitants. According to this theory, there is no advantage, benefit, or good higher than that of the state. Hence, pursuing or defending the national interest, either internally or externally, is conceived as moral or right. Classical reason of state, it should be pointed out, is a rule of conduct in both domestic and foreign policy, and realism as a theory embraces both. From an external point of view, the core of national interest is viewed as national security. This is based on the assumption that other states are likewise pursuing or defending their interests. The usual means include national defense, diplomacy, military alliances, espionage, the balance of power, and other instrumental measures and calculations that disclose states as power apparatuses.

What do these and other prudent means assume about the state whose interest is defended? Defending the national interest makes sense only if that interest entails real value: the state being defended must give or at least be assumed to give expression to the good life. In the early modern dynastic state, the good life included the goods of the ruler and the nobility: their estates. But in theory, it was never confined only to them. Jean Bodin defines a commonwealth as a government that provides public order, and he considers felicity for the sovereign and for the citizen to be one and the same common good.[19] In Frederick the Great's conception of the state, according to Gerhard Ritter, "domestic and foreign policy were guided exclusively by the <u>raison d'état</u>, by the interests of the state. Both prince and people were its servants."[20] In the subsequent version of the state that we are familiar with today, the good life is the life of the nation: the public or common good. The "hard shell" of the modern territorial state, to use an image made familiar by John Herz, is and must be hard because it contains a great store of value, namely a national population living and enjoying its distinctive way of life.[21] There is no point in a hard shell if there is no value, no life behind it. This proposition is not affected by the particular shape of national values but only by the existence of them. Consequently, it can embrace the liberal-constitutional form of state and the social-welfare form of state as well as any other—providing it is of authentic value to the populations involved, which is the usual justification of modern statehood.

One can make a similar argument about Wight's conception of Grotianism, which discloses an image of international relations shaped significantly by diplomatic dialogue and the rule of law. In brief, states in their relations with one another are bound by rules and practices such as equal sovereignty, mutual recognition, nonintervention, reciprocity, and so forth, which they observe by and large most of the time. In their external relations states are right- and duty-bearing units and not merely apparatuses of power. International morality and law are reciprocal: interstatal. This is clear even in Jeremy Bentham's rationalist utilitarian account of international law based on the pluralist principle of the "common and equal utility of all nations," according to which rulers must take into account the good not only of their own nation but also of other nations. This principle, as one commentator puts it: "obliges the state, first, to do no injury and to do the greatest good to other nations, saving the regard that is proper to its own well-being," and it requires in the second place that no state should receive benefit or injury from other nations without taking account of "the regard due to the well being of these same nations."[22] The point of international law (and diplomacy) is not to override state egoism but to "rationalize" it and "moderate" it and thereby enhance the liberty and survivability of states, which are then free to operate domestically according to utilitarian legislation and morality, which is Bentham's "chief value."[23]

But what is assumed about the state by this utilitarian image of international society? Regulating states by international law to avert or reduce the incidence or extent of damaging collisions between them makes sense only if these entities are valuable in themselves at least to some degree: collisions will result in harm to persons and property, perhaps even bloodshed and destruction on a large scale. That is the primary concern of Jeremy Bentham and most international theorists whom Wight labels as "rationalists." The Grotian image of international relations has been likened to an egg carton by R.J. Vincent: the container cushions the eggs to prevent or at least reduce the chance of cracking them and thereby decreasing or destroying their value.[24] There is no point in egg cartons if eggs are not only valuable but also breakable. This proposition is not affected by the particular color or contents of each egg, which only postulates that all eggs are presumably fresh and therefore of authentic value. However, it is affected by the external shape of eggs, which must be able to fit uniformly into the carton and thereby benefit from it. Pursuing the analogy, international society presupposes the intrinsic value of all states and accommodates their inward diversity. But it requires and postulates their outward uniformity and conformity as indicated by their equal legal status and respect for each other's sovereignty. International society is therefore arranged primarily to provide for the independence and preservation of legally equal and presumably valuable states.

In short, the two major versions of classical international theory identified by Martin Wight presuppose states as valuable places where the good life, if rarely realized in full measure is nevertheless a definite possibility in most respects. This is the traditional justification of the state in political thought. International theory, in both its realist and rationalist versions, is a theory of survival only because political theory is a theory of the good life.

Idealism and the Good Life

There is a third version of international theory, identified by Wight as "revolutionism" (or "Kantianism" and what I shall more conventionally label as idealism), about which he evidently has some reservations. This stands for the ideological impulse to universalism in international history as reflected in "the Reformation, the Counter Reformation, the French Revolution, and the totalitarian revolutions of the twentieth century."[25] According to Wight, all these revolutions, despite their profound differences, disclose the imperative to transcend international society as a plurality of sovereign states and to establish either a "pattern of conformity" or a "*cosmopolis*": a universal political authority: solidarism.[26] Idealists are thus inclined to reject the existing system or society of states—pluralism—as an obstacle to the good life of humankind, or at a minimum they are inclined to see *cosmopolis* as "immanent in the existing state structure."[27]

Kant addresses the puzzle of an international state of nature first identified by Hobbes:

> The same unsociability . . . gives rise in turn to a situation whereby each commonwealth, in its external relations . . . is in a position of unrestricted

freedom. Each must accordingly expect from any other precisely the same evils that formerly oppressed individual men and forced them into a law governed civil state.[28]

Whereas Hobbes's solution is deterrence and Bentham's is reciprocity, Kant believes the good life ultimately requires escape from international anarchy by means of an institutional arrangement equivalent to the domestic social contract that instituted Leviathan, namely, a "great federation" of states, which establishes the international rule of law of a "united power" with a "united will": that is, *cosmopolis.* Kant, as Wight points out, "finds the idea of human progress in a 'continuously growing state consisting of various nations' to which 'the federative unions of states' of the Perpetual Peace is a second best."[29] This growth is the fulfillment of the Enlightenment, which is the ascendancy of reason over man's baser instincts. For so long, according to Kant, this growth perpetuated the international anarchy and its "lawless condition of pure warfare."[30] Reason and therefore peace can triumph only in a "law governed civil state" or *Rechtstaat* which, in turn, depends for its existence on an international rule of law and right. This is expressed in the seventh proposition of Kant's "Idea for a Universal History": "The problem of establishing a perfect civil constitution is subordinate to the problem of law-governed eternal relationship with other states, and cannot be solved unless the latter is also solved."[31]

If Kantian idealism is a variant of international theory, then that theory is not limited to the theory of survival, since Kantians are "the subversion and liberation and missionary men" who consider the existing states system as an obstacle to be overcome in the construction of a better world polity for all. Hedley Bull portrays idealism as a project to transform the states system into something more in tune with universal humankind.[32] Revolutionists are thinkers who love the future, who understand the world as a community free of division and discord, and who wish to help bring it into existence as soon as possible. This is because the present international anarchy is not only an unnecessarily rough and inhumane world but it is also an unenlightened world of false knowledge that leads to misunderstanding about the true nature and potential of human beings and human society.

Wight thus considers idealism to be, at heart, a political theory rather than an international theory because it is progressive and not conservative.[33] It thus occupies a contradictory position in his trinity of international theories. Idealists do not presuppose the good life of a plurality of sovereign states. On the contrary, they see the good life in transcending international anarchy. Even for that most liberal of revolutionaries—Kant—the domestic rule of law is unobtainable without the international rule of law. And the latter is unobtainable without a super-sovereign lawgiver of some sort: *cosmopolis*. Revolutionary theory cannot be a theory of survival; it cannot be conservative when applied to the states system. Rather, it is a theory of progress: it seeks an overthrow of that system. By Wight's definition, this means that idealism is a political theory and not an international theory.

International Theory as Political Theory

As far as I am aware, Wight never addressed this irregularity in his international thought. Perhaps that is because he was an historian first and a philosopher second, and would rather abide by historical tendency even at the price of theoretical ambiguity. However, it can easily be resolved if international theory and political theory are both understood to be concerned ultimately with the good life. This overcomes, what I believe, is a false distinction in Wight's thought, namely, that between international politics viewed as a sphere of recurrence and domestic politics as one of progress. His trinity makes no such distinction but instead seems to operate in a dialectical manner, with realism as thesis, idealism as antithesis, and rationalism seeking some kind of synthesis or at least compromise. Each is defined in relation to the others, which means that none can be investigated very profitably in isolation.

> All I am saying is that I find these traditions of thought in international history dynamically interweaving, but always distinct, and I think they can be seen in mutual tension and conflict underneath the formalized ideological postures of our present discontents.[34]

Furthermore, Wight's equation of political theory with progress is not apt. Some of the great political theorists are conservatives. Burke is perhaps the leading example. He is a conservative both internationally and domestically and his ends (civility, tradition, the rule of law) and his means (judgment, moderation, prudence) are the same for each realm. Likewise, it is not difficult to find thinkers who are progressives in each sphere, for example, Kant. Neither Burke nor Kant is inclined to differentiate sharply or fundamentally between these spheres, perhaps because each in his own way operates with universalist ethics.

If the distinction that Wight draws between the theory of survival and the theory of the good life is false and both are branches of one theory of the modern state, where does this leave the academic enterprise of international thought? I believe an answer to this question lies in the political and moral vocabulary of the modern state. There is not one vocabulary for international politics and another for domestic politics. We do not as a practical matter, for example, speak only the instrumental language of power when we engage in international politics and only the normative language of authority when we participate in domestic politics. We speak both languages in both spheres. I am only saying that international relations could no more be conducted exclusively in the language of power than could domestic relations between the state and the citizen be carried on exclusively in the discourses of legality and morality. A statesman or diplomat confined to the idiom of threat and inducement would surely be as handicapped as a domestic politician limited to that of legislation or a citizen to that of rights. Political agents in every sphere have recourse to all the tools of their trade. In practice, each discourse belongs to international and domestic politics alike. And insofar as theories seek, in the Hegelian manner, to give a philosophical account of preexisting practices, we cannot adequately theorize each sphere in only one idiom either.[35] I cannot believe that Martin Wight would disagree, since he resorts to all three discourses in his essays on states systems.[36]

The poverty of international thought in the history of ideas deserves a final comment. There is no denying Wight's observation that the literature of political thought, and especially the works of the great political thinkers, pays little attention to international relations as compared with the relations between the state and the citizen. But as I indicated, this may only reflect the uneven contribution of each dimension of the state to the good life in the past. It does not deny that political goods have always been derived at least in part from international relations. Today, political and moral reflection on international relations is on the rise arguably because the good life is affected more and more by events external to states. The growth of interest in international ethics involving urgent issues such as weapons of mass destruction, failed states, protection of human rights, humanitarian intervention, political reconstruction, economic assistance, environmental protection, and much else is an indication of that. Although most of that upsurge has occurred since Martin Wight's death in 1972, it nevertheless suggests that international theory cannot be restricted in the manner he argued and is constantly breaking any such bounds placed upon it.

CHAPTER 4

Martin Wight's Theology of Diplomacy

> Finality is not the language of politics.
> Benjamin Disraeli

Historian of International Thought

Diplomacy, its practice, its history, and its philosophy, is a preoccupation of Martin Wight's international thought.[1] Modern international society is understood to be a diplomatic system at its core.[2] The various activities and institutions of diplomacy, such as the exchange of resident ambassadors, the activity of communication between states, the practice of diplomatic immunity, the holding of congresses and conferences, the negotiation of treaties and agreements of various kinds, are not only a distinguishing feature but also a foundational element of any society of independent states. When the diplomatic system is absent we are not likely to be contemplating political activities that could accurately be labeled "international." When it is present we are almost certainly witnessing international relations. Diplomacy has a long history and a well-established theory, which is the business of scholars to elucidate in their teachings and writings. Historical and philosophical perspective on international relations is what Martin Wight very largely succeeded in bringing to his scholarship.

Diplomacy is a historical subject: it has a beginning in time. There was no diplomatic system, properly so-called, among the city-states of ancient Greece.[3] *Hellas* was a community of blood, language, and religion. The only principles the Greeks recognized for governing the relations of their city-states were those ordained by their Gods.[4] "There was no Greek Grotius."[5] Europeans in the high Middle Ages (A.D. 1200–1400) understood diplomacy, if they understood it at all, in an uncertain, ambiguous, and intermittent way.[6] Medieval "diplomacy" was not a central institution of a society of states; no such society yet existed nor were medieval states sovereign. It was an activity of a loosely connected ecclesiastical society of Christians, *respublica Christiana*. Medieval "diplomats," if we can use the term, were papal envoys or representatives of rulers of church, kingdom, principality, fiefdom, or city.[7] In medieval England Mayors of distant boroughs met and negotiated "commercial treaties."[8] "The right of embassy was not spoken of in theory or regarded in practice as diplomatic representation, a symbolic attribute of sovereignty. It was a method of formal, privileged communication among the members of a hierarchically ordered society . . . The precise definition of a body of diplomatic principles had to wait for a revolution in men's thinking about the nature of the state."[9] This is evident from English usage of the word "diplomacy," which begins its history in the seventeenth century referring to diplomas, that is, official documents. "Ambassador" dates to the late fourteenth century: Chaucer wrote of them.[10] But "diplomacy" only acquires its standard signification in the late eighteenth century, as the management of international relations by negotiations.[11]

Diplomacy is also a subject of political thought: it raises normative questions as well as instrumental questions.[12] Diplomacy is a specialized political activity between and among selected people who normally are agents and representatives of independent states. The world of the diplomat is a world created and kept in existence by independent governments whose agents and representatives must deal with each other at least from time-to-time and most likely on a standing and regular basis. We cannot separate the world of the diplomat from the states they represent; the one is not completely intelligible without the other. The activity of diplomacy, as Wight sees it, is inextricably connected to the existence and operation of a system or society of states, which has its own special ethics.

Diplomacy is an activity involved in dealing with foreign governments who are independent from ourselves and probably also different from ourselves but whose policies and activities must be of interest and concern to us because we could be affected by them and we do not control them, at least not completely. They are not a part of us, that is, our country. If they were a part of us, diplomacy would not be called for. States cannot choose their neighbors and not every neighbor is a good neighbor. Some neighbors may not be easy to deal with: in Anglo-French relations that would probably be the prevailing historical view from both sides. In Anglo-American relations, after the war of 1812, the history by and large is one of good neighbors and close relations. Diplomats are called upon to deal with neighboring states, both good and bad, regardless. The diplomatic system exists to manage and adjust and, if possible, to reconcile the various interests and concerns involved in the relations of the governments of sovereign states some of which are bound to be in disharmony or even in conflict on certain occasions.

Diplomacy, in its classical *persona*, is not an aggressive activity of crushing neighbors or obliterating them and wiping them off the political map. Neither is it a quasi-religious activity of making them better by converting them into versions of ourselves. This of course happens, for example, during or following wars, revolutions, reformations, or during times of imperialism, or expanding civilizations. But such an international activity exceeds the normal bounds of diplomacy that are confined to accommodation of already existing and usually recognized others. The diplomat possesses a *dignitas*, which derives from the state he or she represents. We speak of war diplomacy in awareness that the activity does not and arguably must not cease during wartime, which creates its own problems of diplomacy. It is usual, however, to think of diplomatic activity as a branch of politics in the service of peace and not war. Diplomats, at their best, are peacemakers and peace-preservers rather than warmongers. Classical diplomacy, Martin Wight's phrase, is a civilized and civilizing activity.

Diplomacy is not only expedient and useful in an ad hoc way but it is also necessary to a working system or society of states: some degree of contact and communication among independent governments is desirable and probably unavoidable. This is because states exist cheek to jowl. Diplomatic activity as such, however, is not a world of necessity or inevitability; it is a world of choice, policy, and decision. The choices involved in diplomatic activity are often difficult choices and sometimes they are very hard choices indeed. But whether they are easy or difficult they are always affected by circumstances the most important of which are the presence and policies of other states with regard to which they are addressed. There is no best or ideal foreign policy choice; there is only the best in the circumstances that exist at the time. The moment will pass and tomorrow the situation may be different. Diplomacy is historically and geographically situated and its arrangements and agreements are provisional. It is not an activity of seeking and journeying to some better world that is free of the problems that beset the international system. Diplomats, conventionally understood, are not missionaries: diplomacy is not an activity of conversion. It is an activity of carrying on and staying afloat in the world of states, whether the international oceans are stormy or calm, and fathoming what is called for at the moment by the circumstances of the day. A diplomat is somebody who knows this in his or her bones.

One of Wight's main purposes in studying diplomacy is to explore this activity in its historical and philosophical depth. In one of his essays he argues that historical interpretations of diplomacy are more likely to capture "the quality of international politics" and "the workings of the states-system" than "much recent theoretical writing based on the new methodologies."[13] Among his examples of historical interpretation is Garratt Mattingly's unsurpassed study of *Renaissance Diplomacy*, which is a good demonstration of Wight's point that the diplomatic system is the heart of modern international society.

Martin Wight's notion of diplomatic study can be summarized as follows. He understood it to be a historical inquiry into the prevailing ideas and ideologies involved in international relations and, in this case, diplomatic relations. The ideas he sought to track down were not so much pragmatic or instrumental as moral and ethical. Diplomacy, as he discerned and studied it, is a sphere of human relations with its own distinctive norms that reflect the complexities, uncertainties, and anxieties of different member states of international society. He was of course profoundly interested in the *pragmata* of diplomacy, the repertoire of expedient diplomatic means and maneuvers, as registered in encounters between diplomats at different times and places. His acute historical sense of these encounters, his intimate knowledge of so many cases in point, of the leading characters involved in the play of diplomatic activity at different times, is a strength of his thought. But he was always more interested in the background ideas and the major thinkers associated with them. These ideas endured while diplomats came and went. Martin Wight's thought at this point echoes that of Edmund Burke, whom he greatly admired.

Wight was clearly fascinated by the thought of those who were involved in the conduct of diplomacy: statesmen's recollections and diplomats' reflections on their own activities and that of counterparts with whom they dealt—especially in the great crises of their day. His reading of political and diplomatic memoirs was extensive and probably unmatched in its scope and depth. He was especially interested in the general reflections of famous statesmen and diplomats, which sometimes contained deep insights: perhaps deeper insights than those achieved by academic students of the subject. This is evident, for example, in the commentaries of Alexander Hamilton, W.E. Gladstone, Guiseppe Mazzini, Otto von Bismarck, Woodrow Wilson, V.I. Lenin, Winston Churchill, John Foster Dulles, and the many other statesmen and diplomats who populate the indexes of his books. But this should not be taken to mean that he ignored leading political and legal thinkers. On the contrary, he shaped his own thinking under the long shadows of the thought of Thucydides, Machiavelli, Suarez, Grotius, Hobbes, Burke, Kant, and Marx, among others. He sought to capture the idea of diplomacy in the most complete way possible—which means that he wanted to understand it historically and philosophically. In this ambition Martin Wight was remarkably successful.

His writing on diplomacy and other subjects of international relations belongs to the *genre* of the history of ideas and particularly the history of international thought. International relations was at base a world of ideas, of thought. He characterized international thought as expressing or illuminating different "traditions." He discerned three recurring traditions, which he labeled as Grotian (rationalism), Machiavellian (realism), and Kantian (idealism) after the names of the leading thinkers associated with each one.[14] It is these persisting ideas and approaches that he endeavored to capture and clarify in his lectures and writings.

Christian and Skeptic

Before we try to retrieve the main elements of Martin Wight's thought on diplomacy, it is necessary to be aware of the intellectual and moral temper of his mind. Unlike most twentieth-century scholars of international relations, he held a view of the subject that was affected if not indeed shaped by Christian theology in the Augustinian tradition.[15] If we fail to appreciate the Christian predilection of Wight's international thought there is a good chance we shall misunderstand it.[16]

Martin Wight was a traditional Christian. A traditional Christian is someone who recognizes the permanent place of sin and grace in human affairs and does not subscribe to any doctrine of the progress and perfection of humankind. Humans may perhaps mature in their moral refinement and they may also progress in the technical sophistication of their lives. There is civilization and there is science, both of which are human achievements of the greatest importance. Nations can advance in both culture and technology—as many have advanced over the past several centuries. Yet, even if some people are well-meaning and sincerely try to do their best, even if human societies can and do move forward at certain times or places, humankind as such cannot progress: the leopard cannot change its spots: human nature is permanently fixed: natural law is engraved in the human heart and mind. The heaviest sin is committed when people think they can create heaven on earth, which is the sin of pride in which they attempt to take the place of God.

One of the most sophisticated and enduring expressions of that traditional Christian theology is found in the thought of Augustine. Martin Wight is an Augustinian in his view of international relations.[17] Hedley Bull draws attention to the importance of Christian theology in Martin Wight's thinking:

> In the Christian's attitude towards the march of history, he thought, two attitudes should go hand in hand: on the one hand, the rejection of secular optimism; on the other hand, the acceptance of theological hope. "Hope," as he once put it, "is not a political virtue: it is a theological virtue." In his 1948 article in the *Ecumenical Review* he attacks the Pelagian belief that "we are on the whole well-meaning people doing our best, who will somehow muddle through," together with secular optimism, "the belief that because we are well-meaning and doing our best, things will therefore tend to come right; or (for optimism sidesteps subtly into fatalism) that what does happen will be for the best anyway." Neither of these beliefs, he says, is Christian. "We are not well-meaning people doing our best; we are miserable sinners, living under judgment, with a heritage of sin to expiate . . . We will not somehow muddle through; if we . . . cast ourselves upon God's mercy we have the promise that we shall be saved—a totally different thing, which carries no assurance of muddling through in this world."[18]

In noticing his deep and abiding opposition to Pelagianism (in its modern idiom of secular faith in progress) Bull locates the religious root of Martin Wight's international thought. Here is how one commentator sums up the doctrine: "We are born characterless (*non pleni*), and with no bias towards good or evil (*ut sine virtute, ita et sine vitio*). It follows that we are uninjured by the sin of Adam, save in so far as the evil example of our predecessors misleads and influences us (*non propagine sed exemplo*). There is, in fact, no such thing as original sin, sin being a thing of will and not of nature."[19] Peter Brown captures Augustine's theological opposition to Pelagianism perfectly: "The deadly perfectionism of the Pelagians was distasteful to him: he also was trying to be perfect; but [in Augustine's words] 'in their exhortations, let them urge the higher virtues; but without denigrating the second-best.' " Wight was critical of the same intellectual arrogance that Hans Morgenthau[20] criticized and Reinhold Niebuhr[21] portrayed as the "ideological taint" of modern social thought, which was and still is a predilection of many European and American politicians, intellectuals, journalists, and academics—including scholars of international relations.

Michael Oakeshott was struck by exactly the same ideological tendency of modern thought. He saw Pelagianism as a distinctive style of modern politics, what he termed "the politics of faith," which contrasted with its opposite number, "the politics of skepticism."

> In the politics of faith, the activity of governing is understood to be in the service of the perfection of mankind . . . Human perfection is to be achieved by human effort, and confidence . . . springs here from faith in human power and not from trust in divine providence . . . Perfection, or salvation, is something to be achieved in this world: man is redeemable in history. And it is on account of this belief that it is both relevant and revealing to speak of this style of politics as "Pelagian" . . . these ideas . . . have an indelibly modernistic appearance.[22]

In Oakeshott's terms, Wight is condemning the politics of faith and invoking the politics of skepticism as the form of action that diplomacy must take if it is to achieve what only diplomacy can achieve in international affairs: mutual accommodation of independent states.

A traditional Christian is somebody who is resigned to human imperfections and flaws and is profoundly skeptical about the possibilities of human perfectibility and the fulfillment of human destiny in the city of man.[23] He or she accepts the second best, or the best in the circumstances. Perfection, for such a Christian, is something that is only attainable in a spiritual world beyond that of the living, *Civitas Dei*.[24] It is only attainable by accepting the teachings of Jesus and the apostles of the Christian church and by devoting oneself to these teachings during one's life. Pelagianism seeks to create heaven on earth, which, for a traditional Christian, is both impossible and profane. Wight takes a dim view of the politics of faith, which he believes is utterly misplaced. Hope is a theological virtue. In politics, and certainly in international politics, we should of course strive to do our best in the circumstances we face. But we should be under no illusions about what we may hope to achieve by our efforts, for all that we can reasonably expect is at best a temporary solution to a recurring problem the root of which is the human animal. In other words, we cannot escape from our flawed selves or from other flawed selves with whom we must deal. "If this is indeed the character of international politics, it is incompatible with progressivist theory."[25]

The traditional Christian's attitude to politics is one of pessimism about what might be achieved and gratitude for what is achieved but it is not one of hope or confidence that anything can be achieved if we only put our minds to it and keep an open heart. Hedley Bull comments on this point in connection with the thought of Martin Wight:

> In his attitude to international affairs he was remarkably free of the impulse that drives so many students of the subject to advocate policies or canvass solutions to the problems of the day. Wight emphatically did not stand for an attitude of what today is called political commitment, and this was because his commitment, while it was very powerful, was not political in nature, but intellectual and moral—and, most fundamentally of all, religious.[26]

Detachment, skepticism, and the ability to hold oneself aloof from the subject that one is studying, in this case diplomacy, while yet appreciating the difficulties and dilemmas that the activity presents to the people involved is a striking feature of Wight's thought. Wight usually does not take sides, and that arguably is because any secular ideology or political position is of limited importance, is transitory, and perhaps trivial, when viewed from the perspective of traditional Christianity. When he takes sides, for example, against deception and machination and against propaganda, he is at the same time affirming at least minimal reasonableness, honorableness, and mutual respect. He is, in this regard, siding with the Grotians whom he portrays as upholding the values of international society.[27]

Ethics of Classical Diplomacy

Wight turns to Harold Nicolson for a definition of diplomacy that he quotes with seeming approval. "Diplomacy . . . in its essence is common sense and charity applied to International Relations; [it is the] application of intelligence and tact to relations between governments . . . The worst kind of diplomatists are missionaries, fanatics, and lawyers; the best kind are reasonable and humane skeptics."[28]

Wight characterizes this as the "classical" conception of diplomacy and says "it is explicitly Grotius's."[29] The harmony with the worldly skepticism of traditional Christianity is easy to discern. International ethics involves recognizing and accepting one's responsibilities to others without sacrificing oneself. It goes without saying that diplomats are in the service of their own government and are responsible for carrying on its foreign policy to the best of their ability. But in addition, diplomats have responsibilities to their international counterparts. The ethics of classical diplomacy emphasize the importance of maintaining the minimum of human decency and reciprocity while upholding as far as that may be possible international peace and security. The vital idea is that of taking fully on board the circumstances of one's diplomatic counterparts and dealing with them in a way that not only defends or promotes the interests of one's own government, but also tries to address the interests of the other parties while seeking to uphold the practices, institutions, and values of international society. The essentials of Wight's conception of classical diplomacy are summarized in the following principles:

Honesty or truthfulness: don't tell lies or break promises, it does not pay and brings its own retribution; establish a reputation for straight dealing.[30]

Moderation and restraint: keeping a sense of proportion . . . requires the absence of assertiveness or national (and personal) egotism, and a readiness to make concessions, to give way on unessentials.[31]

Courtesy: seeking not diplomatic "victories," "triumphs," or "successes," all of which imply a defeated antagonist, but "agreements," which suggests common achievement; or perhaps seeking "victories" which come without being noticed. The art of diplomacy is to conceal the victory: "the best diplomacy is that which gets its own way, but leaves the other side reasonably satisfied."[32]

Respect for the other side: thinking the best of people . . . trying to share their point of view, understand their interests . . . [Anthony] Eden's *Memoirs* are full of examples of his capacity to get inside the mind of his opposite party and understand their interests.[33]

Grotians seek to uphold international society as an end in itself, and they see these principles as serving this end. Wight quotes George Kennan on this point: "The function of a system of international relationships is . . . to isolate and moderate the conflicts to which it gives rise, and to see that these conflicts do not assume forms too unsettling for international life in general . . . this is the task for diplomacy, in the most old-fashioned sense of the term."[34] Telling the truth is a greater expediency than telling a lie, for if the lie is taken for the truth it will return to trouble and upset whatever relations that were previously built up. The same can be said for a policy of extremes and lack of restraint, of discourtesy and disrespect, of disregard or contempt for the other side. Classical diplomacy is a civilizing activity both in itself and in its consequences. Herbert Butterfield captured this characteristic in a recapitulation of Sir Edward Grey's view, which I am certain Martin Wight would endorse:

[I]n diplomacy it was . . . wrong to meet everybody with distrust . . . indeed it was better to err on the side of trust than to be over-suspicious in negotiation. In these ways the art of international politics, in spite of its unpromising basis, can be brought to considerable urbanity and refinement. So much so that in the long run many people, who only see the surface of things, come to forget that there ever had been a sword behind the velvet—and imagine that the world had been naturally civilized all the time, civilized in its original constitution.[35]

As suggested, Wight's diplomatic ethics are not merely ends in themselves but are in addition wise and fitting means. They could be summed up as counsels of prudence and they are in that regard Burkean: they recommend policies and actions that take full account of what one owes to others and full account of the consequences.[36] The stratagems they counsel against clearly are wrong in themselves, but in addition they also have unwelcome consequences that in the end may carry a heavy price. This is evident from a brief assessment of each one. Diplomacy cannot be a deceitful or duplicitous craft or it will perish as an activity itself. To exist and flourish it requires good faith and straight dealing on the part of the statesmen and diplomats involved in it. Without confidence in one's counterparts diplomatic activity is unlikely to begin; if such confidence is lost it is likely to be jeopardized. If diplomacy is necessary, by this reasoning it cannot rest on duplicity. The same could be said of moderation and restraint and the willingness to be conciliatory whenever possible: it is not only right or proper conduct but it also contributes to diplomatic effectiveness in the longer term. It makes diplomatic arrangements and agreements more likely. Displaying courtesy and refraining from triumphalism likewise is not only the mark of civilized diplomacy; it is also necessary for bringing others into negotiation and for moving toward some understanding, agreement, or modus vivendi on matters of common concern. This leads to respect for the other side, for their point of view, and their concerns and interests. This is conduct that recognizes the other party as similar to oneself, as worthy, and as an equal with oneself: the principle of recognition. Dignity and mutual respect are the basis of any durable and fruitful relationship. These diplomatic norms clearly are indicative of a form or style of international relations that is valuable not only in itself but also for what it can help to bring about.

What, then, should we make of the ethics of classical diplomacy? At first glance it seems to be the ethics of British diplomacy or, perhaps, European or Western diplomacy. Wight acknowledges that Harold Nicolson's conception of diplomacy is actually a conception of "British Diplomacy."[37] It might therefore be argued that these practices cannot be recommended for they are not sufficiently general. In an important essay Wight asks: "How can we describe this cultural community? Does it consist essentially in a common morality and a common code, leading to agreed rules about warfare, hostages, diplomatic immunity, the right of asylum and so on? Does it require common assumptions of a deeper kind, religious or ideological?"[38] Is classical diplomacy confined to nations of the West? Hedley Bull commented on this important point: "Wight raises but does not answer the question whether the cultural unity that is a necessary presupposition of states-systems consists simply in a common morality and code, leading to agreement about the basic rules of coexistence among states, or whether it requires common assumptions of a deeper kind—religious or ideological."[39] If it requires a religious foundation then clearly it cannot extend across the entire breadth and length of the states system. A more strictly expedient diplomacy would seem to be required for managing international relations between nations of different civilizations. Martin Wight debated the issue but came to no firm answer: the jury was still out.[40] He did however acknowledge, fully, the place of expediency in diplomacy.

Machiavellians, Kantians, Grotians

For a traditional Christian it would be reasonable to suppose that there are, and there will always be, states whose agents and representatives will disregard the foregoing ethical principles, exploit them, condemn them, or work against them. This would include the following two styles of diplomatic activity: first that of deceit, guile, conspiracy, audacity, and second that of disdain, arrogance, high mindedness, high handedness. Martin Wight identifies the first style as Machiavellian and the second style as Kantian.

Machiavellian diplomats and statesmen can be characterized as those who hold a cynical view of classical diplomacy. They may see it as the comfortable ethos of satisfied states, for example, Great Britain in the nineteenth century, which were ruthless in the past but are now on top and can accordingly indulge norms of honesty and civility that preserve their privileged position. Machiavellianism is registered in negative notions of "diplomat" and "diplomacy": "The ambassador was the man who was sent to lie abroad for the good of his country"; "I can find no better signification for the word which typifies the pursuit . . . than double-dealing . . . It is expressive of concealment, if not duplicity."[41] Machiavellians may see anyone who enunciates the foregoing principles as disingenuous. Only those who are naive would take it seriously. Since naive diplomats and statesmen could not survive for very long such principles must in reality be part of a conspiracy to deceive. One must therefore respond with craftiness, stealth, strength, and boldness in order not to be exploited or bested. Respect for classical diplomatic norms would be irresponsible because that could put at risk the success of one's foreign policy if that policy depended on deception and double-dealing. One cannot trust other diplomats and their governments to the degree required by deference to such principles. They might fail to keep their word and leave us dangerously exposed. Better to betray them before they betray us.

Diplomacy cannot be based on the ethics of a gentleman's club. It can only be based on an instrumental approach that views world affairs as constantly shifting from one set of circumstances to another as determined by chance and contingency. "The Machiavellian conception of diplomacy can be organized under four headings: flux or change; fear and greed; negotiation from strength; and the technique of bargaining."[42] The only genuine ethics of diplomacy is that which counsels the use of vigilance and intelligence to correctly assess changing circumstances according to the opportunities or dangers they present, and to act accordingly in striving for advantage and strength or at least the avoidance of weakness: realism. To adopt this Machiavellian posture is to see the limits and risks of classical diplomacy in a fluid and changing world that is a source of both hazard and opportunity. It is also to grasp the higher responsibility that one owes to oneself and one's country. This is the well-known thesis of Machiavelli's *The Prince:*

> The gulf between how one should live and how one does live is so wide that a man who neglects what is actually done for what should be done moves towards self-destruction rather than self-preservation. The fact is that a man who wants to act virtuously in every way necessarily comes to grief among so many who are not virtuous.[43]

Some may view the principles of classical diplomacy as reflecting the values and prejudices of a conservative international order that leaves little or no room for change, particularly fundamental change, of the states system itself. People who long for change are necessarily impatient with the status quo. They may hold established institutions and traditional values in contempt because they see them as self-serving barriers to progress. It is not that classical diplomatic ethics are window-dressing: the velvet cloth draped over the steel sword. It is that the states system that it serves is standing in the way of an urgently needed international revolution. In this style of international thought, which Martin Wight labels revolutionary or Kantian, there is a better way of arranging and judging international affairs: make states the servants of humankind.[44] In its most revolutionary version, Kantianism is a secular eschatological doctrine of getting beyond the states system and replacing it with an entirely new political age that will finally put a permanent end to war and related predicaments that have always plagued world affairs. It is the theory of the permanent solution. To finally achieve this *cosmopolis* would be to fulfill human destiny on the planet.[45] That, of course, is the international politics of faith.

International revolutionaries reject the classical ethics of diplomacy because it tolerates what ought to be condemned: compromises that may be unfair or may entail inequality, lack of vision of a better world, failure or refusal to promote and pursue such a world. Kantians are people who are working for higher values, who are pursuing a grander vision, and who reject, as a matter of principle, the corrupting accommodations and adjustments of classical diplomacy. Order must be subservient to justice if human destiny is ever to be fulfilled. Furthermore, justice between states—what classical diplomacy also strives for—is not true justice. The latter notion is only intelligible in relations between individuals. Kantians are advocating a moral doctrine that is cosmopolitan, that is, inherently domestic. It is thus antagonistic to traditional diplomatic values, that is, the good of states and the states system. Martin Wight's Kantians are ideologists: their cherished vision of a better world must displace the politically pragmatic and morally compromised arrangements of conventional diplomacy, either Grotian or Machiavellian. Here Kantians disclose themselves as Pelagians. In this connection, Herbert Butterfield aptly speaks of "ideological diplomacy" which he contrasts with the values and institutions of an international order.[46]

The old diplomacy of the balance of power was often a target of international revolutionists. Wight singles out, for particular attention in this regard, the condemnations of President Woodrow Wilson when he occupied the center stage of world politics during and immediately after World War I. He quotes one of Wilson's speeches to Congress made not long after the United States entered the war, seemingly as the savior of Europe and the creator of a new world order: " 'the great game, now forever discredited, of the balance of power' was abolished. 'There must be, not a balance of power, but a community of power; not organized rivalries, but an organized common peace.' "[47] Here Wilson is giving voice to the Kantian ideal in which permanent cooperation and peace rather than persistent rivalry and belligerency between states shall prevail. The old diplomacy of the balance of power had no place in Wilson's vision. It was based on secret negotiation, which was antithetical to a politically desirable and morally defensible world order constituted by "open covenants openly arrived at." Wight refers to Wilson's remarks as revealing a doctrine of "anti-diplomacy": 'the process of negotiation and compromise was repugnant to him . . . his characteristic policy was not negotiation, but an appeal to public opinion, over the heads of the opposite government to *their* public. This follows from the abolition of diplomacy."[48] Hence Wight's sardonic commentary on Wilson's progressivism:

> Diplomacy is the attempt to adjust conflicting interests by negotiation and compromise; propaganda is the attempt to sway opinion . . . Conferences with revolutionary powers tend to be, not meetings where statesmen strike bargains, but forums where positions are asserted, either simply "for the record," or in a direct appeal to public opinion on the other side. It must be noted that Wilson's creed of "open diplomacy" was revolutionary, which was why it aroused suspicion among diplomatists of the old school in Europe.[49]

So it is not clear, in Wight's terms, whether Wilsonian statecraft is diplomacy at all for it attempted to abolish the traditional international order based on the balance of power which classical diplomacy sought to uphold.

The twentieth century witnessed several other versions of anti-diplomacy. Prominent among them were the revolutionist Communist International directed and supported from Moscow after 1917 and the militaristic opportunism and expansionism of the Fascists and the Nazis during the interwar period. After 1919 there was, as well, a proliferation of new states and corresponding diplomatic activities—the diplomacy of the weak and powerless—which also departed, at least in some degree, from conventional notions of the subject.

Machiavellian opportunism was strongly evident in speeches and recorded remarks of Mussolini and Hitler when they were asserting their power and testing the political will of rival states, most especially Britain and France, in the 1930s. But it was Machiavellianism with a difference. Sometimes it had a revolutionary, even a romantic, edge; it echoed Hegelian ideas of war.[50] Or it conveyed unmistakable signs of barbarism; R.G. Collingwood wrote of the Nazis as "the fourth barbarism."[51] Or it carried a message of Social Darwinism as applied to the world of states: the survival of the fittest. According to Hitler "Struggle is the father of all things . . . If you do not fight for life, then life will never be won."[52] Some of it was old-fashioned brinkmanship. According to Ciano, Mussolini's foreign minister, "the Duce considered that the party would win at a conference which was ready in certain circumstances to allow the conference to fail and take into account the eventuality of war as a result of failure."[53] "Thus Hitler constantly raised the price of peace which the League powers so anxiously desired."[54] In other words, warmongers can exploit peace-lovers by threatening to destroy the peace unless their demands are met.

This came to be known as appeasement that marked the limits and defeat of British diplomacy by Nazi statecraft. It made it apparent that classical diplomacy presupposed states that were civilized members of a gentleman's club. Hitler wanted no part of any such club which he characterized as a Western bloc: "The Western Democracies are dominated by the desire to rule the world and will not regard Germany and Italy as in their class. This psychological element of contempt is perhaps the worst thing about the whole business."[55] Some of it exploited the democratic principles of the League. After 1933, according to Wight, Hitler's speeches "appealed to the Wilsonian principle of self-determination . . . and gained their success thereby on the principle of the big lie."[56] Nazi diplomacy took advantage of the right of national self-determination by claiming reunion with Sudetan Germans living inside Czechoslovakia. The "big lie" is the anti-diplomacy of propaganda.

Borrowing Reinhold Niebuhr's distinction between hard and soft utopians, Wight distinguishes between "hard Revolutionists, like Lenin, and soft Revolutionists, like Kant."[57] Lenin saw the international revolution in Marxist terms: "the outcome of the struggle will be determined by the fact that Russia, India, China, etc. constitute an overwhelming majority of the population of the globe . . . in this respect there cannot be the slightest shadow of doubt what the final outcome of the world struggle will be."[58] At Lenin's funeral Stalin proclaimed the oath: "We vow to you, Comrade Lenin, that we will not spare our lives to strengthen and extend the union of the toilers of the whole world—the Communist International."[59] The "union" he referred to was of course the "Soviet Union." Here, then, was a revolutionary vision of a communist world governed from Moscow. But it was a world revolution built on struggle and violence and was, in that regard, about as far removed from Kantianism as it is possible to be. Here Wight is capturing the contradictory dynamics of ideological diplomacy. Both Wilsonianism and Leninism are visionary. But Wilsonianism is about ethics and right. Leninism is about power and force.

So in the twentieth century, Kantianism was not adequate to capture the entire idea of revolutionism which had both a hard and a soft version. Wilsonianism was a recognizable form of Kantianism. But the same could scarcely be said of Leninism. Force and fraud and other dark means were entirely justified by the communists as necessary to bring about their world revolution in which "international politics will be assimilated to the condition of domestic politics" and their goal of universal material equality will be achieved thereby.[60] Leninism was ruthless. But communism was at the same time revolutionist. Here revolutionism is reminiscent of holy war. In marked contrast, the soft revolutionists, liberals to a fault, recoiled from even contemplating and much less employing force to bring about revolutionary change. After World War I they set about arranging "Anti-war Treaties," "Non-Aggression Pacts," and various other renunciations of war. During the Cold War they placed their faith in unilateral disarmament and talk. Henry Wallace, who had been U.S. vice president from 1940 to 1944, claimed in the nuclear weapons debate of the 1950s: "War is impossible because of the H-Bomb: therefore ban the bomb, disarm, and talk."[61] Here Kantianism is scarcely distinguishable from pacifism.[62]

Yet another version of twentieth-century diplomatic activity that Martin Wight tried to capture in his thought was that of an expanding society of new states operating multilaterally via proliferating international organizations and conferences: the diplomacy of the ex-colonial Third World. Wight was a careful student of that development and his thought makes ample provision for it.[63] Here was a world of states that existed largely by courtesy of international society and particularly the major powers. More than most states they relied upon recognition of their sovereignty. Independence was a right more than a fact. They also found themselves in a world divided by the struggle between the Soviet Bloc and the West. These circumstances together with their anti-imperial sentiments (dictated by their status as former colonies) shaped their perspective on the world. "Wherever, whenever, and however it appears, colonialism is an evil thing and one which must be eradicated from the earth."[64] These sentiments were often expressed as a revolutionism that echoed Leninist ideology but lacked Soviet power. The world should be ruled by states representing the majority of its population, not by a minority:

> We can mobilize all the spiritual, all the moral, all the political strength of Asia and Africa on the side of peace. We, the peoples of Asia and Africa, 1400 million strong, far more than half the human population of the world, we can mobilize what I have called the moral voice of nations in favor of peace.[65]

This revolutionary pronouncement by President Sukarno of Indonesia, made at the 1955 Bandung conference of nonaligned states, could have been voiced by any number of leaders of postcolonial Asian or African states. It sought nothing less than to democratize the states system. Ironically, the international majority would consist of mostly nondemocracies (many of them dictatorships), the international minority of mostly democracies.

What the Third World states asserted, as their most fundamental principle, was the doctrine of nonintervention, which presupposed respect for their newly acquired sovereignty and recognition of their legal equality with all other independent states. Here they were following the footsteps of the new states set up in Central and Eastern Europe after the end of World War I. They wanted their weakness to be protected by international society. In that regard they were Grotians at heart. They believed at base in what Wight dubbed "two-dimensional" relations between states. "Revolutionist doctrine embraces a third dimension, which from a diplomatic standpoint is underground: relations between peoples." The Russian and Chinese communists attempted, for a time, to operate with relations of peoples in their clandestine Third World diplomacy, hoping the communist revolution would spread through Asia and Africa. This stratagem worked in a few places but failed overall. Most Third World statesmen insisted on two-dimensional, government-to-government relations in their dealings not only with the Western powers but also with both Moscow and Peking. They were against foreign interference in their domestic affairs from any quarter, East or West. They rejected and repudiated any "three-dimensional" relations of peoples. They affirmed and welcomed the conventional institutions and organizations of international society and they became staunch supporters of the United Nations, especially the General Assembly, whose role in world affairs they wished to expand—for by doing so they would be enlarging their own role.

Martin Wight captured all this diplomatic or quasi-diplomatic activity, and much more besides, in terms of his Grotian, Machiavellian, and Kantian distinctions, the variations of each, and combinations among them. Some of these combinations and deviations were novel. But most of this supposed novelty was scarcely anything more than old wine in new bottles. History had witnessed something very much like it before. The world stage upon which statesmen and diplomats carried on their activities and relations was larger than ever. There were many more minor players and bit players than in the past. There was much more diplomatic activity. There were scores of new international organizations. The management of international society by the great powers was more complicated and more difficult. But all of this is recognizable in terms of the classical ideas of international thought that Wight explored in remarkable historical detail. If international relations scholars bothered to probe beneath the surface of current world affairs, if they took account of history, if they traced ideas to their sources, they would notice many important continuities with the past. They would not mistake repetition for innovation. They would discover that international relations and diplomacy for the most part continued to be variations on familiar themes.

Augustinianism

I have tried to recover the essential outline and content of Martin Wight's thought on diplomacy as found in his texts and lectures and occasionally in those of his most able commentators. It only remains to consider, first his contribution to the theory of diplomatic relations, and second his own position in regard to the international ideas he explored.

What are the contributions and limitations of Martin Wight's thought on diplomacy? He could be criticized for creating little more than a taxonomy or typology without much explanatory power. This might be the core social science critique of his international thought. But it misses the point. He does operate with a typology: Machiavellians, Kantians, Grotians. But the point of this is: these categories are discernible in the ideas and thought of the existential world, they have a life of their own outside the academy; they have a basis in historical fact. His typology is not an a priori social science framework or model that is imposed upon the subject by the researcher and that generates its own "data." His typology is an arrangement and reenactment of "evidence" left behind by the decisions and actions of historical agents. Wight is seeking to interpret the evidence. His evidence is the thought and ideas of others—not his own. He is a historian of international ideas and arguably one of the best. Like any good historian of ideas, Wight is immersed in the thought of others.[66]

The strength of Martin Wight's international thought considered in these terms is also the weakness. What is impressive is his effortless command of the international thought of the past. The breadth and the depth of his historical reading is beyond comparison with any other twentieth-century historian of international ideas I have read. He is particularly gifted in detecting and organizing vital notions and insights scattered in the commentary of numerous statesmen and diplomatic practitioners. He shows how their observations and reflections fit into a larger picture or pattern—of which they themselves are very likely unaware. But these strengths are accompanied by corresponding weaknesses. Two major weaknesses can be singled out here. The first is his evident disinclination to consider the question as to whether his typology of international thought is sufficiently comprehensive and complete. The second is his tendency to prematurely break off from attempts to answer important questions that his approach provokes.

Do the three "Rs"—Realism, Revolutionism, and Rationalism—exhaust the leading ideas of international thought? Machiavelli, Kant, and Grotius, as well as kindred thinkers, have an ample place in his texts. Is any important thinker or body of thought left out? Are there other traditions that go unnoticed or unrecognized or undeveloped in his thinking? Martin Wight studied deeply and wrote extensively on empires and imperialism. These subjects have a large place in his texts. He writes of the Roman Empire and other ancient empires. He writes of medieval Europe in terms of empire. Above all, he writes of modern empires, particularly the British Empire.[67] But imperialism and colonialism do not feature as a systematic category of his international thought—which is surprising given his interest in the subject and extensive commentary on it. He does not gather together his scattered thoughts and comments on empire and fit them into his overall thinking on international relations. The quasi-diplomacy of imperial systems is not worked out, that is, the relations of dependencies to their metropole and to each other. In a similar vein, Wight could be criticized for failing to explore the important distinction between true diplomacy of authentic international relations and quasi-diplomacy of confederations and federations. The thought of Alexander Hamilton on the virtues of federation versus international relations, which comes under his scrutiny from time to time, could have been collected and fitted into the corpus of his diplomatic thinking. In short, the borderland between genuine diplomacy and quasi-diplomacy remains under defined in his work.[68]

Moreover, Wight recognizes a fourth category of international thought that he labels Quaker and places alongside the three "Rs." It seems to be a synonym for Christian pacifism. But it is not developed. He also could have systematized his extensive and insightful commentaries on the political and religious ideas of Latin Christendom, *respublica Christiana*. This would have given him an opportunity to draw a more extensive and precise distinction between a modern secular international world of bona fide diplomacy and a medieval theocratic *imperium* without it, along the lines of Garrett Mattingly's work—which influenced Wight.[69] But unfortunately this systematic analysis of religious thought on states and statecraft is not developed in his texts. This is all the more surprising given the spirit of his international thought, which, as indicated, registers a clear and strong note of traditional Christian theology.

The second major weakness of Martin Wight's contribution to diplomatic thought is the absence of sustained argument on some questions it raises. Wight frequently does not push his insights and reflections to their conclusions. After tracking down his quarry he breaks off the hunt and leaves it for others to catch. This may disclose excessive intellectual diffidence or perhaps a conviction that the subject does not lend itself to any final conclusions. Both of these tendencies are evident in his texts. His work in that regard compares unfavorably with that of Hedley Bull.

What I have in mind is evident in Wight's justifiably celebrated "Western Values in International Relations" which, although only an article in a book, nevertheless is a *tour de force*. The account of intervention and international morality given in the article is unrivaled by any other short study I am familiar with. But even in this outstanding essay important questions remain unanswered and arguments are not pursued to any conclusions that are intellectually satisfying. For example, at the end Wight raises the vital question of justice versus survival in international affairs, by introducing the maxim *Fiat justitia et pereat mundus*. He remarks: "The maxim has been applied in many different circumstances, and with many different interpretations both of 'justice' and of 'the world perishing.'" He points out noteworthy instances of contradictory use: "Perish the interests of England, perish our dominion in India, rather than that we should strike one blow or speak one word on behalf of the wrong against the right." "If the welfare of England requires it, international agreements can go to the Devil."[70] Wight speculates that nuclear weapons may change all this: "It is indeed only since 1945 that it has been possible to imagine that the price of justice may literally be the ruin of the world."[71]

The implications of this for diplomacy obviously are profound. It also raises fundamental issues for a traditional Christian. But it is left hanging in the air. He remarks that between the two quotations, which obviously represent extreme and opposing positions, "lies the moral sense we are considering." He is alluding to Grotianism. But that intermediate "moral sense," its pertinence for grasping this mind-boggling issue, is not investigated to the point of drawing conclusions. Instead, we are left with a tantalizing reflection: "These assumptions seem to lie within the province of philosophy of history, or belief in Providence, whither it is not the purpose of this paper to pursue them."[72] Presumably for Wight, the traditional Christian, it rests in belief in Providence. On this issue, as well as others he investigates, Wight leaves his reader wishing he had persisted in his inquiry to the end. One might compare this reticence in Wight's thought with Herbert Butterfield's writings, which also disclose the sensibilities of a traditional Christian commentator and the empirical knowledge of a very good historian. Butterfield wrote at length and far more robustly and conclusively on judgment, fear, righteousness, tragedy, and other foundational elements of traditional Christian teaching—including providence—as it applies to diplomacy, war, and other recurrent features of international affairs.[73]

Finally, what were Martin Wight's own leanings as regards the theoretical ideas he explored? He operates with remarkable detachment as regards the traditions he identifies: his predilections for any one of them are placed under very strict scholarly discipline. He admires Hobbes. Thucydides receives pride of place as the greatest international thinker in one of his essays.[74] He is a friend of Grotius and he gives natural law the respect it deserves. Kant also has a valued place in his thought. Marx and Lenin are approached with composure. Even Hitler's pronouncements are examined with detachment.

But some Kantians come in for heavy criticism. Woodrow Wilson in particular is a recurrent target of Wight's scarcely concealed hostility. He is fighting hard to keep his account of Wilson's statecraft cool and scholarly. Why Wilson who is, after all, a man of peace and an academic as well? I think it is because Wilson personifies the failure of many intellectuals and academics to recognize that the international world is deep, old, complex, and—at many points—incomprehensible. It does not readily surrender to abstract theories about it. Theory and history go their own different ways. Nor is it plastic. It cannot easily be shaped at will—including good will. It is one thing for scholars to prefer their neat theories to the cloudy and perplexing world of political reality. Their theories have no power to do any real damage. At worst they mislead their students. But when a professor of political science, namely Woodrow Wilson, becomes the president of the United States and tries to apply his academic ideas to American foreign policy—that is deeply worrying. One is reminded of Burke's well-known comment on university professors:

> A statesman differs from a professor in a university; the latter has only the general view of society; the former, the statesman, has a number of circumstances to combine with those general ideas, and to take into his consideration . . . A statesman, never losing sight of principles, is to be guided by circumstances; and, judging contrary to the exigencies of the moment, he may ruin his country forever.[75]

Wight's critique of Wilson can be construed as revealing a realist *persona*. But it also discloses his rationalism. Wight is a man of the middle ground and the middle way. He declared himself to be a Grotian.[76] He acknowledges the perennial tensions between natural law and state sovereignty. But the middle way is no highway, it is more like a meandering trail through forest and heath and it is easy to lose one's way. The theorist and practitioner to whose thought Wight is particularly drawn, in this regard, is Burke. His thought is Burkean more than anything else. Edmund Burke, M.P., surely would have subjected President Woodrow Wilson's international pronouncements to scornful criticism. Wight makes the following comment after quoting from Burke:

> Politics is the perpetual movement from one stage of the provisional to another. There are no complete solutions, only the constantly repeated approximation towards the embodiment of justice in concrete arrangements, which do as constantly dissolve with the passage of time. Thus to be a Rationalist politician is to exist in a state of moral tension between the actual and the desirable.[77]

Wight regarded this situation as the permanent predicament of political activity which history cannot erase. All the good will in the world is not enough to change it. Here Wight is speaking his own mind on the subject. Wight's position in this important regard, it should again be noted, is very near to that of Reinhold Niebuhr and Herbert Butterfield. The former saw political and diplomatic activity as permanently poised between human ideals and difficult circumstances: the tragedy of the human condition.[78] The latter saw tragedy and other basic human predicaments as lodged in the nature of international relations and as resistant to any ideologies or policies that might seek to overcome them.[79] Perhaps the best term for capturing their thought is Augustinianism.[80] The final point then is: unless we take hold of the religious dimension of Martin Wight's thought on diplomacy and international relations more generally we will not understand it.

CHAPTER 5

Changing Faces of Sovereignty

> A sovereign power may choose to subscribe to limitations without ceasing to be sovereign.
>
> F.H. Hinsley

The Syntax of Modern Politics

Sovereignty is one of the foremost institutions of our world: it has given political life a distinctive constitutional shape that virtually defines the modern era and sets it apart from previous eras. As A.P. d'Entrèves puts it: "The importance of the doctrine of sovereignty can hardly be overrated. It was a formidable tool in the hands of lawyers and politicians, and a decisive factor in the making of modern Europe."[1] And not only Europe: in the past century or two, sovereignty has become a cornerstone of modern politics around the world. It was originally an institution of escape from rule by outsiders and to this day it remains a legal barrier to foreign interference in the jurisdiction of states. Basic norms of the UN Charter (Articles 2 and 51) enshrine the principle of equal sovereignty, the doctrine of nonintervention, and the inherent right of self-defense.

The institution is, shall we say, a basic element of the grammar or syntax of modern politics.[2] It exists as a normative premise or working hypothesis of political life. It may not always be explicitly acknowledged as such and may, like an iceberg, be mostly hidden from view. But it silently frames the conduct of much of modern politics nevertheless. Sovereignty is like Lego: it is a relatively simple idea but you can build almost anything with it, large or small, as long as you follow the rules. The British (English) used sovereignty to separate themselves from the medieval Catholic world (Latin Christendom). Then they used it to build an empire that encircled the globe. Then they used it to decolonize and thereby created a multitude of new states in Asia, Africa, and elsewhere. Then they used it to enter the European Union (EU). It has other uses besides these.

My purpose is to investigate sovereignty in international relations in basic outline. Limitations of space dictate that this chapter can only be an abridgement of a large historical subject. The main questions, although by no means the only ones, which can and I believe should be asked about sovereignty are the following: What is sovereignty? What is its character and modus operandi? Who are the principals and agents of sovereignty? Who are the subjects of sovereignty? What would be involved in going beyond sovereignty in world politics? What are the values that sovereignty can be seen to uphold? The chapter is devoted to suggesting some responses to these questions, starting with the first and ending with the last.

Independence and Supremacy

What, then, is sovereignty? To begin, it is a constitutional arrangement of political life and is thus artificial and historical; there is nothing about it that is natural, inevitable, or immutable. Sovereignty is a juridical idea and institution. A sovereign state is a territorial jurisdiction, that is, the territorial limits within which state authority may be exercised on an exclusive basis. Sovereignty, strictly speaking, is a legal institution that authenticates a political order based on independent states whose governments are the principal authorities both domestically and internationally.

A caveat is necessary. Sovereignty is not an economic notion as it is sometimes made out to be. The expression "economic sovereignty" is a conflation of two different concepts that are best kept in separate compartments if we wish to be clear. A better term might be economic autonomy. This is not to say that sovereignty and economics are unrelated. Obviously they are related. It is merely to point out that the relation is a contingent relation and not a conceptual relation. Economic autonomy is the notion that a country's economy is insulated from foreign economic influence, or involvement, or control. This may or may not be desirable in any particular case. But it is a matter of policy and not one of definition. Rather than speak of the decline or loss of "economic sovereignty" it would be more to the point to speak of the difficulties that independent governments face in trying to pursue nationalistic economic policies, especially in our era of globalization.

Thus, like all independent states, Canada has the sovereign authority to issue and manage its own currency. The United States does not have the authority to do that in Canada. But for Canada and presumably for all states in similar circumstances of economic interdependence that right is a bit hollow. The Canadian government does not have much room for maneuver in that regard, because although monetary policy is set in Canada, the value of the Canadian dollar is heavily dependent on American monetary policy and on international currency markets. Hence although Canada has the right to its own currency, it has limited power or capacity to determine the value of that currency. Canada is a sovereign state but it does not possess very much economic autonomy.

Sovereignty is the basic norm upon which a society of states ultimately rests. Sovereignty is thus a precondition of international society properly so-called. If states were not sovereign, political life would have to rest on a different normative foundation, such as suzerainty, empire, or theocracy as was the case prior to the revolution of sovereignty, for example, the ancient Chinese suzerain-state system, the Roman Empire, medieval *respublica Christiana*, and so forth. A conceivable future world of non-sovereign states would have to be based on an alternative normative foundation of some kind, for example, global federation. But in a world of independent states certain norms are necessarily basic: norms of self-defense, equal sovereignty, nonintervention, reciprocity, and so on. This is the normative logic of the institution. J.L. Brierly identifies the following basic norms of sovereignty: "self-preservation, independence, equality, respect, and intercourse."[3] These norms are radically different from those that are basic in a world of Chinese suzerainty, Roman imperialism, or medieval theocracy, that is, state inequality, dependence, intervention, paternalism, nonreciprocity, and so on. In the absence of sovereignty the normative shape of world politics would be significantly different and in all likelihood it would be fundamentally different. In a world federation, for example, countries might resemble American "states," which under the U.S. constitution hold sovereignty jointly with the federal government, but they do not hold it exclusively by themselves.

F.H. Hinsley captures the core meaning of sovereignty: it is "the idea that there is a final and absolute political authority in the political community . . . and no final and absolute authority exists elsewhere . . . ."[4] In another place, he notes "sovereignty . . . is an assumption about authority."[5] We might say that sovereignty is the basic assumption concerning authority of modern political life, domestically and internationally. By "authority" I am of course referring to a right or title to rule. Sovereignty is the assumption that the government of a state is both supreme and independent. Regarding insiders, sovereignty is disclosed by the supremacy of a governing authority over everybody who lives in its territorial jurisdiction and is subject to its laws and policies. Internal sovereignty is a fundamental authority relation within states between rulers and ruled, which is usually defined by a state's constitution. Regarding outsiders, sovereignty is disclosed by the independence of a governing authority from other governing authorities. External sovereignty is a fundamental authority relation between states, which is defined by international law. Thus, as seen from inside a state, sovereignty is paramount authority, and as seen from outside it is independent authority.

Most of the time there is an established and recognized set of states in the world whose title to sovereignty is not contested to the point of serious uncertainty. There are of course occasions when things are not taken for granted and sovereignty is anything but habitual. These are moments when political life gets interesting from an academic point of view. There is a chameleon-like narrative of sovereignty that this chapter attempts to recapitulate briefly. Sovereignty, in that respect, should be understood as an institution that is periodically renovated to respond to new historical circumstances. There are of course limits to the renovations that can be made to any institution, including sovereignty, beyond which it is changed out of all recognition and it can no longer be said to exist as such. But viewed historically, these limits are rather broad and flexible. And no such fundamental change has occurred as yet.

Because sovereignty is so fundamental, so much a fixture of modern political life, these occasions when questions are raised about sovereignty are likely to be highly contentious and sometimes even combative moments. In Canada, the sovereignty of Quebec has been raised in recent decades with increasing political intensity. There is a deep division of public opinion on this issue, which has been disruptive of Canadian political and economic life. A similar question, posed by certain Slovak politicians, led to the peaceful break-up of Czechoslovakia into two successor states after the Cold War, the Czech Republic and Slovakia. A comparable partition could yet happen in Canada. These are peaceful episodes whose international dislocations are local and minimal. This might not be the case if an existing sovereign is not only called into question peacefully but is also opposed by force. After the Cold War armed secession movements were mobilized by Chechens in Russia, by Serbians in Croatia, by both Serbians and Croatians in Bosnia, and by Albanians in Kosovo (Serbia-Montenegro)—to cite only a few well-known cases. The latter conflicts disrupted international relations in the Balkans region.

We should probably regard periodical reshuffling of the title to sovereignty, even major redistribution, as something to be expected from time to time. This could dislocate the political life of certain states and regions for a period. But it would not challenge the institution itself. The extensive reshuffling of sovereignty after the Cold War in the former Soviet Union and the former Yugoslavia was disruptive. These episodes not only challenged and overturned the existing territorial distribution of sovereign states. But they also confirmed the popularity of the institution. Sovereignty clearly is something that many people want to keep and many others want to acquire.

However, there are moments in world politics when the current modus operandi of sovereignty, that is, the existing rules and norms of the institution itself, are placed in some degree of doubt. The history of sovereignty has involved occasions of that sort, for example, when national self-determination became a basic norm of sovereignty or when colonialism became illegitimate and illegal. On both of these historical occasions the constitutional shape of sovereignty was altered significantly. This has happened in the past. It could happen again in the future: for example, if the doctrine of humanitarian intervention and international reconstruction of failed states becomes a generally accepted practice rather than occasional episodes. There may someday even be another occasion, reminiscent of the "Grotian moment" of the seventeenth century that may come to be regarded as the end of sovereignty and the beginning of some fundamentally different post-sovereign arrangement of world politics. Some scholars believe that that revolutionary time has already arrived.[6] (This point is pursued in chapter 7.)

A basic inclination of the society of sovereign states, however, is to prevent international revolutions and to keep international reformations to a minimum. International society is fundamentally conservative. Sovereignty is a historical institution and change has therefore to be met, but the encounter does not have to be a capitulation on the part of sovereignty. Nor could it be without putting the state system at normative risk. This conservative bias is a striking feature of the arrangement. It is justified by reference to political values that the institution is seen to underwrite and indeed foster. Among the most important of these values is international order and stability. As international circumstances change, however, requirements for order and stability also change, and the practices of sovereignty must change too. In the beginning, sovereignty was dynastic and imperial. Then it became popular and nationalist. In the second half of the twentieth century, in many parts of the world it became anti-imperial. After 2001 a hint of imperial sovereignty returned in connection with the American-led war on terrorism. The particular manifestations of sovereignty changed over time but the core notion as political independence remained the same.

Political Authority before Sovereignty

Because it is so easy to take sovereignty for granted it may be useful to recollect, if only in brief outline, the European political world before sovereignty became a standard of conduct in the relations of principalities, republics, monarchies, confederations, and so forth—what we refer to as states and the states system. If we can understand what that older historical world was basically like, and what the political change from medieval to modern essentially involved, we will be in a better position to grasp the operational meaning and significance of sovereignty.

A striking impression that the Middle Ages convey to anyone looking back from our vantage point at the dawn of the third millennium is one of astonishing diversity concerning political authority. By comparison our international world has a remarkable degree of uniformity centered on the institution of sovereignty, which is now global in extent. The only uniform institution that existed across Western Europe and by far the most important institution was the medieval theocracy—Latin Christendom—which was at one and the same time both a religious and a political organization. *Respublica Christiana* (defined below) holds the key to our understanding of that time.

In the late Middle Ages and early modern era, political life was not sharply differentiated from other departments of social life. Government authority was not clearly public; in most places a king's (public) realm was also in significant part his or her (private) estate.[7] Medieval commentators distinguished "the king's two bodies," his or her personal body and the body politic.[8] Rulership was in many places largely the private affair of dynastic states. But in other places, it was the corporate activities of religious foundations or commercial organizations and in yet other places it was the communal property of cities, towns, guilds, or estates. There were many different kinds of "political" authorities whose relations were ambiguous and whose responsibilities and activities could easily conflict. Sometimes and indeed quite often it was difficult to distinguish political and religious authority. Even to try to make such a distinction risks misconceiving the medieval world in which the political was entangled, inextricably, in the theological. Some of the leading political authorities were bishops or heads of religious orders who controlled extensive semiautonomous territories.

The late medieval and early modern map was not a territorial patchwork of different, sharply defined, colors that represent separate countries each under its own sovereign government. Instead, it was a complicated and confusing intermingling of lines and colors of varying shades and hues. "Europe was not divided up into exclusive sovereignties, but was covered by overlapping and constantly shifting lordships."[9] "Lordship" involved "a proprietary right to territory" but it did not imply sovereignty: a duke, a city government, or the head of a religious order could exercise lordship, which was not restricted to noble families—although most lordships were the hereditary tenures of such families.[10] Kings and other rulers were the subjects of higher authorities and laws. They were neither supreme nor completely independent. And much of the time local rulers were more or less free from the rule of kings: they were semiautonomous but they were not fully independent either. "The people" did not exist as such. Most people were vassals of superiors and some people were chattels of ruling families far more than they were subjects of independent states. Only rarely were they citizens of states, and only the wealthy class enjoyed citizen status, for example, the rich mercantile citizenry of the Venetian Republic.

It was unusual for a king's realm to be concentrated and consolidated at one place. A ruler's territory would often resemble an archipelago: peripheral parts were scattered like islands among the territory of other rulers; core parts were perforated and interrupted by the intervening jurisdictions of other authorities. Some rulers held fiefdoms within the territorial domains of other rulers that gave them the status of semi-independent vassals. Many dynastic states were composites or conglomerates. Rulers had more than one country under their sovereignty.[11] Rulers also frequently occupied different offices in their different territories, which affected the way they had to rule these territories, such as the kings of Prussia, who were absolute monarchs in Konigsberg but were imperial vassals of the Holy Roman Emperor in Berlin, or the Habsburg's themselves, who later were autocrats in Vienna and Prague but were constitutional monarchs in Brussels.

If we can stretch a word and speak of "sovereignty," in the first instance, the sovereign was God whose commands were generally acknowledged by Christians as requiring obedience. In the second instance, it was the pope, the bishop of Rome and Vicar of Christ, God's representative on earth, who presided over Christendom.[12] The core political idea was that of *respublica Christiana*: the notion that secular authorities no less than spiritual authorities were subjects of a higher authority, God, whose commandments were expressed by the precepts of Christianity. Both secular and religious authorities were Christ's subjects and servants. According to St. Paul: "The state is there to serve God . . . The authorities are there to serve God . . . All government officials are God's officers."[13] *Respublica Christiana* was based on a joint structure of religious authority (*Sacerdotium*) headed by the pope and political authority (*Regnum*) headed by a secular ruler designated as emperor (in the late Middle Ages and early modern era that office was held by the head of the Habsburg dynasty). In short, if there was a "sovereign state," it was the Christian Empire, *respublica Christiana*. Before a system or society of such states could fully emerge, the superior authority of the papacy and the imperial office had to be extinguished or at least rendered superfluous.

Respublica Christiana was thus a *universitas* rather than a *societas*. A *universitas* is a human association that has a commanding authority and an overriding purpose, which is the standard against which all conduct is judged. *Respublica Christiana* was a unified authority in theory, however shaky in practice, which was devoted to the overarching purpose of Christian redemption and salvation.[14] The medieval *universitas* was a community of Christian believers, which was the duty of the pope and the emperor, of kings, barons, bishops, priests, and indeed of every Christian to uphold. Christian rulers were defenders of the faith. Latin Christendom was a religious–political community that encompassed all social divisions, including those of political jurisdiction, and gave at least minimal unity and cohesion to Europeans, whatever their language and wherever their homeland happened to be.[15] Even if the actuality of unity varied widely from one place or time to the next and was sometimes nonexistent "the belief in unity was deep-seated and died hard."[16] Since it was based on the Christian religion there was no room in Latin Christendom for Greek, Coptic, or other Christians, for Christian dissenters, reformers, or heretics, or for pagans or nonbelievers, not to mention followers of other religions. Medieval Christians thus drew a sharp line to separate their world of true faith from the false Christian, the non-Christian and the anti-Christian world. This boundary was not only personal; it was also territorial. A similar border was drawn later to separate the European and then Western world of sovereign states from the non-Western world that was deemed to be incapable or unworthy of sovereignty and was thus a candidate for European imperialism and colonialism.

Respublica Christiana presided loosely over European political–religious affairs not only by means of the papacy and the office of the emperor, but also by means of periodic councils of the church. One of the most important conferences in the emergence of sovereignty was the Council of Constance that put an end to the "great schism" (1378–1417) in Latin Christendom when there were several popes each claiming to be the Vicar of Christ and to represent the authority of the papal monarchy.[17] This conciliar intervention in papal authority was followed by the Council of Basle (1449), which finally gave up on the attempt to reestablish the unity of the Western church by conciliar means. This opened a way for the emergence of states with greater authority than had existed previously.[18] Here, arguably, was the first clear intimation of a postmedieval political world based on the *societas* of sovereign states as the defining and unifying institution.[19] Unlike a *universitas*, a *societas* accommodates different authorities and is thus governed not by any commanding agent or purpose but, rather, by a general rule, or norm, which those authorities recognize, are subject to, and are expected to subscribe to. Following this reasoning, international *societas* consists of a variety of states each free to devote themselves to their own national interests provided they observe international law, which is a set of general norms that vouches for the authenticity of sovereign states.

The Medieval ecclesiastical–political order began to fall apart during the sixteenth century under the dual shocks of the (initially Italian) Renaissance and the (initially German) Reformation that occurred at about the same time. The Renaissance involved the emergence of independent Italian city-states, which formed a regional state system that soon spread north of the Alps. Other European rulers took their political cue from the Italians and the arts and sciences of the Renaissance, including the political art of independent statecraft, spread to all of Western Europe. Crowned rulers of dynastic and absolutist states claimed for themselves the divine right to rule that previously belonged to the pope. Subsequently, <u>raison d'état</u> and more narrowly <u>realpolitik</u> or in other words the morality of the interests of the state became the primary and sometimes the only justification of state-craft.[20] By the sixteenth century the papacy itself had become a state: one among several rival Italian powers.[21] If the pope was now an Italian states-man could he still also be the presiding authority of *respublica Christiana*?

The Reformation involved a struggle for religious freedom (by Reformers, later called Protestants) against religious orthodoxy (by Catholics) and simul-taneously for political authority (by secular rulers) over religious matters, which meant freedom from outside interference. The political theology of Protestantism disengaged the authority of the state from the religious sanc-tion of *respublica Christiana*.[22] One of the clearest instances of disengage-ment was King Henry VIII of England's divorce not only from Catherine of Aragon, which the pope refused to sanction, but also simultaneously from *respublica Christiana*, as registered in the Act of Supremacy (1534) that abolished papal authority and elevated the King to Supreme Head of the Church.[23] The Church in England became the Church of England. The notion of sovereignty is systematically explored at length and in depth for the first time in the French vernacular in Jean Bodin's sixteenth century political treatise *Les six livres de la Republique* (1576).[24] This was not a study of *respublica Christiana*. It was a study of the French monarchical state as a freestanding and self-regarding political entity. "It is most expedient for the preservation of the state that the rights of sovereignty should never be granted out to a subject, still less to a foreigner, for to do so is to provide a stepping-stone where the grantee himself becomes the sovereign."[25] This political counsel was a rejection of the Middle Ages.

Westphalian Sovereignty

The great transformation from medieval to modern thus involved at its core the institution of the sovereign state and the corresponding *societas* of states. When, exactly, this happened is a subject of debate among scholars. Martin Wight sees its tentative beginnings in the conciliar movement of the fifteenth century.[26] F.H. Hinsley sees its full historical manifestation only in the Concert of Europe in the 1820s.[27] Most scholars, however, see the seventeenth century and particularly the Peace of Westphalia that settled the bloody Thirty Years War (1618–48) as the best historical marker for symbolizing that fundamental turn in European political life.

It is important to understand the Westphalian moment from the perspective of that time and not from the present time, insofar as that is possible. The conceptual and linguistic categories available to the statesmen at Westphalia were those of the late medieval era.[28] In spite of their confessional differences, as Catholics or Protestants, they had a notion of being members of one community, the basis of which was the Christian religion.[29] They still spoke of "Christendom" and of their peace congress as the "senate of the Christian world." They expressed their agreements in Latin. The peace treaties do not specifically include much evidence for the claim that Westphalia is the crucial turning point in the emergence of sovereignty. Westphalia was an important stage, perhaps the most important, in the long retreat that lasted over several centuries during which time *respublica Christiana* was obliged to surrender more and more authority to the emergent states of Europe. "At Westphalia the states system does not come into existence: it comes of age."[30] Westphalia is not a literal moment of political transformation but, rather, the symbol of this change.

After Westphalia the language of international justification gradually shifted, away from Christian unity and toward international diversity based on a secular society of sovereign states that acknowledged common practices and principles of international law. By the time of the Peace of Utrecht (1712–13) the rulers of Europe understood each other as "essentially . . . self-determining actors, none of which was entitled to dictate to others."[31] The treaties of Westphalia and Utrecht still referred to Christendom but they were among the last to do that. For what had come into historical existence in the meantime was a secular European society of states in which overarching political and religious authority was no longer in existence in any substantive sense. The arch constituted by *respublica Christiana* had been broken. An anarchical society of sovereign states had taken its place. Europe displaced Christendom. Europe was now conceived as a plurality of territory-based political systems each with its own independent and supreme governing authority. What had been a political–theological *universitas* became an international *societas* of sovereign states. This is what Westphalia stands for.

The institution of sovereignty sorted out the uncertainty and indeed the confusion around the question of authority that existed in the later Middle Ages. The new sovereign state escaped from the medieval system of dispersed authority and successfully established and enforced its own centralized authority. The state captured its territory and turned it into state property, and it captured the population of that territory and turned them into subjects and later citizens. Internally, there was no room for semi-independent territory or people or institutions. Territory was consolidated, unified, and centralized under a sovereign government. As indicated, in many cases the Christian churches, Catholic and Protestant, fell under state control as rulers claimed a divine right to rule their territories.[32] The population of the territory now owed allegiance to the sovereign and had a duty to obey the laws of the land. Externally, there was no room for any intervening overarching authority comparable to the pope or the emperor. *Rex est imperator in regno suo*: king is emperor in his own realm. The familiar territorial patchwork map was brought into being in which each patch was under the exclusive jurisdiction of an independent state. All territory in Europe and, eventually, all territory around the world was partitioned by sovereign governments and placed under their independent authority. Although the Christian Empire survived formally until the early nineteenth century, it had long been reduced to a hollow shell. *Respublica Christiana* was displaced by a *societas* of independent states that operated according to common norms of self-defense, equal sovereignty, nonintervention, reciprocity, and so forth.

Imperial Sovereignty

When a government exercises supreme authority over a foreign territory, it can be said to possess imperial sovereignty. A foreign territory is somebody else's homeland. Imperial sovereignty is thus a denial of local sovereignty in foreign countries. Sovereignty gave imperial states independent status not only in their homelands but also in their foreign territories while simultaneously imposing a dependent status on the populations of those same territories. This denial of equal status is often the seed of the demand for political independence on grounds of national self-determination.

After the Westphalian revolution, imperialism within Europe carried a taint of medieval feudalism and was contrary to the political norms of a *societas* of independent states. There were of course empires and indeed many of them. But Europe was no longer an empire. The empires that remained within Europe were dynastic states, most of which occupied territory outside the core area of the West European *societas*, for example, the peripheral lands in Central, Southern, and Eastern Europe of the Hapsburg (Austrian) Empire which was the remnant of the Holy Roman Empire. As indicated, attempts to reinstate an overarching empire across the heartland of *societas* Europe, for example, by France on several occasions, were resisted and prevented. But empire building by European states outside Europe was the fashion until the twentieth century. European governments saw commercial and military advantages in holding non-European territory in the Americas, Asia, the Pacific, Africa, and so forth. Many European states projected their military power and commercial enterprises into non-European oceans and continents, where they inevitably made contact and frequently come into conflict with local non-European political systems. The historical outcome was most often victory for the Europeans. Conquest, colonization, and other actions to extinguish the independence of non-European political systems were lawful in the eyes of Europeans. In their acquisition of non-European territory, the European states were guided by Roman principles and practices, that is, occupation of *terra nullius*, cession, prescription, inheritance, accretion, and conquest.[33]

When European states began to penetrate non-European continents and oceans, usually in competition with each other, sovereignty was conveniently available as an institution for annexing new territories. The imperialists understandably preferred a recognized title to foreign territory, rather than the uncertainty of holding it by force in competition with each other. European states consequently recognized each other's empires while agreeing not to recognize non-European political authorities. European imperialism was initially sanctioned by the *respublica Christiana*: for example, the pope's jurisdictional division of the Americas between the Portuguese and Spanish crowns in the early sixteenth century. But the notion that territorial occupations could be authorized by someone other than European sovereigns themselves; this idea disappeared. When the East India Company and the Hudson's Bay Company asserted claims to territories in South Asia and North America they did so by reference to royal charters they obtained from the British Crown. Sovereignty was a means of instituting the European states' claims to imperial authority over the rest of the world. Sovereignty was then understood to be a distinctly European institution. European states did not extend a right of membership in their *societas* to political authorities outside Europe; their international association was closed to outsiders. Non-European political systems were regarded as lacking legitimate or credible claims to sovereignty and were consequently subjected to unequal treaties and other discriminatory measures. The justification for this discrimination had a medieval ring: it was the right and indeed the responsibility of Europeans to rule non-Europeans and other peoples of different and by implication lesser civilization than their own. There was believed to be a "standard of civilization" to which non-Western societies had to measure up before they could make a legitimate and credible claim to sovereignty. The high point of European imperial sovereignty, in this regard, was reached in the second half of the nineteenth century. It is captured in the rationalization of a prominent British international lawyer published in 1880:

> International law is a product of the special civilization of modern Europe, and forms a highly artificial system of which the principles cannot be supposed to be understood or recognized by countries differently civilized . . . .[34]

Thus, in the relations of European states to each other Westphalia inverted the practices of medieval Europe. But in the relations of European states to political authorities outside the European heartland and in the rest of the world Westphalia reiterated medieval practices that asserted the superiority of Latin Christendom or Western civilization, the moral inequality of peoples, the right of intervention, the right of conquest, and ultimately the right of colonization and conversion to Western ways. The old medieval boundary between Christendom and the non-Christian world was redefined as a line between the civilized Western world and the not yet fully or properly civilized rest of the world.

European states that acquired imperial possessions governed them in the manner of a *universitas* with each one managing its own empire with a view of enhancing its own military or commercial interests. Some European Empires held numerous dependent territories abroad that were dispersed in a fashion reminiscent of the empires of medieval Europe. The British Empire is an excellent example of such a conglomerate state which consisted of its homeland, Great Britain, the British Dominions (Canada, Australia, New Zealand, South Africa), British India, and an assortment of crown colonies, colonial protectorates, protected states, and—in the twentieth century—mandated and trust territories scattered around the world.

In the late nineteenth and early twentieth centuries, European imperial states adopted a posture of paternalism in which they assumed the responsibility of educating their non-European subjects in the arts and sciences of Western civilization. This is evident in the General Act of the Berlin Conference (1884–85) which sanctioned the partition of Africa and called upon "all the Powers exercising sovereign rights [in the continent] . . . to watch over the preservation of the native tribes, and to care for the improvement of the conditions of their moral and material well-being . . . bringing home to them the blessings of civilization" (Article VI). It is evident in the League of Nations Mandates System that spoke of non-Western "peoples not yet able to stand by themselves under the strenuous conditions of the modern world" whose "tutelage" "should be entrusted to advanced nations" (Article 22). And it is evident in the UN Trusteeship System that aimed "to promote the political, economic, social, and educational advancement of the inhabitants of trust territories, and their progressive development towards self-government or independence as may be appropriate in the particular circumstances of each territory and its peoples . . . ." (Article 76). The aim was clearly to eventually erase the normative distinction between the West and the rest of the world thereby making a global *societas* of states not only desirable but also possible. But this was expected to take time and probably a long time in some cases. In the meantime imperialism or international trusteeship was necessary.

What proved fatal to the institution of imperial sovereignty, however, was the liberal political idea that there was something inherently wrong about a government that laid claim to foreign territories and populations—even if its intentions were benevolent. Increasingly it was felt that there was no longer any room in international society for governments that asserted a right to govern foreign territories and their populations. The *societas* of states was now understood as an institution in which membership could not be denied on grounds of religion, civilization, geography, race, and so on. This presupposed an intrinsic right to sovereignty, which is usually portrayed as a right of national self-determination. In spite of the thorny problem of determining who ought to exercise that right or in other words what is the nation for purposes of political independence in particular cases—which is anything but straightforward—that came to be virtually the only valid ground for asserting and claiming title to sovereignty. After centuries of legality, imperial sovereignty became unlawful. This is explicitly registered in various UN General Assembly resolutions, including Resolution 3103 (1973), which portrayed colonialism as nothing less than "a crime." It now takes special effort to remember that less than a century ago Western imperialism was a global institution that seemed destined to continue indefinitely.

Popular Sovereignty

By "popular sovereignty" I refer to the notion that sovereignty resides in the political will or consent of the population of a territory, rather than its ruler or government: that is, the independence of the people considered as a political community. Sovereignty begins its career as dynastic sovereignty. Political authority is autocratic or absolutist: "I am the sovereign, and I shall exercise authority over my subjects, wherever they live, at home or abroad." Sovereignty logically would seem to end its history as popular sovereignty. Political authority is democratic or at least representative: "We are sovereign over ourselves. Nobody else has any right to intervene in our country and exercise sovereignty over us without our consent."

The doctrine of popular sovereignty is anything but new. The idea was registered in the French and American revolutions of the late eighteenth century. It was evident in the American Declaration of Independence (1776) and the U.S. Constitution (1787). The American Federalists spoke of the virtues and advantages of "popular government" even while recognizing the vices and dangers.[35] The French constitution of 1791 declared "Sovereignty is one, indivisible, unalienable and imprescriptible; it belongs to the Nation; no group can attribute sovereignty to itself nor can an individual arrogate it to himself." The shadow of Rousseau's "general will" is not difficult to make out. Martin Wight sees the seed of popular sovereignty in the challenge to dynastic and absolute monarchy in the English "glorious revolution" of 1688–89.[36] One could argue, however, that the seed was already planted by the revolt against *respublica Christiana* and the creation of independent territorial realms—even if it took about three centuries for the flowering of the idea that state authority is rooted in the people who make their home in the territory.[37]

The explicit principle of national self-determination came much later in the history of sovereignty. President Woodrow Wilson's efforts to promote a notion of sovereignty based on consent made national self-determination a primary consideration in the formation of new states in Central and Eastern Europe in areas of the defeated or disintegrated Habsburg, Hohenzollern, Romanov, and Ottoman Empires. In the Atlantic Charter (1941), with Nazi occupied Europe in mind, the United States and Britain called upon sovereign states to "respect the right of all peoples to choose the form of government under which they will live." Popular will dictated sovereign right. The UN Charter committed its members to "friendly relations among nations based on respect for the principle of equal rights and self-determination of peoples" (Article 1). In 1950, the UN General Assembly "recognized the right of peoples and nations to self-determination as a fundamental human right." If the people or nation were easy to recognize in practice the story might end there. But this is not the case. This can come as no surprise after a moment's reflection on the relationship between peoples and territory. That is usually an awkward fit even at the best of times. The practical problem of determining who shall count as composing the people is anything but easy to solve. Even if it is clear who the people are, the problem still remains that territory and people are not usually neatly aligned. Furthermore, it is always problematical, both politically and morally, either to redraw territorial borders or to relocate people in an effort to achieve alignment. This is one of the big lessons not only of the attempt to create new national states in Central and Eastern Europe at the end of World War I, but also of various territorial partitions (e.g., Ireland, India, Palestine, Yugoslavia, etc.) and population transfers (e.g., at the end of World War II in Europe or in British India at the moment of independence in 1947).[38]

This is perhaps most evident from the issue of national minorities. When the people or the nation, rather than the ruler or the government, become the referent for sovereignty, the issue of national minorities arises at the same time. Point 12 in President Wilson's famous Fourteen Points speech (1918) acknowledged that postwar Turkey should be "assured a secure sovereignty," but he immediately added "the other nationalities which are now under Turkish rule should be assured an undoubted security of life and an absolutely unmolested opportunity of autonomous development." This came to be read as political independence. New nation states were subsequently recognized in those areas outside the Anatolian heartland of the Turkish nation. As it turned out, however, it proved impossible to draw sociologically rational borders that perfectly divided nationalities into separate territorial compartments of their own without domestic societal overlap, for example, Greece and Bulgaria had Turkish minorities. The same problem arose in the partition of the Habsburg Empire into new states. Redefined Hungary ended up with Slovak and Romanian minorities, Romania had a Hungarian minority, Czechoslovakia had Hungarian and German minorities, and so on.[39]

The issue of national minorities alerts us to the problems that surround the principle of national self-determination in a *societas* of sovereign states organized, fundamentally, on a territorial basis. National self-determination, strictly speaking, is realized in practice only in a relatively small number of cases of sovereign statehood. Most sovereign jurisdictions include several nations and peoples, and some jurisdictions contain many of them.

Uti Possidetis Juris

Does the existence of a discernible people determine the sovereignty of a territory, or does the existence of a recognized territory define the sovereign domain of the people who live there? The latter situation is nearer to historical reality. The current practice is to vest sovereignty in a bordered territorial homeland rather than a distinctive people or nation. This should not be surprising insofar as sovereignty is an institution that expresses a territorial definition of political authority.

In the twentieth century, the political map of the world was frozen in a territorial pattern shaped by the outcome of World War II and also by the colonial borders established in the non-Western world by European imperialists. These jurisdictions defined the postwar and postcolonial territorial status quo. Existing borders became sacrosanct and lawful border change correspondingly difficult. The right of territorial conquest was extinguished in the twentieth century. No longer could states acquire territory or lose territory by means of armed force. Nor, for all intents and purposes, could territory any longer be purchased, exchanged, rearranged, or altered in any way without the agreement of all affected states parties. In short, the current territorial boundaries of states acquired entrenched legality and corresponding rigidity.

The League of Nations Covenant undertook "to protect and preserve . . . the territorial integrity and existing political independence of all Members" (Article 10). The League failed but the UN Charter upheld the same juridical principle using identical language (Article 2). The 1960 UN Declaration on Granting Independence to Colonial Territories and Countries stated "any attempt aimed at the partial or total disruption of the national unity or territorial integrity of a country is incompatible with the purposes and principles of the Charter of the United Nations." The 1975 Helsinki Final Act expressed the principle "frontiers can [only] be changed, in accordance with international law, by peaceful means and by agreement." The 1990 Charter of Paris for a New Europe reiterated the same principle. It was the basis of the Dayton Agreement signed between Bosnia-Herzegovina, Croatia and Serbia. The two key articles read as follows:

The parties . . . shall fully respect the sovereign equality of one another . . . and shall refrain from any action, by threat or use of force or otherwise, against the territorial integrity or political independence of Bosnia and Herzegovina or any other state. (Article I)

The Federal Republic of Yugoslavia and the Republic of Bosnia and Herzegovina recognize each other as sovereign independent States within their international borders. (Article X)

The territorial status quo has been preserved almost without exception even in the face of armed challenges. In Europe, the major apparent exception is the unification of East and West Germany. It should be noted, however, that the external post-1945 borders of former East and West Germany were not altered in the slightest degree by reunification. It might be thought that the new states that emerged after the Cold War in the territory of former Soviet Union and former Yugoslavia contradict the juridical practice. But the external borders of each federation were not altered, and the internal borders were used to define the territorial jurisdiction of the successor sovereign states. The latter were subsequently upheld even in the face of armed efforts to change them: for example, in Croatia, Bosnia, Russia (Chechnya), and Serbia (Kosovo). The only case where that was in doubt at the time of writing was Kosovo, which could become independent. In the postimperial world it seems that boundaries cannot be modified even to punish an aggressor state. Iraq retained its borders despite having committed the crime of aggression and having suffered an overwhelming military defeat in the Gulf War (1990–91). By this logic, any partition of post-2003 American-occupied Iraq into a Kurdish state, a Shia state and a Sunni state would be out of the question.

Almost all new states of the Third World previously were colonies or other territorial jurisdictions created by Western imperialism. Not only in Africa but also in Asia and the Middle East existing borders are virtually identical to those of the colonial era. The exceptions are minor and few. In Africa that is all the more surprising in light of the profound weakness of the existing states most of which are seriously deficient in political stability and country-wide unity. Even the old colonial frontiers of the Middle East that divided the Arab "nation" into multiple territorial jurisdictions are now regarded as legitimate and lawful by almost every Arab government.

The conservative principle involved is that of *uti possidetis juris*, according to which existing boundaries are the preemptive basis for determining territorial jurisdictions in the absence of mutual agreement to do otherwise. The principle seeks to uphold the territorial integrity of states by demanding respect for existing borders unless all of the states that share them consent to change them. If consent is not forthcoming and change must occur, as in the disintegration of Yugoslavia, then the external border of the former state shall remain in place and internal borders shall be used to determine the jurisdictions of the successor sovereign states. This is the accepted norm for determining international boundaries in ex-colonial situations and in the break up of states. This principle originated in nineteenth-century Latin America.[40] Colonial administrative boundaries were largely followed in drawing international frontiers in the absence of any alternative territorial norm that could secure general acceptance. Thus the Spanish colonial territories of Peru, Chile, Ecuador (Quito), Columbia (Caracas), and so forth became independent states.[41] The same norm was recognized in Africa at the time of decolonization in the 1960s: colonial borders were the only generally acceptable basis for determining the new international frontiers of the continent. When colonial territories proved unworkable for self-determination and self-government, as in the cases of French West Africa and French Equatorial Africa, internal administrative borders that had also been defined by the occupying colonial powers were raised to the status of international boundaries. In both Latin America and Africa *uti possidetis juris* was closely connected to the search for a normative foundation for regional peace after colonialism. In 1991, the EU created an Arbitral Commission chaired by Robert Badinter, president of the French Constitutional Council, to rule on the validity of various claims for political independence in former Yugoslavia. The Commission underlined the crucial importance of *uti possidetis juris*: "The territorial integrity of States, this great principle of peace, indispensable to international stability . . . has today acquired the character of a universal and preemptory norm. The people of former colonial countries were wise to apply it; Europeans must not commit the folly of dispensing with it."[42]

In late twentieth and early twenty-first century world politics the "self" in self-determination is juridical and not sociological. Ernest Gellner points out that in the approximately 200 sovereign states of the contemporary world, 8,000 languages are spoken.[43] Virtually all the new states that were created or resurrected (Poland) in Central and Eastern Europe in the aftermath of World War I were multinational in social composition. Many nationalities that could not secure independent statehood were internationally recognized as national minorities.[44] The new state jurisdictions of ex-colonial Asia and Africa were also multiethnic and usually contained significant minority communities but they were not recognized internationally. Most of the world's numerous ethnonational communities have no international status, either as independent states or as recognized national minorities. They remain submerged within or divided between existing state jurisdictions. One important consequence of this is a world of multiethnic states. In short, neither ethnonationality nor any other exclusively sociological definition of the collective self is, by itself, a valid basis for a claim to sovereignty in the current practice of international society.

The twentieth-century principle and policy of national self-determination unleashed a revolutionary expansion of international society that multiplied the number of independent countries in the second half of the century. But the previously outsider groups who became sovereign insiders had, in almost every case, an immediate prior existence as a juridical entity of some sort. Acquisition of sovereignty almost always involved straightforward elevation of the legal status of a territory. It rarely involved recognition of a sociological people, which would have been far more difficult and disruptive. Most of these elevated jurisdictions formerly were either colonies of empires or internal administrative units of federal states. The principle of national self-determination thus became subordinated to the practice of *uti possidetis juris*: the juridical–territorial clearly and decisively trumped the sociological–national.

Beyond Sovereignty?

Sovereignty, as that idea has been employed in this chapter, is a distinctive status that opens the door for a government to engage lawfully in certain political activities, domestic and international. Sovereign status qualifies a government to participate in the *societas* of states. Canada can participate but—so far—Quebec cannot. This is not because Canada is more worthy or more capable than Quebec: there is no significant difference between the two entities in this regard. Rather, it is because this is the way it was decided historically. In this traditional way of thinking, sovereignty is a prescriptive right of membership, intimated and defined by a preexisting but non-sovereign territorial status, in a very exclusive political club.

The *societas* of states is the most exclusive political club in the world and has been so for several centuries. There are always more polities that seek membership than have it, and states that presently enjoy membership are almost always unwilling to part with it. Given this universal appetite for sovereign statehood and the premium conservative value placed on the existing distribution of territorial sovereignty it would seem rather surprising if any states were prepared to surrender their sovereignty either in whole or in part. It has happened in the past. The political unification of Italy and Germany in the mid-nineteenth century is an instance of smaller states and statelets transferring their sovereignty, either voluntarily or under military duress, to a government of one larger resultant national state. Nationalism was a powerful impetus in each case.

Another example is the American colonies who, after liberating themselves from the British Empire, elected to form a larger sovereign state, the United States of America, and thus to constitute and exercise their newly acquired independence jointly instead of each colony becoming independent on its own territory—as usually happened in twentieth century decolonization. Americans were determined to avoid what they understood were the lessons of European history, namely, that state systems foster incessant conflict and warfare. According to Alexander Hamilton, "to look for a continuation of harmony between a number of independent, unconnected sovereignties in the same neighborhood, would be to disregard the uniform course of human events, and to set at defiance the accumulated experience of ages."[45] So to avoid the errors of Europe, the American ex-colonies formed a federation.[46] This constitutional arrangement has had one or two predecessors and a few imitators, for example, Switzerland, Canada, Australia, and so on. North America is noteworthy for its two transcontinental federations, its paucity of sovereign states, and its poverty of international relations. But most of the world's states have been determined to hold sovereignty exclusively rather than divide it and hold it jointly with somebody else. Almost every postcolonial federation in Asia, Africa, and the Caribbean collapsed into its constituent ex-colonial parts not long after independence. *Societas* Europe and not federalist America was the wave of the future in most parts of the world.

Sovereignty clearly is not a status that is lightly surrendered or easily foregone. The most noteworthy instances of the widespread transfer of sovereignty (discussed above) are those in which imperial states gave up sovereign title over what had been their colonial territories. But these same states retained sovereignty over their homelands. They relinquished some of their territorial sovereignty when they could no longer decently or effectively hold on to it—usually the former. It is all the more interesting, therefore, that in Western Europe since the 1950s steps have been taken by a growing number of sovereign states, including several former imperial states, to establish a European Union in which the question "Who is sovereign here?" has increasingly come to be asked.

There is a continuing debate on this question that cannot be investigated in any detail. But the main arguments can perhaps be reduced to the following two opposing views. (1) There is something that is fundamentally new in the EU: its member states have come together to form a European political and legal authority which is constitutionally distinct from those same states that have limited their sovereign rights and prerogatives in certain important respects. This is a fundamental political change that moves Europe some distance beyond a *societas* of states and toward an emergent *universitas*. (2) There is nothing new in the EU: the member states of the EU have merely formed an international organization devoted to improving their socioeconomic conditions and enhancing their civil society, which does not involve any permanent and irrevocable transfer of sovereignty. The EU is a "union of sovereign states" and nothing more.

The EU, according to the first argument, is not merely an international organization but, rather, it is a polity of a novel kind whose member states have relinquished some of their independent jurisdiction with the effect that EU Europe is in certain important respects moving beyond the *societas* of states in its political life. The European Court of Justice can rule on the validity of national legislation in certain areas of common policy, such as social and economic policy, some aspects of which have been placed under the jurisdiction of the Treaty of Rome and subsequent EU treaties.[47] The Court has ruled that the various EU treaties have established "a legal order of a new and unique kind to which the member states have freely transferred certain of their sovereign rights."[48]

The EU is a new kind of polity in the following ways. On the one hand, the member states are no longer fully independent; they have endowed the EU with some of their sovereign authority, especially as regards the making and conducting of social and economic policy. Common obligations under EU law remove from member states some of their previous freedom of action in these policy areas. On the other hand, the EU does not constitute a fully sovereign entity either, at least not yet. The relations between the EU and its member states have been characterized as "co-coordinately valid legal systems" in that each side of the relationship "for certain purposes presupposes the validity of the other." There is not so much a sharing of sovereignty as a mutual acknowledgment of coordinate jurisdiction between the EU and its member states in certain policy areas in which the states used to enjoy exclusive jurisdiction.[49] In this regard, it is argued, the EU is an important instance of Europe going "beyond the sovereign state."[50]

In the same vein, the EU is seen to be fostering a "supra-national citizenship." This argument has been made in connection with a celebrated case of the European Court of Justice (the Van Gend en Loos case), which found that EU law imposes direct obligations and confers direct rights on individual Europeans regardless of the member states of which they are citizens. Here again the EU is seen to constitute a new legal and political order in which member states have "limited their sovereign rights" within certain areas. The subjects of this new constitutional arrangement are not only the member states but also their nationals who are becoming, in a somewhat awkward arrangement, citizens of Europe while still remaining citizens of their own country.[51] Some legal scholars argue that the EU should therefore be understood as not merely "an agreement among States" but also as "a 'social contract' among the nationals of those States."[52] One such analysis concludes: "It is not inevitable, but it is possible, that what we are now embarked on in Western Europe is a thoroughgoing transcendence of the sovereign state as the essential model for legal security and political order."[53] This image of the EU as an emerging polity that is more than the sum of its partner states is reminiscent, somewhat, of the old European *universitas* with the Christian religion replaced by a secular European civic identity and with EU citizens, like their medieval Christian ancestors, retaining a significant attachment to their individual homelands. Here, too, is an intimation that Europe has seen the light and is now belatedly following in the footsteps of Alexander Hamilton's federalist America.

The EU, according to the second argument, is still basically an international organization: we might call it the European "union of sovereign states" view. According to this way of thinking, the member states have authorized all its basic rules, institutions, and organizations. If we probe the constitutional basis of the EU, in an effort to discern the justification for the authority of EU law, what we find is a familiar and traditional norm of a society of states, namely *pacta sunt servanda* or in modern terms the principle of reciprocity between equally sovereign EU member states who remain fully in charge of the EU. The sovereign governments in Berlin, Paris, Rome, Madrid, Lisbon, Athens, and so forth are not out of the picture. Far from it: they are the principal players. On this view, the international agreements upon which the EU is built are entirely consistent with treaty law that rests squarely on the institution of sovereignty.[54] The EU is the child and not the parent or even the sibling of its member states. In short, there is nothing new about the EU.[55] Europe continues to be a *societas* of states rather than an embryonic *universitas*.

Let us suppose, for the sake of analysis, that the first argument is more accurate. An important element of this argument is the claim that territory in Europe is being redefined and reconstituted, away from the states and toward the EU.[56] If the EU were to become an independent polity there would then be fewer states in the world and, possibly, one new superpower. Europe would look more like North America. This would be a revolutionary change for Europe. It would also realign the balance of power in world politics. But it would not alter the *societas* of states on a global scale in any fundamental way. In this regard, it would not be a revolution or even a reformation of the sovereign state system. It would recollect comparable changes in the past that significantly reduced the number of sovereign states, such as the mid-nineteenth century unifications of Italy and of Germany. A politically united Europe would still be part of a world of sovereign states.

The first argument is sometimes supplemented by a globalization thesis concerning the withering away of sovereignty in the face of rapidly increasing economic transactions and traffic around the world. The thesis basically turns on a notion of sovereignty that is economic in character. In this vein, Robert Keohane views sovereignty as a "bargaining resource."[57] Sovereignty is considered to be the same as autonomy: that is, the capacity to insulate oneself or protect oneself from outside influences and forces. The common market regulations or common policies on economic competition or common currency—are seen to entail a loss of economic sovereignty for its member states. The states that adopted the Euro as their currency no longer have their own exclusive national currency. Keohane speaks of states "bargaining away" their sovereignty to the EU as if it is something that is instrumental rather than constitutional.[58]

If we think about sovereignty in this way, there is no question but that the EU involves a voluntary loss of sovereignty on the part of its member states. But this is a misleading way to think about it. The EU states that are opting to join the "Euro" currency zone are deciding to exercise their sovereignty in this way. This is a matter of policy and not of sovereignty. Their sovereignty is being used to authorize certain common rules and activities in cooperation with other EU member states. EU members have decided to limit their sovereignty in some areas of common policy. Their sovereignty has not been transferred in the permanent, nonrefundable way that British sovereignty over its colonies was transferred. The EU does not involve a one-way and irreversible transfer of sovereignty. There is nothing that prevents Britain from legally withdrawing from the EU. There are of course policy considerations that might make this unwise. Sovereignty is not a resource to exchange. It is not an instrumental relation or commodity. It is a status: that is, a legal standing and thus a right to participate, to engage in relations, and to make agreements with other sovereign states. Rather than speak of the decline or loss of "economic sovereignty" it would be more to the point to speak of the difficulties that independent governments face nowadays in trying to pursue nationalist economic policies in a rapidly integrating global economy.

In whatever way we decide to understand the EU, either in the first way or in the second way, there is no doubting that it is a very significant development in European politics. Even if the first argument is more accurate, the EU as an embryonic *universitas* should be understood against the background of earlier periods of European history. That Europeans would give up on their *societas* might come as a surprise when we recall that it was they who conceived of sovereignty in the first place, ran with it for centuries, and in the course of doing so expanded the *societas* to the rest of the world. But it is less surprising if it is understood against the background of European medieval and Roman history. Maybe Europeans are again leading the way, either backwards or forwards depending on how we view the endeavor, to a more politically and legally integrated world, perhaps along institutional lines of confederation or federation. But that too has happened before.

The Values of Sovereignty

The final question to be addressed, the most fundamental, is a value question. Why is sovereignty pursued so constantly and possessed so jealously? Why do the people of the world, or at least their political leaders, either want to hold on to it if they have it, or to obtain it if they do not have it? Where governments are prepared to submerge some of their sovereignty in a larger community, as perhaps in the EU, why do they immediately turn around and safeguard their newly united jurisdiction against external encroachments by drawing a sharp line on the map between EU insiders and EU outsiders? In short, why is sovereignty and the *societas* of sovereign states so deeply ingrained in world affairs? This surely is because, like any basic human institution, it is an arrangement that is particularly conducive to upholding certain values that are considered to be of fundamental importance.

Whenever a human institution survives for a long time and is adopted on a wide scale, some basic values are likely to be involved. The core values of sovereignty are the following: international order among states, membership and participation in the society of states, coexistence of political systems, legal equality of states, political freedom of states, and pluralism or respect for diverse ways of life of different groups of people around the world. There may be other values involved, but these do seem to be the most fundamental.

International order is one of the basic values of the anarchical society, and for some scholars it arguably is the most basic.[59] How does sovereignty fit into that value? A clue is given by James Madison in *The Federalist* number 51 in which he justifies a constitutional separation of powers for a republican government: "In order to lay a due foundation for that separate and distinct exercise of the different powers of government . . . it is evident that each department should have a will of its own; and consequently should be so constituted that the members of each should have as little agency as possible in the appointment of the members of the others . . . The interests of the man must be connected with the constitutional rights of the place."[60] A parallel and even stronger argument along these lines can be made about sovereignty and international law: the interests of the rulers, or government, must be connected with the constitutional rights of the country and its people. Sovereignty and the *societas* of states provide that connecting juridical framework. It is a norm that prohibits one state from acting authoritatively within the jurisdiction of another state. It is an arrangement, of a constitutional kind, against outside involvement or interference.

It is important to add that this legal arrangement is not based on fairness: as indicated, many political communities are arbitrarily denied recognition as sovereign states. Why should Nigeria be recognized as having interests and rights internationally, but Biafra (Eastern Nigeria) should not be? Why should Canada be sovereign but not Quebec? Why India and Pakistan but not Punjab? Madison would probably say: it is not about fairness or justice; it is about convenience, prudence and power as arranged and managed historically. Nigeria was the entity that conveniently and historically emerged out of British colonialism. It would have been risky if not dangerous to partition Nigeria in order for Biafra to be recognized as a sovereign state. Canada was a remnant of British North America that remained after the American Revolution. Quebec might have become independent but history said otherwise. It had been conquered by the British in the Seven Years War (1756–63), and that determined its subsequent fate as a constituent part of Canada. British India was partitioned between India and Pakistan and Punjab divided along with it. That was the way it was in the circumstances at the time.

The *societas* of sovereign states has been referred to above as a political "club," the most exclusive political club in the world. Politicians and polities of diverse interests, concerns, beliefs, ideologies, and so on want to participate in world politics, they want their voices to be heard, which means they want to be inside the room and around the table. They want that opportunity even if their voice is not as weighty as some other voices. It is their presence in those places that sovereignty makes possible. It is an issue of inclusion. Sovereignty based on state equality is inclusive: it underwrites the value of representation and participation in world politics.

The *societas* of sovereign states accommodates, imperfectly, the diversity of human social organization around the world that must be taken into account if the world political system is to have some general basis of validity. Montaigne famously put the point as follows: "Let every foot have its own shoe."[61] This could mean a different law for different states.[62] Each sovereign state constructs and operates its own constitutional and legal system. But it could also mean a law sufficiently general to embrace human diversity. This is what Montaigne is driving at: "the most desirable laws are those that are rarest, simplest, and most general."[63] This is what sovereignty is. Notwithstanding its very real limitations and imperfections, to date the *societas* of sovereign states has proved to be the only generally acceptable and practical normative basis of international affairs on a world scale. At present there is no other worldwide political institution that can perform that service for humankind. Another way of putting this is to say that the above-noted values are among those very few values around which the world can unite politically even if that union is a minimalist one.

CHAPTER 6

Knots and Tangles of International Obligation

In the house of human history there are many mansions.

Isaiah Berlin

Realists claim that questions of obligation have little or no place in international relations, which they portray as a world of power politics: <u>raison d'état</u>, <u>realpolitik</u>. Diplomatic and commercial relations between sovereign states, not to mention military encounters and acts of war or intervention, are instrumental activities calculated to advance or defend national interests. Issues of obligation—issues that demand or require acts of performance, observance, or compliance as a matter of duty or responsibility—are confined to states and do not extend across international borders. The state is the terminal political community: there is no community beyond the state. Political obligation is the duty to uphold and abide by the constitution, laws, and regulations of the state. It involves the most fundamental demands the state can lay upon its officials and citizens: allegiance to the constitution, obedience to the law, conscription, taxation, and education are among the most important.[1] The notion of international obligation is a flight of the imagination. Worse than that, it is a misunderstanding and misrepresentation of international relations. Sovereign states are not in a position to demand or require acts of performance, observance, or compliance from each other as a matter of duty or responsibility. They cannot bind each other in the same obligatory way they can bind their officials and their citizens—when the state is effectively institutionalized.

I shall argue, to the contrary, that international relations do involve questions of obligation: the normative language of duty and responsibility has a place alongside the instrumental language of power and interests. However, this must be immediately qualified, because international obligations are looser and more pluralistic with divergent, overlapping, and contradictory elements. They follow a crooked course, with many twists and turns, which disclose the complexity, ambiguity, and uncertainty of the subject.[2] They are also more contingent on circumstances, which weigh heavily in world affairs. The following have been among the most prominent international obligations historically: preserve the society of states, uphold the balance of power, abide by international law, accommodate international trade and commerce, and respect human rights. International obligation is a sphere of greater complexity, ambiguity, and uncertainty than that of domestic political obligation, which means that such norms come into conflict more readily and are resolved with greater difficulty, owing to the weakness or absence of authoritative bodies that exist for that purpose. Often they are not resolved. They are tolerated or endured.

International obligation is a wide-ranging and many-sided subject. I can only touch on some of the more important issues by way of introduction. My approach is a middle way between those who deny there is any place for questions of obligation in world affairs and those who claim there is an overarching moral and legal order by reference to which such questions are to be judged. The middle way is that of the society of states and international law. This way is not a highway. It is not a Roman road running straight as far as the eye can see. It is a low road, of broken pavements, winding its way across an ever-changing landscape, encountering many interruptions and obstacles.

Political Obligation

First it is necessary to clarify the notion of "obligation" and to examine, briefly, the idea of political obligation. An obligation is a binding norm or standard of conduct by reference to which human activities are demanded or required. To be under an obligation is to be legally or morally *bound* to take an action or refrain from taking one, such as to perform a duty, to observe a requirement, to comply with a demand, and so forth. An obligation is a notion of whom we *ought* to obey. It is a component of a normative framework of some sort (moral, legal, religious), to which we are expected to conform in our policies and activities.

Questions of obligation do not concern who we actually obey. This is a different question, and under certain circumstances we may obey somebody we have no duty or responsibility to obey: for example, we are likely to do whatever a person holding a knife at our throat demands. Being obliged to do something, or to refrain from doing it, under a threat or act of force—or any other means of compulsion—is not to be obligated. Coercion and force can slice through the normative bonds and ties of obligation. This can happen not only in relations of individuals but also in relations of states. In April 1940, Nazi Germany invaded Denmark, then a neutral country, without any valid international justification and, in effect, held a knife at the throat of the Danish government and people. Compelling power, especially armed force, in the hands of independent governments is a standing provocation to any notion that independent states can be subject to norms or standards of international conduct. The international system is often characterized as an arena where coercion and force have a determining role. Threats and acts of war are the paradigm instance. This characterization is apt in many important respects, for there is no doubt that international relations offer wide latitude for instrumental stratagems and activities, including those involving coercion and force.

Questions of obligation address the categorically different idea of whom we *ought* to obey. Who *should* we obey? Who are we morally or legally *bound* to obey? Such questions invoke a duty or responsibility: a demanded or required action or restraint of action that is not open to free choice.[3] The idea of obligation excludes the notion of freedom to choose, in the sense that I am not at liberty to decide whether or not to carry out my obligations. If I am under an obligation I am bound to do what it requires, whether I want to or not. What that obligation is and where it is located in a normative framework, for example, constitutional law or international law or some other body of norms is another important question. Our obligations are not subjective: we do not personally decide what they shall be and whether we shall obey them. On the contrary, they are part of a social order that we are involved with in such a way as to be morally or legally bound by it. This is indicated, not least, by the standard meanings of the word in the English language.

The main historical usages of "obligation," as recorded in the *Oxford English Dictionary*, provide insight into the concept and what is at stake in its use.[4] Four usages in particular are worth noting:

1. *General.* The action of binding oneself by oath, promise, or contract to do or forbear something; an agreement whereby one person is bound to another, or two or more persons are mutually bound; also, that to which one binds oneself, a formal promise.

2. *Legal.* An agreement, enforceable by law, whereby a person or persons become bound to the payment of a sum of money or other performance; the document containing such an agreement; a written contract or bond under seal containing a penalty with a condition annexed. Also, the right created or liability incurred by such an agreement, document, or bond.

3. *Moral or legal constraint.* The condition of being morally or legally bound; a moral or legal tie binding to some performance; the binding power of a law, moral precept, duty, contract, and so forth

4. *Action.* An act that one is bound to do; a particular duty.

Obligation is a fundamental concept of political and legal thought.[5] Why that is so requires a few preliminary remarks. Humans are social or political animals: that is, they live in groups, which means they must depend on each other, at least up to a point. Mutual assistance, and the assurance that travels with it, cannot be left to chance. It cannot be left to inclination or goodwill—or even to offers, incentives, or rewards. It must be arranged and underwritten, in advance, by a system of duties and responsibilities to which the people involved are morally or legally tied.

A common way of providing for that is via the state. Aristotle saw the state—the *polis*—as a natural political body for enabling people to live together in concord.[6] Here we approach a fundamental raison d'être of the state. In legitimate and capable states political obligation is a positive habit of obedience, of both rulers and ruled, to the demands and requirements of the state, that is, its constitution, laws, regulations, policies, and so forth.[7] Proceeding from the two last dictionary usages of "obligation" noted above, we could say that the state is a moral and legal framework that constrains its officials and citizens to perform or avoid certain actions. Thomas Hobbes argues, famously, that people must be bound by means of a social contract to put the state and its laws on a solid foundation of constituted authority, the sovereign state.[8] If we wish to enjoy the benefits of an effective state, for example, security, welfare, and so on we must bind ourselves to it by accepting duties or responsibilities it places upon us. We cannot dodge the obligations and still expect to enjoy the benefits. If we try to evade or get around them, the state must be authorized and equipped to stop us. Political hierarchy—overarching governmental authority and power—gives substance and reinforcement to the bonds of obligation between state officials and citizens. The law of the sovereign state is monistic: it issues from a single, ultimate authority within the country.[9]

International Obligation

The system or society of states is not a political hierarchy. It does not have its own centralized power and authority. It is not sovereign *in itself.* International law is not monistic. Instead, as indicated, each state is bound by its own framework of political obligation, usually a constitution. The system or society of states is pluralistic.[10] The underlying idea is that sovereign states exist in a condition of freedom vis-à-vis each other: international anarchy. They are free to arrange their own domestic affairs and govern themselves in whatever manner or fashion they decide. They are free to defend themselves and they possess a right of war. They are also free to arrange international law and other norms, practices, and organizations between themselves, as they see fit: an international society. This freedom of sovereign states is primordial, in the sense that it comes before any international relations they may enter into. International obligation, therefore, is not itself primordial. Rather, it is secondary and subject to state sovereignty.

The historical existence on the planet of numerous sovereign states that govern themselves, rather than one greater sovereign that rules over all lesser states, makes international obligation, at the very least, more open to question and less binding than domestic political obligation.[11] International law, as conventionally and historically understood, derives from sovereign states that constitute international society. Practices of diplomacy, military alliances, commercial treaties, international organizations, and much else besides—are constructs and creatures of states. Sovereign states, patently, are not constructs and creatures of international society. International law is not set above constitutional law. It is produced by the will and consent of sovereign states. To regard international law otherwise, for example, by seeing it as a supreme body of norms to which state constitutions are subordinated, would presuppose a normative arrangement of world affairs that does not exist in any discernible and recognizable sense.

If international law were such a body of norms there would be no anarchical system or society of *independent* states, and thus no *international* relations properly so-called. Instead, there would be some form of overarching political authority and power, such as universal empire or world federation, in which the state units are subordinate rather than independent. This was the theory, if not fully the practice, in premodern Europe when states— *regna*—were subordinate to the overarching authority of pope and emperor: *respublica Christiana*. But no such entity has existed in any substantial way since the seventeenth century, and it scarcely existed even then. In the late eighteenth century, Immanuel Kant envisaged a future "federation of free states" on a global scale. But, as of yet, no such entity exists nor is it likely to exist in the foreseeable future.[12] Instead of universal empire or world federation, what has existed, what still exists, and what is likely to continue in existence is a system or society of sovereign states, of widely diverse domestic constitutions, laws and institutions, which now extends around the world and embraces the entire family of humankind, and one of the important elements of which, but only one, is international law.

International law, for our purposes, can be defined as a body of norms that sovereign states contract (by entering treaties) or observe (by following customs) in their communications, interactions, and dealings with each other.[13] At most, international law is *between* states. Treaties are legally binding because states have entered into them and expressly acknowledged acceptance of their terms. Customs are valid because they are generally and avowedly observed by states.

Yet for some states, such as the United States at least from time to time, international law is conceived to be subject to domestic law.[14] There is a recurrent debate in American international jurisprudence between those who hold "treaties are binding internationally" and others who claim "treaties are simply 'political'."[15] Here the expression "political" means discretionary and not obligatory. According to the latter realist view, American governments are at liberty to observe and enforce international law, or to disregard it, in accordance with their reading of the national interest. However, they patently are not at liberty to observe or enforce the U.S. constitution and laws. On the contrary, they are legally bound to do that. Yet even according to the former view, treaties are binding "not because international law is 'higher' than U.S. law, but because it imposes a separate set of obligations voluntarily undertaken and owed from one or more countries to other countries."[16] This international law, entered into by the United States, becomes part of American law. This makes international obligation something of a hostage to the political will, policies, and actions of sovereign states, especially the great powers. But it does not make it a fiction or flight of the imagination.

One can dodge one's obligations more easily in international affairs than in domestic affairs. This is particularly so for the great powers, who are often free to decide for themselves whether to enforce or circumvent international law. Powerful states may go as far as to make domestic laws that dictate to foreigners: for example, by forbidding foreign companies from engaging freely in international commerce, and imposing penalties and privations for doing so. This is evident in the U.S. Helms-Burton Act (1996) that sought to exercise extraterritorial jurisdiction in evident violation of international law (GATT, WTO, etc.) by threatening to punish companies or citizens of

Mexico, Canada, the European Union countries, and so on for engaging in economic relations with Fidel Castro's Cuba.[17] Here international obligation is revealed as a duty or responsibility of states to forbear from interfering with the commercial freedom of foreign companies or governments.

Yet, in spite of such difficulties and limitations, most sovereign states disclose, time and again, the political will to respect and honor their international obligations. This is registered in diplomacy, treaties, alliances, commerce, and other interactions and engagements between states, many of which have long-term existence and stability. The world of international relations is far from being only a world of capricious powers acting exclusively according to their own dictates. It is a world, however, where states, irregularly undermine or breech the international bonds to which they have subjected themselves. That vulnerability, or exposure, to the independent and self-serving political wills of sovereign states is probably the biggest limit placed on international duties and responsibilities. It does not nullify international obligation, but it does qualify it in a very important way. States enter into foreign obligations of various kinds, but they do that as a matter of policy and not because they are internationally bound to do it. This places in sharper perspective a basic feature of international obligation: it reflects the free will and consent of sovereign states, for example, by becoming signatories to international treaties or by observing customary international law.

When states commit to international agreements they do not surrender their sovereignty or even reduce their sovereignty. Instead, they put it to use. By definition, international law does not and cannot involve any surrender of sovereignty on the part of its states subjects. If that happened it would create a different kind of law: for example, constitutional law, as in the 1787 Federal Constitution of the United States of America according to which the "states" of the federation are not sovereign in the international meaning of the word. By constituting themselves as a federation they abandoned any prior independence they possessed and acquired a greater, united sovereignty: *e pluribus unum.*[18]

State sovereignty is primordial. This is recognized by the UN Charter Article 51 that acknowledges an "inherent right" of self-defense that resides with all sovereign states regardless of the international agreements they have contracted with each other.[19] The international world is one of limited obligation in correspondence with the foreign policies of states. International bonds of duty and responsibility are also subject to circumstances. So much is that the case that one of the most fundamental principles of international law is *rebus sic stantibus*: the doctrine that treaties are binding only as long as the circumstances that gave rise to them remain unchanged.[20] The states subjects of international law are voluntary subjects, unlike the citizen subjects of the domestic laws of the state, who are compulsory subjects. Citizens of effectively institutionalized states ordinarily have little or no choice except to obey the law or suffer the penalty for failing to do so. This cannot be said, at least not nearly as readily, of sovereign states with regard to international law, especially the more powerful. This obviously is a fundamentally important difference that should always be kept in mind when trying to understand the character and substance of international obligation.

Thus far our discussion has focused on the international obligations of sovereign states, which is the core of the subject. That is not the whole story, however, because international obligation involves other right and duty-bearing agents besides states, including individuals, non-state actors, and collectivities that are not sovereign. At this point the story becomes more intricate and tangled. It involves individual human beings and their relations understood as distinctive from their civic identities and relations as citizens of particular states. Today there is an elaborate body of international humanitarian law that lays down rights and duties of human beings as such. Those humanitarian obligations may come into conflict, from time to time, with obligations of state sovereignty and citizenship. Some of those conflicts can pose difficult questions and even dilemmas of international obligation: for example, questions involved in humanitarian intervention or questions involved in individual responsibility versus collective (state) responsibility for war crimes.[21]

There is a closely related issue of freedom in world affairs, a space in which people are at liberty, as individuals or as members of non-state organizations, to move about the planet and undertake relations or engage in transactions across international borders. This idea has been prominent historically with regard to freedom of the seas. Grotius wrote a book on the subject in a seventeenth-century debate with the Englishman, John Seldon.[22] It was debated whether the seas and oceans could be subject to exclusive territorial jurisdiction of sovereign states. Grotius argued for freedom of the seas and in so doing made room for the idea of free and unobstructed international commerce. Kant makes provision for freedom of commerce as well as human mobility in his notion of a "community of reciprocal action" (*commercium*).[23] This is a classical-liberal idea of an open world of human interaction and transaction. It is equivalent to "don't walk on the grass," which presupposes freedom to walk anywhere that is not explicitly prohibited. According to that idea, the world is not closed generally and only opened specifically: it is not a world of specific permissions: an unfree world. It is not equivalent to "only club members are allowed on the grass," which presupposes a regulated sphere of licenses and privileges. The world is open generally and only closed specifically.

That notion of an open world society may apply without too much difficulty to the seas and oceans, which individuals and non-state actors may transit more or less at will—except during times of war. But on land it runs up against the primordial right of sovereign states to regulate and police their own territorial jurisdictions, including offshore waters and airspace, allowing and disallowing movements of people and goods across their borders. States decide who shall enter and operate in their territory. They are not bound to open their doors to free trade or mobile people. They are at liberty to do so, or not, as they see fit.

Finally, international obligation involves non-sovereign groups or collectivities that extend across international boundaries. This brings us to yet another issue of normative divergence and discord: to whom do I owe allegiance? My fellow citizens? My family or dynasty? My church or mosque? My ethnonation, tribe, or race? Such confusions occur within states, of course. But they are more likely in international relations, which multiply the different and sometimes incommensurate duties and responsibilities to which people can be subject. Some of these issues are addressed later in the chapter.

Classical Theories of International Obligation

The various duties and responsibilities discernible in world affairs are reflected in different theories of international obligation. The main ones are intimated in the discussion thus far: anarchical theories, cosmopolitan theories, and consent theories. They have in common a modernist (postmedieval) focus on states, individuals, and the society of states. But their emphasis is different and indeed distinctive. It is only possible to give a summary of each one.

"The safety of the people is the supreme law."[24] The primary responsibilities of sovereign rulers, according to Hobbes, is that the people "be defended against foreign enemies" and "that peace be preserved at home."[25] Rulers lawfully possess "the sword of justice" or "the right of punishing" for ensuring domestic peace, and "the sword of war" or the right to "compel citizens to take up arms" and provide "expenses of war" for ensuring national defense.[26] The ruler is the exclusive "judge of what is necessary for the peace and defense of his subjects."[27] The ruler must be the sole judge because otherwise controversies and quarrels are likely to ensue within the state over questions of obligation which would be to the detriment of the people's security. Here, in summary, is one of the most enduring ideas of political obligation in the history of political and legal thought. These political responsibilities remain unchanged, for we still live in a world that presents both dangers from outside the borders of the state and disorders from inside. Obeying the laws of the sovereign state, which are held to be conducive to safety or security, is the most important duty of the citizen. Law and the state are coterminous.

Hobbes's theory is a classical realist account of political obligation: it confines obligation to the state; a legally binding relation between government and citizens. Each social contract results in separate and independent states within each of which political and legal obligation exists. Beyond the state there is no law or justice. The international world is a wholly instrumental sphere devoid of any normative bonds and ties between states. Hobbes portrays this external world as "a state of nature," a condition of permanent war, with only one fundamental norm, the right of self-defense. This is a theory of international obligation at one extreme, which denies the existence of any foreign obligations owing to the absence of an overarching super state to impose them and enforce them. I shall refer to it as the anarchical theory of international obligation.

Immanuel Kant provides a view of international obligation from a pole nearly opposite that of Hobbes: the universal responsibilities of free people under the rational law of human intercourse rooted in human reason. Kant is sketching a cosmopolitan liberal idea of a world community resting on a universal moral principle that is obligatory and binding on all people and every government at all times. International obligation is a prior *human* relation that neither sovereign states nor any other authorities or agents have the right or power to extinguish. It is based on a law far more fundamental than that of the sovereign state: the "universal law of right" planted in human reason.[28] Kant speaks of "international right" as a bond or tie that involves "not only the relationship between one state and another *within a larger whole*, but also the relationship between *individual persons* in one state and individuals in the other or between such individuals and the other state as a whole."[29] This not only blurs the normative significance of international borders. It effectively erases them by postulating a moral community beyond and above the state; not only a community of states but also a community of humankind; world community. In one sentence Hobbes's international state of nature is swept away and replaced by a universal sphere of human obligation that applies to both individuals and states, both within and beyond their own state. We are all fellow humans despite our citizenship. Kant thereby opens up questions of obligation that Hobbes denies and excludes.

Kant develops his argument under the rubric of *jus cosmopoliticum*: the right of all nations to unite "for the purpose of creating certain universal laws to regulate the intercourse they may have with one another."[30] His theory of international obligation at this point comes very near to being indistinguishable from natural law.[31] Unlike that of Hobbes's, Kant's social contract does not foreclose on international obligation; it builds a bridge to it. This bridge does not stop at international obligations between states but extends to cosmopolitan obligations between human beings everywhere: the community of humankind. Kant's social contract is a way by which global civil society is brought into existence. The notion that the world is a constitutional "whole," that is, a juridical community of both states and individuals, is a badge of Kantian international thought. I shall refer to this view as the cosmopolitan theory of international obligation.

As indicated, Hobbes and Kant present ideas of international obligation very nearly at opposite poles: the Hobbesian pole confined to particular states, and the Kantian pole extending to every human being on the planet. But many issues of obligation, probably most issues, fall somewhere between. There is a large area of international obligation that is expressed in diplomatic practices, legal arrangements (mostly treaties), and international organizations. It can be characterized as a positive legal order of *international* obligation properly so-called: obligations contracted by sovereign states in relations with each other. This is a world that Hobbes does not consider to be one of genuine political obligation, because it lacks an overarching sovereign and thus fails to get beyond his anarchical notion of a lawless "state of nature" in which the only recognized right is that of self-defense. This world of contracted obligation between states is one that Kant also dismisses, on surprisingly similar grounds, as hollow and meaningless, because it fails to provide reliable guarantees against breakdown and war. It does not pursue the permanent abolition of war, what Kant refers to as "perpetual peace." Indeed, it stands condemned for justifying war as an international institution: *jus ad bellum* and *jus in bello*. Hugo Grotius, Samuel Pufendorf, Emerich de Vattel, and other classical theorists of international law are, for Kant, "sorry comforters" who create a false image of a world of law. This world does not exist and will not exist until the basis of obligation becomes a political order of the community of humankind and not merely an accommodation and arrangement of sovereign states. As Kant points out: "diplomatically formulated codes do not and cannot have the slightest *legal* force, since states as such are not subject to a common external constraint."[32]

The classical international lawyers spell out grounds of international obligation that are denied by Hobbes as nonexistent and debunked by Kant as having no authoritative effect and thus no value as constraints on war. Yet what stands out in the lawyer's conception of international obligation is an empirical view of states and statesmen as reasonable agencies and agents that are able and often willing to meet each other halfway, or at least somewhere in the middle and thereby avoid unnecessary belligerence and disorder in their relations. It is a positivist notion of international law. It is empirical in that it takes into account international practices, procedures, and organizations that actually exist, having arisen historically in the evolution of state sovereignty and the encounters and engagements of existential states.[33] Positive international law is nothing more, nor less, than an outward aspect of sovereign states, none of which exists in splendid isolation but rather all exist in relation to each other. Together they form a distinctive society of their own, with special rights and duties.

This international society theory is clearly evident in attempts to delineate legal obligations of states to each other, such as the Draft Declaration on Rights and Duties of States of the International Law Commission.[34] In that definition, states are primordial: they have rights before they have duties, including most fundamentally rights of sovereignty. "Every State has the right to independence" (Article 1) and "Every State has the right to exercise jurisdiction over its territory" (Article 2). The duties of states follow from and are keyed to those fundamental prior rights: "Every State has the duty to refrain from intervention in the internal and external affairs of any other State" (Article 3) and "Every State has the duty to refrain from fomenting civil strive in the territory of another State" (Article 4). States are primordial in the sense that they come before the society of states and before the international law of that society: sovereign rights come before international duties. This is one very important reason why Kant does not consider the society of states and international law as a valid basis of obligation. Obligation, for Kant, is fundamentally a question of duties of individuals and not one of rights of states. Human beings are primordial, and not sovereign states.

I shall refer to this argument of the classical international lawyers as the consent theory of international obligation. It is based on consent in two respects: first, in that there is no higher authority to demand or require conformity with international norms; second, in that states possess authority, that is, sovereignty to enter into agreements with each other, to observe common standards of conduct, to form alliances, to establish international organizations, and so forth. State sovereignty is both necessary and sufficient to give consent. The doctrine that treaties are binding because states consent to them is central to the theory: *pacta sunt servanda*. Consent is evident, for example, in the status of international tribunals, such as the International Court of Justice, which exercise jurisdiction over states parties in international disputes "only by virtue of their consent."[35] Treaties disclose an international world based on consenting sovereign states.

Some international legal scholars say "an act of consent is not a sufficient condition for creating an obligation." Prior to and beyond any such act is a body of law that is said to be necessary to make an act of consent a binding obligation: that is, "nonconsensual rules . . . of customary international law."[36] This is an image of a world of law above the society of states: a cosmopolitan image reminiscent of the traditional doctrine of natural law. But arguably this image is misleading: these "nonconsensual rules" only exist in virtue of their observance by sovereign states; otherwise they have no existence and are merely theoretical ideals of speculative legal theorists. States are prior to the rules of customary international law, which they create by their common observance. Without state observance no such law could exist in any meaningful sense of the word. This is the view of the classical international lawyers whom both Kant and Hobbes dismiss.

The consent theory of international obligation is arguably more plausible and less controversial than the consent theory of domestic political obligation. The latter is exposed to the inescapable fact that people seldom consent, even tacitly, to the laws of their governments, yet they obey them willingly nonetheless.[37] It is almost exactly the reverse in international relations, where sovereignty establishes a right of consent for all states, and where international law only exists because states have willed its existence. To the extent that one can speak intelligibly of international obligation, by most accounts it is in terms of consent. This is what treaties fundamentally involve, this is what diplomatic relations are premised upon, and this is what international organizations are built upon. International consent is based upon state sovereignty, which long has been and arguably still is the political and legal foundation of international relations.

Yet consent theory runs up against real limits in international relations: the limits of power. Sovereign states are, at most, loosely and incompletely bound by international law, the framework of consent. Raymond Aron thus writes of "the silken thread of legality" that is necessarily thin because it must bind states without destroying their freedom.[38] Kant was overly pessimistic and very nearly cynical in his contemptuous dismissal of international law. But he had a point, namely, that the independent political will and power of states, especially the great powers, is a standing menace to the international rule of law if those states choose to disregard it or refuse to enforce it. This was made abundantly clear in the failure of the League of Nations in the 1930s, which led to World War II: the most devastating great power conflict in history. Two recent although far less significant instances are: the 1999 war over Kosovo and the 2003 invasion and occupation of Iraq. Each of these episodes divided international society at its great power core. The bonds of international consent are not to be overlooked or dismissed as to their significance and effect. For example, the resolutions of the UN Security Council are significant and are usually taken seriously by major powers. But they are definitely limited.

An important issue in consent theory is the responsibility to uphold a political equilibrium among the great powers, in particular a balance of military force, as a necessary condition for the existence of the society of states and international law. There have never been more than a few states in a position to bear this heavy burden. They are the "great powers." This is an old-fashioned expression but it is better than any other for identifying this most exclusive group of states. Its membership changes over time. At the start of the twentieth century it included Great Britain, Germany, France, Russia, Austro-Hungary, Japan, and the United States. By mid-century it was confined to the United States and the Soviet Union. At the start of the twenty-first century it was not clear whether a balance of power existed or made any sense, because the United States seemed to be the only great power still standing.

That is largely besides the point of this discussion, however, which seeks to clarify, as far as possible, the obligations involved in the balance of power. Arguably its purpose is to defend and promote peaceful coexistence between sovereign states, which is seen as a fundamental value. It can thus be understood as upholding a pluralistic international society. It is a response, as well, to the dictate of prudence out of regard for the same value: the concern to prevent any one power from posing a threat to individual states and the society of states itself. That aim was registered historically in the nineteenth-century concert system of Europe, in which there was a deliberate effort to defend the society of states by the allied wills of the great powers to maintain a balance of power.

The UN Security Council is a departure from that pluralist doctrine in a monist direction by seeking to give substance to the idea of collective security.[39] The core idea is the use of force by the Security Council, operating as a police power of international society, to suppress acts of aggression or other threats to international peace and security. Under the authority of the UN Charter (chapter VII) the Security Council, meaning its five permanent great power members, can set aside the sovereign right of state consent and dictate to states at moments of grave danger to international peace and security. The primordial rights of individual states can thus be sacrificed for the common good of the society of states. This elevated collective authority inclined

Martin Wight to characterize the Security Council as a Hobbesian international sovereign.[40] This is clearer in theory than in practice, however, for the council has only performed this role on a few occasions and rarely with unqualified success in apprehending and punishing aggressors. The first Gulf War (1990–91), in which a UN military coalition drove the Iraqi army out of occupied Kuwait, is perhaps the only unambiguous instance. The council has no armed capacity of its own and must rely on various military powers to carry out its international police activities. The council does nevertheless possess exclusive superior authority, and it has tried with some degree of success to exercise its responsibility to uphold international peace and security, particularly in troubled areas, such as the Balkans since the end of the Cold War.

Here, then, are three accounts of obligation in world affairs upon which I believe it is possible to build, by following lines of argument initially laid down by Martin Wight and Hedley Bull.[41] This traditional international society approach acknowledges the pluralism of international obligation: that there are different, often divergent and even conflicting norms and standards of conduct by reference to which international activities are demanded or required as a matter of duty or responsibility.

Encroaching Forms of Obligation

The trinity of anarchism, cosmopolitanism, and consent captures the leading theories of international obligation. But it does not take into account the greater diversity of the subject, particularly the various forms of obligation that qualify, conflict with, undermine, or disrupt the modernist perspectives. Four are noteworthy: fideism, paternalism, race, and ethnonationalism. Each one is strongly evident historically. None is explicitly international but all have international implications and repercussions. They can only be discussed briefly in passing.

Michael Donelan draws our attention to fideism or the obligations of the faithful in world affairs.[42] Here the overriding duty is to serve God and the one true monotheistic faith (e.g., Christianity or Islam) and to defend the community of the faithful by fighting pagans, infidels, and heretics, wherever one finds them. Members of the faith—both rulers and ruled—are in the service of their religion. They both have a duty not only to uphold this one true faith but also to spread it by bringing it to people in lands as yet outside the community of the faithful: for example, outside *republica Christiana* or *Dar' al Islam*. The goal is to expand the community of the faithful, so that with prayer, devotion, sacrifice, and struggle it may eventually encircle the earth. This goal has been pursued historically, by both Christians and

Moslems, and by arms as well as by preaching.[43] It thus involves activities of both peaceful conversion and militant crusading or holy war. This sort of thinking, characteristic of the Middle Ages, runs counter to modern theories of the state and international law, as discussed above. Here the Church or the Mosque asserts moral, legal, and political supremacy over the state. This was evident in medieval Latin Christendom, when secular rulers and regimes (*regna*) were not considered to be sovereign. Only God and his Vicar on earth (*sacerdotium*, the pope) were sovereign.[44]

The end of the Middle Ages in the West is marked by the decline and defeat of the monist doctrine of *respublica Christiana* and the ascendancy of the modern pluralist doctrine, initially in the shape of the divine right of kings, which expresses itself internationally as two fundamental principles. The first is the principle that *rex est imperator in regno suo*: the king is emperor in his own realm. This was a repudiation of papal and imperial Christian authority over European kingdoms. The second is the principle *cujus regio, ejus religio*: whoever is the ruler shall determine what the religion of the realm shall be. There can be different Christian confessions in different states and religion cannot be a *causus belli*. Further developments of these doctrines are: the subordination of the church to the state, as in King Henry VIII's Church of England, and the separation of church and state, as in the First Amendment of the U.S. Constitution. In the West, fideism has thus been fundamentally transformed and greatly restricted, in the evolution of the modern society of secular states, into a matter of private conscience: a development that is famously summarized by John Locke: "The care of each man's salvation belongs only to himself."[45] The only thing that should concern government is to ensure that that is so by upholding religious liberty.

Islam has not followed that course, at least not to the same conclusive extent. Instead, even at the present time, many Moslem faithful have set out to define and control the state as dictated by Islamic theology and law. Here the ruler is in the service of Islam and the worldwide community of Islamic believers: the *umma*. One can discern an echo of medieval Christian theology. In some places in the Middle East, an uneasy modus vivendi exists between the mosque and the state. In a few places Islamic states have existed, for example, in Pakistan (at least for a time following independence in 1947), in Iran (after the 1979 Islamic revolution), and in Afghanistan (under the Taliban). In other places the mosque was subordinated to the state by governments that were attempting to fit their country into the modern secular world, for example, in Turkey, in Egypt, in Iran (prior to 1979), and in Lebanon until civil and international war, riddled with local sectarianism, destroyed the secular, constitutional state (in the 1970s). In some places politicized Islam rose up in reaction to the existence of a neighboring state defined, at least in part, by a different religion: Israel and Judaism. The idea of fideism, or something like that, is necessary to understand the role of religious devotion in international relations, not only in the past but also in the present. The secular society of states evolved, in significant part, in response to an encounter with the great monotheistic religions, which historically it has endeavored, with great success, to subordinate to its authority. Recent events rooted in the Middle East indicate that this history is not yet complete.

Outside the West that encounter involved European imperialism and colonialism, and was justified by some version of paternalism: a regime that regards and treats its subjects as children who are not yet ready to accept full political responsibility for themselves.[46] Colonialism rested on superior military and economic power. But power has to be justified, and an important justification of colonial government was the assertion of an obligation to rule on the grounds of having to look after colonial subjects who were allegedly unable to look after themselves.[47] This often involved Western education and conversion to Christianity. That was particularly evident in the Americas, the South Pacific, and sub-Saharan Africa. Imperialism and colonialism refused to regard non-Western peoples as entitled to enjoy state sovereignty and belong to the society of states. Before that could occur they had to be educated in the ways of the modern state and states system. Paternalism was evident in colonial policy of the various European Empires in Asia, Africa, and beyond. It was evident in the enforced subordination of native North Americans, indigenous South Africans, and aboriginal Australians to the intruding European settler states: the United States of America, the Dominion of Canada, the Union of South Africa, and the Commonwealth of Australia. It was evident, as well, in the international law of trusteeship. Article 22 of the League of Nations Covenant and Article 73 of the U.N. Charter repeated this justification. The twentieth-century revolt against the West by colonial subjects and peoples was justified by the political ethics of consent and also by anti-paternalism both of which converge in doctrines of national self-determination.

The ethos of paternalism was not very far removed from that of race. Race is a "uniquely modern" idea that enters international relations via the imperialist encounter of Europeans with peoples of the Middle East, the Americas, Asia, Africa, and Oceania.[48] Initially Europe and then the West was a Christian idea that later became an idea of civilization.[49] Only in the nineteenth century did it become, at least in part, an idea of race: that is, different categories of humans distinguished and ranked by physical characteristics. Race was supposed to determine ability and thus responsibility. People of non-European race were deemed incapable of participating in the society of sovereign states, membership in which was restricted to peoples of the European cum Western world. They had demonstrated their racial superiority by inventing modern science and technology and by conquering and controlling the rest of the world.

The European Empires and colonies could be characterized in racial terms at least in part. The rulers were fair-skinned Europeans or peoples of European descent: Spanish, Portuguese, Dutch, English and later British, French, Belgians, Americans, Canadians, Afrikaaners, Australians, and so forth. Their subjects were darker skinned Asians, native Americans, Africans, Australian aborigines, and so on. A huge category of international outsiders defined by racial criteria—most of the population of the world outside the West—was constructed by nineteenth-century Europeans and persisted in their international thought and activity well into the twentieth century. In some places, the concept of race was later turned on its head and used to demand self-government. People of European descent had no rights or responsibilities to be involved in the African continent as either colonial rulers or governments of independent states. Africa was for the Africans.[50] Africans must cast the Europeans out of Africa. By that reasoning the white settler states of Algeria, Kenya, Rhodesia, and South Africa must be either dismantled or destroyed.

The historical emergence of nation-states, initially in Europe, involved forms of political obligation that sometimes dovetail with the sovereign state and sometimes clash with it. We might refer to this as political obligation based on a notion of self-determination of the people. The less ambiguous and more manageable cases are those where the state defines and even creates the people: for example, the civic nations of the West: Britain, France, and the United States. An individual's nationality is determined by the political territory where he or she is born or "naturalized": *jus soli* in international law. The more ambiguous and awkward cases are the ethnonations of Central and Eastern Europe, beginning with the unification of Italy and Germany in the mid-nineteenth century and extending eastward after the defeat or collapse of the German, Russian, Austro-Hungarian and Turkish Empires in World War I. In at least some of these cases, such as the Germans and the Italians, an individual's nationality is determined by his or her parentage: *jus sanguinis* in international law. The policy seeks to make the state territory fit the ethnic nation either by redrawing the map or by forcibly relocating people (ethnic cleansing) or both: ethnonationalism.[51] It can also involve the protection of national minorities, defined by language or religion, and the launching of treaties and institutions that attempt to bring that about, such as the minority rights guarantees of the League of Nations and more recently the High Commissioner for National Minorities of the Organization for Security and Cooperation in Europe.[52]

These four doctrines of obligation disturb and even disorder the conventional forms of international obligation of the modern world, which are blind to claims of religion, paternalism, race, and ethnonationality. Fideism recollects a premodern mode of obligation that was defeated in the West historically by the secular state system. But it remains significant in the Middle East where it conflicts with the secular authority of sovereign states that emerged from the ending of Western Empires. Paternalism appeared to be abolished by decolonization but it is lurking beneath the surface, although never acknowledged as such, in connection with largely Western efforts to rebuild "failed states." The racial idea cannot be proclaimed openly but it can be masked and promoted by ideas of development and democracy in accordance with Western standards. The ethnic idea of political community is widespread across the world and gives little indication that it will surrender to the opposite notion of civic nationality.

International Pluralism

This pluralist argument might seem, at first glance, to be entirely consistent with realist doctrine. It identifies states as the primary political units of world affairs. It attributes to states the characteristics of sovereignty or political independence. It recognizes, indeed emphasizes that states have national interests that they seek to defend and which they have a right to defend. It also recognizes that states are, to a very considerable extent, self-help organizations. But it is more than a realist argument, indeed much more. Realists deny the existence of valid international norms to which states subject themselves: for example, international law as demanding or requiring observance as a matter of duty or responsibility. Realists acknowledge the existence of international law, of course, but they see international law as wholly instrumental and thus without any normatively binding claim upon the sovereign states that contract into it (treaties) or observe it (customary international law). At the extreme, realists see the laws and institutions of one state as, in principle, equivalent to the laws and institutions of any other state. The realist world is normatively relativist. Realists do not discern any obligatory norms between states: in a world of sovereign states there cannot be any true international society. What they see is international anarchy: a literally lawless world.

The modern political world, the postmedieval world, is not and never has been composed of political entities that are entirely self-regarding and self-sufficing. Pluralist thought does not see international relations as mere anarchy. Pluralism is not relativism. Pluralists see state sovereignty as not only a domestic political arrangement, but an international arrangement as well: the two are inward/outward aspects of one overall idea and institution.[53] They see sovereign states dwelling in an international society that they themselves compose and constitute. They see international law as (part of) the constitution of that society. They see diplomacy, international organization, war and other societal elements of the relations of states in the same light. The society of states, like any other association, is a membership body to which one belongs and as a member of which one enjoys rights and has responsibilities. Pluralists see international society, most fundamentally, as an institution for the freedom, security, and happiness of human beings who form themselves into sovereign states. This is shining the brightest light upon it. But that nevertheless is the normative ideal underlying state sovereignty and the society of states.

The assorted international obligations noted in this chapter suggest themselves because they reflect historical and contemporary experience. Pluralism is acknowledgment and accommodation of a diverse and varied global reality. Bernard Williams puts the pluralist point well: "we use a variety of different ethical considerations . . . if only because we are heirs to a long and complex ethical tradition, with many different religious and other social strands."[54] He is saying that about ethical thought in general but it applies particularly well to international ethical thought. Any realistic discussion of international obligation must be prepared to face the fact of moral and legal diversity, which is facing up to normative pluralism. A pluralist world is one where genuine dilemmas between divergent and sometimes conflicting normative principles are to be expected. Looking at it historically, this would certainly include the dilemma between the secularized state and the theocratic state, or that between state sovereignty and human rights, or that between national economic protection and international free trade, or, again, that between national industrialization and international environmental protection. These and many other such conflicts and dilemmas are an inescapable feature of world affairs. There is no universally acceptable principle or method of resolving them.

> In the house of human history there are many mansion . . . There are many objective ends, ultimate values, some incompatible with others, pursued by different societies at various times, or by different groups in the same society, by entire classes or churches or races, or by particular individuals within them, any one of which may find itself subject to

conflicting claims of uncombinable, yet equally ultimate and objective, ends. Incompatible these ends may be; but their variety cannot be unlimited, for the nature of men, however various and subject to change, must possess some generic character if it is to be called human at all.[55]

That quotation from one of Isaiah Berlin's essays can perhaps be supplemented by a final comment that shall serve as a conclusion. That the world has many mansions, whose members contemplate human ends according to their own enlightenment, could be seen as an insurmountable obstacle to international obligations of any kind. Some moral philosophers and even some international lawyers may see it that way. Berlin is referring to natural law when he speaks of the "generic character" of human beings. This, for him, is the silver thread that knits humanity together. But there is a more empirical and historical way by which human beings constitute a world of obligation. That is by forming themselves into separate sovereign states that are locally controlled and thereby respond, imperfectly, to the diversity of human values and beliefs. Those same states are also, simultaneously, component units of a great human association, a *societas* of states, that today is global in extent.[56] And it is to diverse humanity that those associated states give political voice when they operate as they are supposed to, that is, as agencies for the freedom, security, and happiness of their people. That is the human taproot of international pluralism.

CHAPTER 7

Jurisprudence for a Solidarist World: Richard Falk's Grotian Moment

The cosmopolitan society which is implied and presupposed in our talk of human rights exists only as an ideal, and we court great dangers if we allow ourselves to proceed as if it were a political and social framework already in place.

Hedley Bull

That the contemporary world may be entering another "Grotian moment" for legal scholarship is a thought-provoking idea closely associated with the work of Richard Falk.[1] Reduced to fundamentals, it is the claim that a transformative change in the organization and <u>modus operandi</u> of international life is presently occurring that is reminiscent of a revolutionary change three or four centuries ago that was captured by the jurisprudence of Hugo Grotius. A useful purpose might be served by assessing this idea with a view to its heuristic value for helping us understand world jurisprudence as we settle into the twenty-first century.

The approach I shall take is that of the traditional international society school associated with scholars such as Martin Wight and Hedley Bull.[2] Their perspective is broadly in touch and even in tune with many of the historical, legal, and philosophical assumptions about world affairs that Falk's argument rests upon. The conclusions they reach are fundamentally different, however. Richard Falk is an advocate of a solidarist conception of international society in which the global community of humankind has normative priority and the society of states is in conflict with it. The international society school views the society of states, and its connected law of nations, as the only practical institution through which the values and interests of humankind can be defended and advanced. According to that approach, Hugo Grotius is the legal theorist par excellence of international society. The first section comments briefly on Grotius's life and the original Grotian moment. The second section reviews Falk's basic argument that a second Grotian moment is underway. The final section presents a pluralist interpretation of neo-Grotian jurisprudence that leads to different conclusions than those put forward by Richard Falk.

Grotius and the Original Grotian Moment

The notion of a Grotian moment directs our attention to the remarkable historical changes underway during Hugo Grotius's lifetime which, with the advantages of hindsight, we recognize as the transformation from the Middle Ages of theocratic politics based on the Christian religion to the modern era of sovereign states and the law of nations. But who was Grotius? And what was his moment?

Huig van Groot in Flemish, or Hugo de Groot in French, was a Dutch Protestant, a late Renaissance humanist, and a legal publicist and diplomatist whose lifetime (1583–1645) spanned some of the revolutionary political changes in Europe that were spawned by the Renaissance and the Reformation.[3] He was educated at the University of Leiden and graduated with the degree of doctor of law. Some of his noteworthy roles and activities in a very active life were: historiographer for the States General of Holland, advocate for the Dutch East India company, political prisoner in Holland (his wife orchestrated his escape from prison), refugee in France, pensioner of the king of France, and ambassador to France for the king of Sweden during the Thirty Years War (1618–48). Throughout his life Grotius was a prolific and celebrated author, managing to write a number of books on various religious, political, and legal topics, including among others: *De jure praedae* (the law of prize), *Mare liberum* (freedom of the sea), *De veritate religionis Christianae* (the truth of Christianity), and, most famously, *De jure belli ac pacis* (the laws of war and peace).

Hugo Grotius was a wide-ranging Renaissance thinker whose thought was not confined by any means to the narrow study of that specialized subject we make reference to as "public international law." One thing in particular should be emphasized: Grotius was not a secular thinker in the modern sense of that term. The emerging international society that he captured in his jurisprudence was not only strictly European but also exclusively Christian in its membership. Grotius's international thought was permeated with religious concerns and conceptions that were characteristic preoccupations of his time: like many other publicists in that era of disruptive and disorienting social and political change, Grotius struggled to bring Christian morality and secular life into agreement. He was a liberal Calvinist. Not all of his writings were published in his lifetime, yet by the time of his death in 1645 Grotius nevertheless was famous throughout Europe. He was one of several brilliant political and legal commentators of the early modern era whose names include the French thinker Jean Bodin and the English philosopher Thomas Hobbes who are widely regarded as the founding political theorists of the modern sovereign state. Grotius's international jurisprudence, especially his notion of natural rights, was "particularly significant" for Hobbes's political theory.[4] The law of nations and the modern state are close relatives that were born at virtually the same time and were connected inextricably via the then innovative and compelling idea of sovereignty. International jurisprudence and political theory have remained in close company ever since.

It is also worth noting that Grotius was writing within an established tradition of jurisprudence that included the names of other famous Renaissance contributors to the emergent subject of international law, such as (to mention only the most famous) Francesco de Vitoria, a Spanish Dominican friar, Francesco Suarez, a Spanish Jesuit, and Alberico Gentili, an Italian Protestant exile who became an Oxford professor. Grotius has been referred to not as the founder of the law of nations, but "as the last genius of the Spanish school" that was launched by Vitoria half a century before Grotius was born.[5] Garrett Mattingly brilliantly captures the seminal contribution of these legal commentators in his unsurpassed study of Renaissance diplomacy:

> A chasm was opening in the European tradition. The public law of Christendom was crumbling and sliding into the gap . . . They had to discover a new foundation for whatever remained. They had to reshape the familiar concept of a law of nations, a *jus gentium*, governing the relations of individuals and public authorities within the commonwealth of Christendom, into the notion of a law for sovereign states, a law, that is, not *of* but *among* nations, *jus inter gentes* . . . it is literally true that "international law" was something which the publicists of the later Renaissance were obliged to invent.[6]

Mattingly provides a fitting historical context for understanding the original Grotian moment that Grotius and these other legal commentators were trying to capture in their writings.

Among Hugo Grotius's many influential writings *De jure belli ac pacis* stands out as one of the great books, if not the greatest, in the canon of international jurisprudence.[7] This is not the place to explore the often subtle and sometimes obscure arguments of that justly famous work on the law of nations. But at least a few comments about that are called for. This book raises the issue of Grotius's scholasticism. It is a difficult and even frustrating experience to figure out exactly what the author is trying to argue. One of the biggest irritations is Grotius's almost endless citation of authorities upon which he tries to rest his case, for example, classical texts, biblical sources, medieval traditions and customs, scholarly commentaries, and so on. Grotius is notorious for the pedantic medieval habit of scholasticism: compare the lucid modernist texts of Machiavelli or Hobbes or even Vattel. Voltaire said that Grotius is boring. But if that is a crime all philosophers, most legal scholars and social scientists, and even many historians should be arrested as academic criminals. Martin Wight writes of "trying to pick a path . . . through the baroque thickets of Grotius's work, where profound and potent principles lurk in the shade of forgotten arguments, and obsolete examples lie like violets beneath gigantic overgrown rhododendrons."[8] And Hedley Bull has remarked: "Few of us have the stamina to pick this kind of path."[9] Bull and Falk happen to be among those few scholars.[10]

Then there is the problem of Grotius's political persona. Rousseau said Grotius favored tyrants.[11] He was given refuge by one absolute monarch and he ended up working for another. But whether or not the king of France and the king of Sweden were tyrants seems besides the point in judging Grotius's contribution as a legal thinker. B.V.A. Roling, an influential twentieth-century Dutch legal scholar, accused Grotius of sanctifying European expansion and imperialism.[12] This is a more telling criticism for it is clear that some of Grotius's legal thought justified the colonial activities of the Dutch East India Company. But Grotius was a creature of his time. He lived in an age of imperialism, and the Dutch were already building their overseas empire in competition with the Portuguese and the English in what is today Indonesia. Many Western liberals have accused Grotius of being hostile to notions of popular sovereignty or national self-determination. He did support Dutch independence from Hapsburg Spain, however, which has been characterized by J.L. Brierly as "the first great triumph of the idea of nationality, and the successful assertion of the right of revolt against universal monarchy." In this regard he was anti-Medieval and wholly modern in his outlook.

What, then, can the word "Grotian" signify for our purposes? Although Grotius's celebrated work on the law of nations was published over 375 years ago it is possible to retrieve two fundamental normative ideas about international conduct from this famous study. The first idea is the notion that all humans are subject to natural law, which is revealed to them by their rational faculties and is independent of their religious beliefs. The second idea is the notion that all sovereigns are subjects of the customs and practices of international positive law—what he referred to as "human volitional law."[13] In Grotius's thought the former norm has moral priority, but the latter norm is a political reality. The crucial problem for Grotius, as for so many other early modern political and legal thinkers, is reconciling these seemingly contradictory norms when they come into conflict as they are bound to do from time to time. This is still our problem today (see chapter 6).

The fundamental normative element in Grotius's conception of international law is the law of universal human nature: "natural law." This is the notion that humans are social creatures who must live together but in order to do that in a morally defensible way they must recognize and respect each other as equal members of the community of humankind. According to Hedley Bull, "natural law theories assert the existence of rules that are valid universally and are not confined to particular societies and cultures."[14] Every male and female human being across the world and at all times without exception has a natural right of self-defense, and wanton assaults that trespass on this right, that is, acts of aggression, cannot be justified. This is the universal ethics of Hugo Grotius.

He saw clearly that medieval Christendom was breaking up and the states of Europe, monarchies as well as republics, were not only asserting their independence but were demonstrating it. There no longer was an overarching religious-political hierarchy throughout Europe as there had been, at least in theory if not always in practice, in the Middle Ages. The Protestant Reformation had shattered the theocratic unity of Christian Europe, and there was a growing international anarchy of independent or semi-independent governments. An alternative foundation was required upon which a modicum of order and justice between those governments could be established. Even though the sovereign rulers of the newly emerging anarchical society of Europe were independent of each other, they were still subjects of the law of nature and were duty bound to obey it just like everyone else. This is the heart of natural law doctrine in the Grotian law of nations. Yet sovereign rulers, unlike everybody else, were also authors and subjects of positive law. The second main normative element of Grotius's conception of international law is the accepted customs and practices of states and sovereigns in their relations with each other. These customs and practices, by virtue of their acceptance and use, have the authority of law. This is Hugo Grotius's positive law of nations: the *jus gentium inter se*.

In expanding on the foregoing answer to the question posed above, I shall follow the lead of Hedley Bull. In his view Grotius is the founder of the notion that "states and rulers are bound by rules" and consequently that they "form a society or community" among themselves: an "international society" based on "the law of nations." As indicated, the modern horizontal "society of states" was displacing and destroying the vertical "medieval empire" (*respublica Christiana*) during Grotius's lifetime. This momentous transformation from the medieval world to the modern world is marked (symbolically if not quite historically) by the treaties signed at the Peace of Westphalia in 1648, which expressed (implicitly if not always explicitly) the following three principles.[15]

> *Rex est imperator in regno suo*: the king is emperor in his own realm. That is what King Henry VIII of England said to Pope Clement VII when he divorced Catherine of Aragon without Papal permission and married Ann Boleyn in 1533. That is what national governments continue to say about their territorial sovereignty.
>
> *Cujus regio, ejus religio*: the king decides the religion; no intervention on religious grounds. That is what the Protestant Elizabeth I of England, daughter of Henry and Ann, in effect said to the Catholic King Philip II of Spain in 1588 when the English fleet defeated the Spanish armada.[16] That is what many European states, Catholic as well as Protestant including the victorious alliance of Catholic France and Protestant Sweden, said to the defeated Hapsburg emperor of Christendom at the end of the Thirty Year's War in 1648. That is what national governments continue to say about their domestic jurisdictions, as in Article 2 (7) of the UN Charter.
>
> *Magna communitas humani generis*: the great society of all mankind; the sanctity of all human beings regardless of their gender or culture or nationality. That is what enlightened thinkers have always said and continue to say when human beings are subjected to abusive treatment at the hands of national governments or anybody else. That is the moral principle underling the Universal Declaration of Human Rights.

The first two principles (of "human volitional law") are basically the same as the legal positivist principles of equal sovereignty and nonintervention that are still very familiar in international jurisprudence today. This is the "pluralist" or state-focused image of international society: an international society of sovereign states. The last principle (of "natural law") is basically the same as the principle of human rights and humanitarianism, which is so familiar in international jurisprudence today. This is the "solidarist" image of international society: a world society of humankind.

There is an obvious problem here: what shall take precedence when pluralist norms of state sovereignty come into conflict with solidarist norms of human rights? This normative conflict is built into the kind of international society that we have been living in for the past 350 years. As Richard Falk comments: "the tension between domestic jurisdiction and human rights is as old as the persecutions of the Huguenots or Puritans and as contemporary as the persecution of Soviet Jewry. The question as to whether deference to state sovereignty should take precedence over efforts to rescue victims of governmental abuse remains necessarily ambiguous and controversial in each context."[17] The sovereign rights of nation-states coexist with human rights, and the long history of international relations and law suggests that there is no principled way of determining which takes priority when they come into conflict. People involved in world affairs are bound to be confronted, from time to time, by situations that present normative dilemmas in which the right course of action to take is not self-evident. We see those international dilemmas all the time: for example, in connection with the issue of humanitarian intervention in Somalia, Bosnia, and Kosovo, or with that of "regime change" in Iraq. If we are convinced that there is a moral high ground in world politics as represented by one of these normative principles to the exclusion of the other—either state sovereignty or human rights—we are only deluding ourselves.

It is obvious that the problems Hugo Grotius addressed in his international jurisprudence are still very much with us, and there is a clear sense in which his Grotian moment is also our Grotian moment because the international world that he discerned before almost anybody else is still very much in evidence today. In addition to the original Grotian moment is there also another Grotian moment of international change that in some sense parallels, but this time in reverse sequence, the transformation from medieval to modern? Is there an emerging transformation from modern to postmodern, from a pluralist society of states to a solidarist community of humankind, with the latter taking on characteristics reminiscent of the legal principles of the medieval era without their religious clothing? Is the world entering a "new medievalism"?[18]

Another Grotian Moment in International Relations?

Richard Falk argues that international life is undergoing a "transformative" reorganization that will result in "drastic modifications of the world order system that has prevailed since the Peace of Westphalia."[19] However, the currently unfolding world order is a "reversal" of the earlier transformation. The first Grotian moment was the culmination and completion of a gradual historical change that had been underway for several centuries before Westphalia: from "nonterritorial central guidance," based on the medieval Papacy and feudal loyalties, to "territorial decentralization," based on the system of sovereign states. The second Grotian moment involves a transformation from the anarchical society to a new world order of increasing "central guidance" and expanding roles for "nonterritorial actors" thus reinstating two organizational principles of the medieval era. The national "loyalty and legitimacy" upon which the state, and also the society of states, could previously depend is "relocating" away from the state: upward to the center of the globe, or the world as a whole, and downward toward the local community. The role of the individual and also that of "subnational movements for self-determination" is expanding. Religious and political movements with "cosmopolitan identifications" are growing rapidly and it is now possible to speak intelligibly of a "planetary community." In short, individuals, groups, and the world as a whole are breaking free of the state system.

Richard Falk speaks of this world historical change as a "juridical revolution."[20] Just as Hugo Grotius correctly grasped the first Grotian moment from medieval to modern, the correct intellectual grasp of this second world order transformation in international jurisprudence is the task that Richard Falk sets for himself and his colleagues. "Today, as in the seventeenth century, the time is ripe for preliminary efforts to give juridical shape to a new paradigm of global relations, one that corresponds more closely than statist thinking to the needs, trends, and values of the present state of global politics."[21] He seeks to provide a world jurisprudence, a juridical "paradigm," which will not only comprehend the transformation but will also provide the basis for guiding it in a benevolent direction—away from power elites, whether those of statist international politics or those of capitalist global economics, and toward populist human goals. To give such direction is, according to Falk, an important role that legal scholars can perform.

Richard Falk identities four alternative models that set out different historical paths that the second Grotian moment could take: (1) "utopian legalism" that envisages and pursues "world government," (2) the "geopolitics of great powership" or a "concert of great powers" presumably under U.S. direction,

(3) the "geoeconomics of the multinational corporate elite" or a "concert of multinational corporate elites" in which transnational global capitalism is predominant around the world, and (4) "global populism" or a cosmopolitan world order based on "human solidarity" in which ordinary men and women take precedence over both great power statism and global capitalism.[22] Falk gives an assessment of each model. The problem with the first model, as he rightly notes, is its naïveté: it fails to grasp the nature and significance of power in world politics and, particularly, the relationship of power to "benevolent ends." The problem with the second model is its tendency to foster destructive wars that can be seen to derive from international anarchy based on state sovereignty. The problem with the third model is that it is driven by the ideology of a powerful "multinational corporate elite" who seek "to subordinate territorial politics" to their transnational economic goals "just as the papacy . . . sought to place the spiritual sword of the Church above the secular sword of national kings."[23]

Richard Falk identifies the fourth model as the only one that should be encouraged by progressive world jurisprudence. That, in any event, is how he conceives of his own role. For he is not content merely to analyze legal change as a detached scholar. He seeks to become politically engaged with the process by trying to provide intellectual guidance. The fourth model is explicitly based on the solidarist conception of an emergent world society of humankind. "The central feature of the normative challenge that I would propose . . . rests upon an acceptance of human solidarity and all of its implications, especially a shared responsibility to seek equity and dignity for every person on the planet without regard to matters of national identity, territorial boundary, or ideological affiliation."[24] Falk emphasizes that the fourth model thus aims at "the well-being of the species as a whole" and in that regard it is responsive "to the objective realities of the misery that afflicts most of the human race." The fourth model, unlike any of the other three, is the only one that can respond to "populist claims for peace, economic equity, social and political dignity, and ecological balance." In other words, it can overcome the normative conflicts and dilemmas of an international society composed of sovereign states. It is in connection with the possibility of this fourth model that Falk speaks of another Grotian moment.[25]

It is difficult to disagree with Falk's assessment of the first model as politically naive and there is little that can be added to that point. However, problems arise in his assessment of the other three models. Nobody who is even slightly aware of the history of world politics could dispute the fact that the state system has been a cockpit of warfare that has produced enormous human suffering. But war is not the uncomplicated and unmitigated political evil that Falk implies. War is a producer of both good and evil, and some wars can be justified more readily than others: in that regard we might compare World War II with the Vietnam War and the war in Iraq. Very few countries have ever been prepared to give up their right to wage war and hardly any countries have ever existed that did not possess armed forces. War is an institution of the state system. Some scholars also suggest that there is a positive and reinforcing historical connection between war and prosperity in the modern states system.[26] Those states that have produced the highest standards of living in human history have been militarily proficient: the historically unprecedented prosperity of developed countries has, ironically, occurred alongside the most devastating wars in human history in which those same states fought mainly against each other. Or they fought against non-Western peoples in imperial competition with each other.

What can be said of the institution of war can also be said of modern nation-states and the system of states: they are sources of both good and evil, prosperity as well as misery. At a minimum states are justified as a necessary evil to provide basic security and safety. This is Hobbes's sovereign state. At a maximum they are seen as an essential institution for achieving and enjoying the good life for the greatest number of people. This is the communitarian ideal of Bentham's and Mill's nineteenth-century public utilitarian state and of most socially conscious thinkers' contemporary welfare state. The fact is that people who live within the ramparts of some modern nation-states, regardless of the ideologies of the parties in power, have enjoyed standards of living that are the highest in all of human history. Citizens of the developed Organisation for Economic Co-operation and Development (OECD) states on average live longer, healthier, more comfortable, more varied, and more enriched lives than any large population groups in history. It is nevertheless also a fact that the contemporary state system contains other states whose populations suffer extremely low living standards: the lives of the vast majority of the people in Africa are wretched by comparison with the lives of most people of Western Europe, North America, and Japan. Which sort of state should we take as a baseline for evaluating the contemporary state system—those of the North, or those of the South? The only reasonable answer is of course: both. Richard Falk resists such a balanced view of the sovereign state and the state system.

Anybody who is aware of global capitalism can recognize elements of truth in Richard Falk's portrait of the third model. The problem is, however, that it seems to postulate a disjuncture between the states system, on the one hand, and global capitalism, on the other hand, which cannot be sustained. There is a well-rehearsed political economy argument, expressed by Karl

Marx no less than by Adam Smith, to the effect that global capitalism operates in tandem with global statism and not in fundamental opposition. There have been times when the state has sought to manage the economy and has gained the upper hand in that regard—as in the mercantilist era of the later seventeenth and the eighteenth centuries and again in the neomercantilist era of the mid-twentieth century. Adam Smith argued against state-dominated economies. However, there have been other times when the relationship was reversed: in the early nineteenth century, markets broke free of states and transformed national governments into advocates and even auxiliaries of global capitalism. This happened again in the late twentieth century. Karl Marx argued against market-dominated economies.

We appear to be living in an era when global capitalism, now based on postindustrial technology, is again reducing the autonomy of the sovereign state in the sphere of economics. Richard Falk compares our era of global markets to the medieval era in Europe when the Christian church stood above kings and other secular rulers. But the medieval church was a centralized clerical bureaucracy, whereas the global market consists of numerous rival business firms, from large corporations to small entrepreneurs. Perhaps a more apt comparison is with the early modern era of merchant capitalism, when Dutch and English commercial adventurers, including investors as well as traders, were building the first world economic system still relatively free of the dictates and demands of nation-states.[27] This is the world that Grotius was living in. Our world of postindustrial capitalism offers some parallels. Globalizing capitalism did not lead to the decline of sovereign states in the seventeenth century; it led to the expansion of European sovereign states via imperialism and colonialism to the four corners of the world. And while states are clearly working in the service of markets today, this reflects a recognition of the inescapable reality of globalism and the electronic technology upon which it is based. It also reflects a cold calculation that this may be in the best interests of states and their citizens. Richard Falk makes no allowance for the possibility of a new modus vivendi between states and markets.

However, it is toward the fourth model that Richard Falk directs his intellectual energies and ideological concerns as an international legal scholar working in the tradition of prescriptive jurisprudence founded in the 1960s by Myers S. McDougal and his colleagues at the Yale Law School.[28] In this "world order perspective" the traditional separation of law and politics is abolished. The legal scholar ceases to be academically detached. Instead, he or she takes on the *persona* and the role of the politically engaged rhetorician and activist. This is not the place to discuss that school of international jurisprudence, but their ideological support of populist causes in world affairs is an essential background for understanding Falk's efforts to guide the second Grotian moment in a solidarist direction. What, then, are the merits of this model that Richard Falk advocates as a goal worthy of a politically progressive world jurisprudence? As indicated, the model rests on the desire to direct international legal studies toward a populist global condition in which every man, woman, and child on earth can live in peace and harmony, can be confident of social and political dignity, can enjoy economic equity, and can live in a balanced natural environment. No enlightened person would disagree with any of these goals. Problems only arise in attempting to know how best to pursue them. Should they be pursued within the framework of the state system? Can they be pursued outside that framework?

Richard Falk argues that the state system is an obstacle to global human solidarity which must be populist and not statist. He poses a fundamental conflict between populism and statism. He believes that worldwide human solidarity can only be achieved outside the framework of the state system. But is there really a fundamental conflict between solidarism and statism? Even if there is, which is debatable, is it reasonable to suppose that populism would or even that it should triumph?

Richard Falk believes that to overcome this statist barrier to human progress it is necessary to distinguish between "the well-being of governments and the well-being of peoples or their countries." There is certainly no question but that governments can abuse their sovereignty and large numbers of people can suffer as a result.[29] What is questionable is Falk's implication that this state-produced suffering is a defining feature of the state system rather than a contingent feature of many states. As indicated, the fact is that the contemporary state system is composed of member states whose domestic living conditions vary enormously, from the affluence in Switzerland at one extreme to the destitution in Ethiopia at the other extreme. The state system based on international anarchy is associated with both conditions, and not just with one of them. The people of Switzerland, and the populations of all other comparable developed countries, enjoy their high living standards as members of those particular states. Sovereign statehood and human well-being go together in these cases. This is indicated not least by the flow of global human migration in the direction of these countries. Millions of people are hoping to better their living conditions by moving across international borders.

Even if we take Richard Falk's negative view of the modern state, the fact remains that the contemporary state system is dominated and controlled by the developed OECD states and it is highly unlikely that either their governments or their citizens are going to do anything out of regard for global human solidarity that would place their national living standards at risk. It is equally implausible that stateless global humanity could oblige them to do that. The fact is that the only political organization available to humankind on a global scale is the state system and probably the only way to effectively promote human well-being worldwide is via that same state system. The possibility of a non-state political organization of humankind that could rival and somehow displace the state system seems far-fetched to say the least. The desirability of such an eventuality is also open to question. It should be obvious from the foregoing analysis that Richard Falk's argument about "global populism" belongs to the same quixotic genre as arguments about "world government," which he rightly debunks.

It may be useful at this stage to recollect some remarks of Hedley Bull about other conceivable future alternatives to the society of states.[30] Bull devotes most of his discussion to the possibility that international society might be yielding to "a secular reincarnation of the system of overlapping or segmented authority that characterized medieval Christendom." He takes note of many of the same developments that Falk calls our attention to: that states in some parts of the world are coming together in projects of regional integration, that some states elsewhere are coming apart internally, that private international violence is on the increase, that transnational organizations are expanding, and that the technological unification of the world is well underway. But the conclusions that Hedley Bull arrives at are almost exactly the opposite of those of Richard Falk. Bull concludes in a detached and skeptical vein that none of these developments, taken either individually or collectively, have the effect of rendering the pluralist society of states obsolete.

The society of states began its historical existence as a parochial political institution in a small corner of the world, namely Western Europe. During a period of about four centuries this originally Christian and European system evolved and expanded to become the basic secular political institution of humankind the world over. Hedley Bull draws our attention to "the continuing vitality of the states system" that has adapted to social change time and again over a period of centuries. Many of these changes were as disruptive and disorienting as the changes we are witnessing at the present time. Among such historical changes are: the long range sailing ship and new navigation techniques that made possible the European "discovery" of "new worlds" overseas beginning in the late fifteenth century; the merchant capitalism of the sixteenth and seventeenth centuries that followed on the heels of those European discoveries and exploited them; the scientific revolution of the seventeenth century; the enlightenment of the eighteenth century; the concurrent emergence of political nationalism and industrial capitalism in the late eighteenth and nineteenth centuries; the development of the mass mobilization warfare state and welfare state of the nineteenth and twentieth centuries; the mass consumption society of the twentieth century. The state system accommodated itself to all of these historical transformations, many of them revolutionary in their consequences.

There are at least two fundamental reasons for the successful political adaptation of the state system. The first is its decentralization. Being pluralistic and, thus, already decentered it cannot be broken the way that the Renaissance and the Reformation broke the medieval *respublica Christiana* or the way the "barbarian" tribes of Europe broke the Roman Empire. The second basic reason for the continued vitality of the state system is given special emphasis by Hedley Bull: "the tyranny of the concepts and normative principles associated with it," which constitutes an intellectual prison from which escape is difficult. This is because it is very hard to think about convincing alternative images of international life, including globalist and solidarist images, without employing the categories and concepts, indeed even the language, associated with it. Richard Falk underestimates the evolutionary adaptability of a pluralistic society of states, which, if history is anything to go by, should be expected to rise to the challenges of globalism as it has risen to comparable challenges on many occasions in the past. He also underestimates the hold that statist concepts and language still have on the minds of people: not only the minds of international legal and political scholars but, far more importantly, the minds of statesmen and everybody who deals with them.

Pluralism and Solidarism in World Jurisprudence

The argument of Hedley Bull leads to an interpretation of Grotianism that is sharply different from the interpretation advanced by Richard Falk. But it is consistent with the basic jurisprudential ideas of Hugo Grotius concerning state sovereignty and natural law. Grotius is not a premodern theorist of the European Middle Ages. Neither is he a postmodern theorist of a "global populism." Grotius is the legal theorist *par excellence* of international society, which means that he is a theorist of the state centric and human focused world that has been evolving for the past three or four centuries and continues to evolve. If there is a Grotian moment, it is measured by that entire span of time.

The second half of the twentieth century is reminiscent of Grotius's own time before the pluralist doctrine of legal positivism had taken almost exclusive possession of the idea of the law of nations, receiving its definitive intellectual shape in the eighteenth-century jurisprudence of Vattel. J.L. Brierly has commented on this point: "This exaggerated emphasis on the independence of states had the effect in Vattel's system of reducing the natural law, which Grotius had used as a juridical barrier against absolute conceptions of sovereignty, to little more than an aspiration after better relations between states."[31] The pluralist doctrine of state sovereignty remained prominent in public international law, both in theory and practice, through the eighteenth and nineteenth centuries. But the solidarist element was never obliterated, and in the twentieth century it was recovered and given new institutional clothing.

It would be generally accurate to say that the twentieth century, especially the post-1945 era, is a neo-Grotian era insofar as solidarist principles have been reinvigorated.[32] At the same time, however, pluralist practices have not been abandoned or even downgraded. On the contrary, they continue to be fundamental to international politics and international law. The solidarist doctrine was reinvigorated largely in response to the monstrous crimes against humanity of the Fascist powers before and during World War II. Solidarism is imperfectly evident in the Nuremberg and Tokyo tribunals (1946–47), the Universal Declaration of Human Rights (1948), the UN Convention on the Prevention and Punishment of the Crime of Genocide (1948), the Geneva Conventions (1949), the International Covenants of Human Rights (1966), and many other human rights and humanitarian initiatives of the post-1945 era. Yet despite the revival of solidarism after 1945, it remains a historical reality that pluralist principles are still powerfully present in contemporary world affairs. This is evident, not least, from the prominence given to the doctrine of state sovereignty in the UN Charter and other international covenants, both universal and regional, whose basic norms are considered almost sacred to the vast majority of the world's independent governments and especially those of the recently independent Third World. I refer to the doctrine of nonintervention, the inviolability of international borders, the sovereign state as the framework within which human welfare and development is pursued, and so forth.

Can any conclusions be drawn from this long-standing historical dialectic of pluralism and solidarism in world affairs? The balance between pluralism and solidarism in international relations obviously changes over time in response to new historical situations. What is most noteworthy about this changing balance is the fact that neither norm has ever monopolized international political life to the complete and permanent exclusion of the other. Since the time of Grotius, the world has never been able to give up completely on either natural law and human rights or positive law and state sovereignty. The link between these norms is the underlying universalism of the state system, which existed from the beginning at least as a potentiality, and the moral premise of inclusion of the world's entire population in that system. In other words, the law of nations was potentially universal right from the start. In historical fact this process of inclusion took over three centuries to achieve and I rather doubt that Grotius ever envisaged a global society of sovereign states and human rights. But it was always implicit in the doctrine of natural law that Grotius saw as the basic moral restraint that had to be placed on the sovereign state. The doctrine of natural law is universal by definition.

I think it is reasonable to conclude from the historical evolution of international society that state sovereignty and human rights belong together and cannot permanently be kept apart. This is arguably one of the most important conclusions of Grotius's international jurisprudence even though he never anticipated a global society of states. If there is a Grotian moment in world jurisprudence perhaps this is it. A final conclusion is linked to this one: the thought of great thinkers often leads to important historical destinations that they themselves could never have foreseen.

CHAPTER 8

Dialogical Justice in World Affairs

Justice should not be construed as some simple unconcern with one's own interests, but as a lively recognition of other men's interests alongside one's own.

J.R. Lucas

Justice between States?

A study of justice in world affairs should begin with a skeptical question: is there such a thing? Hobbes would answer "no."[1] Contrary to the assertions of realists and other skeptics, I shall argue that justice is constitutive and regulative of social life generally and that various principles and practices of justice are operative in international relations. My aim must be confined to sketching the character and modus operandi of the idea.

"The arguments of justice," as Lucas points out, "are essentially dialectical."[2] Justice is interlocutory. It involves conversation, discussion, communication, intercourse, conferral, inquiry, parlay among parties with rival claims who seek an acceptable, at least tolerable, or passing accommodation between themselves. Justice is dynamic rather than static: it is a dialogue involving arguments for or against; it is giving a hearing to all legitimate parties involved. This dialogue can be conducted in many different places but the usual context is the state and the society of states. In domestic political affairs it can take place in courts, in legislatures, in cabinets, in councils, in ministries and departments, and so forth. In international affairs, it can take place in foreign ministries, in embassies, in international organizations, in conferences, and so forth. International justice is usually claimed and meted out in less structured places than courts or legislatures. But this does not mean that it is not claimed and meted out. It only means that international justice is more controversial and provisional than domestic justice. And when meted out it is often a rougher justice. This is particularly the case in war.

Justice involves dialogue. International justice is virtually defined by conversation and negotiation between the parties involved, often conducted via diplomacy, which is perhaps the most important intercommunicative activity of states. Justice between states is channeled and shaped by institutions, practices, and activities that we label "international" and that centrally involve contact, communication, and negotiation. But it is constrained by circumstances, such as military force or economic resources, and by considerations that impinge on international agents and their activities and have the effect of making mutual accommodations between states that much harder to arrive at. The international world is well known for being a sphere of difficult decisions and hard choices. But facing a hard choice is not the same as having no choice at all. And if there is room for choice there is room for justice as well. Justice is an activity that involves approaching and accommodating other people's interests and concerns without repudiating or sacrificing our own.

Justice between states, such as we find it to be, is not the same as justice within states and among individual people. We cannot treat a state as we would an individual because this would lead to moral expectations that would be difficult if not impossible to meet. Justice is never easy. But justice between private parties and even justice in domestic political affairs is easier than justice between states. The international sphere is significantly different from the domestic sphere, and that difference must be acknowledged if we hope to arrive at a correct understanding of the character and *modus operandi* of international justice. Many scholars of international relations avoid the study of justice in the conviction that it is a domestic subject by and large and therefore has little or no place in relations of states, which are considered to involve power for the most part. This view of the subject ignores the effects of states on each other and their entanglement and involvement with each other, which can provoke issues of justice. Power and its agents and instruments are facts of international affairs, but they are not the only facts. The uses and consequences of power do not exist in isolation from moral and legal judgments about them. War, diplomacy, trade, finance, intervention, sanctions, and much else involve such judgments, which are part of international relations, not separate from it.

The vocabulary of international relations includes "society," "sovereignty," "security," "recognition," "equality," "freedom," "responsibility," "appeasement," "aggression," "preemption," "noncombatant," "immunity," "nonintervention," "humanitarianism," "human rights," "terrorism," "free trade," "fair trade," "development," "foreign aid," and countless similar words and expressions. Normative ideas are conveyed in the meanings and usages of such terms. The instrumental discourse of power and the noninstrumental discourse of legitimacy and legality are both operative in the conduct of international affairs—often employed by the same agents at the same time in regard to the same event. Human interactions and transactions are set in motion by various inclinations and aversions: self-interest, ambition, pleasure-seeking, pain-avoiding, hope, fear, concern, expectation, apprehension, loyalty, fraternity, affection, jealousy, dislike, disgust, hate, among many others, which bring people into conflictive or cooperative contact. Our elaborate social vocabulary is testimony to the diversity and complexity of our relations. In these relations, justice operates primarily as a qualification or quality of human interaction as expressed by such words as "fair," "impartial," "disinterested," "unbiased," "equitable," "even-handed," and so forth.[3] If justice is operative among people, such English words—or their equivalents in other languages—enter their discourse. One empirical way to study justice, therefore, is to look at the dialogue of the players.

In the grammar of social and political discourse, justice is adverbial or adjectival: a quality of action or condition; that which is right or at least not wrong, good or at least not bad. Such considerations or concerns are normative in character. Power also is a quality of action or condition: that which is efficient, effective, productive, expedient, sufficient, satisfying; such considerations or concerns are instrumental in character. Power politics, for example, is instrumental political activity: it caters for self-interests. This is not the end of the matter, however, for self-interested political activity is very likely to provoke normative questions, including questions of justice. Because power can produce pain as well as pleasure it is far too important for human well-being to be left to its own instrumental logic and techniques—such as those outlined by Nicollo Machiavelli in the sixteenth century.[4] Power can of course be checked or balanced by power, threats of coercion or acts of force can be responded to in kind—in short, self-interest can be regulative. This is a basic proposition of domestic politics. It is also an elemental feature of international politics. However, the fabric of political life is fashioned from morality and legality as well as self-interest and expediency: if we confine the study of international relations to instrumental questions, we sell our subject short by arbitrarily and I believe unrealistically excluding a crucially significant noninstrumental part. We end up with only half the knowledge that we would otherwise possess (see chapter 1).

Martin Wight speaks of a "dialectical interdependence" of Machiavellian and Kantian theories.[5] Military power should be employed for defending or enhancing our self-interest: this is a Machiavellian maxim. Military power should not be employed except to enforce the categorical imperative—the universal, morally preemptive, principle of right: this is a Kantian injunction.[6] We are both Machiavellians and Kantians: we calculate our interests but we also consider our obligations, which usually comes down to recognizing the legitimate interests and rights of others. This dialectical process (which is also the middle way of Grotius) is central to the practice of international justice. It ought to be at the center of any study that aims to capture this practice in fitting theoretical terms.

Demands for justice (or protests against injustice) are not misunderstandings about the reality of power in human affairs. Nor are they idealistic dreams of utopia. Nor, again, are they merely "window dressing" or masquerades on ulterior motives. They are reasonable responses to real situations that are concerned with subjecting power to noninstrumental requirements and regulations. Justice is not least about moderating and civilizing the uses of power in human affairs. This is what just war doctrines are concerned with: *jus ad bellum, jus in bello, jus ante bellum*. This is what equitable procedures and rules of international trade are concerned with: *pacta sunt servanda*, the most favored nation principle. Practices and acts of civility, that is, observing noninstrumental rules that respect others, and abstaining from actions that would harm or damage others without justification, are a requirement of all international conduct but especially of the strong in their relations and dealings with the weak.[7]

Consequently, to study justice in world affairs is not to ignore power or downgrade its importance. On the contrary, it is to give power pride of place by focusing on fundamental normative questions that various instrumentalities and acts of power raise. Normative considerations cannot be too far from instrumental calculations; otherwise they will be unworldly hopes rather than operative elements in human affairs. This is as evident in world affairs as it is in any other sphere of human activity, in all of which the normative and the instrumental must be in close dialogue if minimal human conditions are to be defended and not defeated and a truly human life is to be lived. Justice and power must be in close dialogue because we are referring to a human world and not a mechanical world or a world of beasts or a world of saints or Gods. Humans are intelligent and willful creatures that are devoted to enjoying pleasure and avoiding pain, but they are also fully capable of being conscientious and reliable agents in their dealings with each other. How else would flourishing human societies be possible? But justice is never automatically forthcoming in human affairs because temptations to engage in aggressive, arbitrary, contemptuous, selfish, or ruthless uses of power are always present. Humans are less than perfect moral agents. This Augustinian point is no less valid today than it was in the past.

The Idea of Justice

In recent writings one idea of justice has commanded particular attention: fairness. The foremost writer on the subject in the latter half of the twentieth century—the American philosopher John Rawls—regards justice as a fundamental moral idea that invokes the practice of "right dealing between persons," as in "fair games," "fair competition," "fair bargains," and so forth. "A practice will strike the parties as fair if none feels that, by participating in it, they or any of the others are taken advantage of, or forced to give into claims which they do not regard as legitimate."[8] Another prominent thinker—the English philosopher J.R. Lucas—focuses on the reverse idea of injustice, which is the wrong or the evil that is committed by taking unfair advantage of anyone or otherwise injuring or damaging anyone in violation of their rights or legitimate interests.[9]

These conceptions have the merit of disclosing justice as an operative element of human relations: a normative standard that can help to elicit and to sustain the myriad interactions and transactions that are necessary for a flourishing human life. This is perhaps why many philosophers, past and present, give justice a central place in their political and ethical theories. Aristotle regarded justice as that which is both lawful and fair: the "supreme" virtue.[10] Rawls speaks of justice as "the first virtue of social institutions."[11] To act unfairly is to act in a way that violates or otherwise offends against common moral standards and expectations. Justice according to Hobbes is "giving to every man his own."[12]

We predictably become indignant at injustice, which indicates that we expect to be treated with due regard, recognition, and respect. Justice is integrative and injustice is disruptive and destructive, as Plato pointed out long ago: "injustice has this effect of implanting hatred" and making "any set of people . . . incapable of any joint action."[13] Injustices provoke outcry. Those that are not corrected drive people down into their private existences, leaving the state as merely a residual world of arbitrary power: tyranny, despotism, dictatorship, totalitarianism, and so forth. When we are out only for ourselves we are involved in a project that excludes considerations of justice. Hence Augustine's famous remark: "states without justice are but robber bands enlarged."[14] We still say this about some states today. Yet we should not forget David Hume's postscript: "Robbers and pirates, it has often been remarked, could not maintain their pernicious confederacy did they not establish a new distributive justice among themselves and recall those laws of equity which they have violated with the rest of mankind."[15] Hobbes and similar realists are in effect saying the same thing of states, where there is justice, in contrast to the anarchical system of states, where there is no justice. Yet if we look we shall find justice there too. Justice of some sort is essential for all flourishing societies, including international society.

Justice consists in fair play, impartiality, evenhandedness, due process, equal consideration, and similar other-regarding practices that invite rather than discourage sustainable involvement of human beings with each other. Justice, as Lucas well puts it, is "the bond of society," which serves as a check on expediency, efficiency, productivity, arrogance, pride, bias, disregard, contempt, hostility, hindrance, and all other instrumental, self-interested, self-indulgent, self-seeking, and one-sided expectations and actions of people. Protests against injustice are indicative of such bonds. The bond is a shared conception and mutual expectation of at least minimal, tolerable, or passable fairness and equity. One crucial and historically commonplace home of such expectations is the state conceived as a framework of just laws for its citizens: the state as covenant. International law, diplomatic practices, international organizations, and other such arrangements can be conceived as spheres of justice or fair dealings between states: the bonds and covenants of international society.[16]

To sum up thus far: power and justice are companion and interactive ideas. Calculations of power and considerations of justice do not exist or operate in separate watertight compartments. On the contrary, they exist and operate in tandem. Instrumental actions are likely to provoke, at some point, normative issues or concerns, including those of justice. I conceive of that interactive relation as sometimes a dialogue or conversation, at other times a disagreement or dispute, between two categorically different ways of contemplating and taking actions: that which is in one's self-interest versus that which gives at least minimally owed regard or consideration to the legitimate interests and rights of others. This dialectic between power and legitimacy is often going on among the same people at the same time in regard to the same episode. To focus exclusively on the former to the complete neglect of the latter, as implied by such expressions as power politics or realpolitik, is to overlook or ignore a crucial normative element that is a close companion and interlocutor of power and interest not only in domestic political life but also in world politics and, indeed, in all human interactions and transactions. No sphere of human relations is exempted from considerations of justice and fair play. When we engage in international relations we do not cease to be human in our dealings with each other. We only find it more difficult because of what separates us.

Realist Skepticism

The belief that there is little place for justice in the actual conduct of foreign policy, and that to search for it is merely to display a faulty understanding based on naive idealism, is usually associated with the realist school of international relations. I rehearsed several narratives of classical and modern realism in chapter 2 and I shall not repeat that exercise here. Instead, I shall be content with stating and replying to five long-standing realist propositions concerning justice in world affairs.

(1) People and states are motivated and moved exclusively by power and narrow self-interest, that is, opportunities, inducements, desires, fears, threats, compulsion, and so on. Hobbes said humans are driven by a desire for felicity but above all by a fear of death.[17] Resist and defend or be defeated and destroyed. Although statesmen speak and act in the name of rights, duties, commitments, honor, and similar norms, these are merely consoling words and at the end of the day it is power driven by narrow self-interest—realpolitik— that moves them. One is again reminded of Hobbes's remark about the state of nature between sovereigns: "The notions of right and wrong, justice and injustice have there no place . . . Force, and fraud, are in war the two cardinal virtues."[18] This is the archetypal thesis of realist international thought.

(2) Because security can be realized within separate state frameworks it is unnecessary to set up an overarching superstate for that purpose based on an international social contract. The pressure on sovereign states to do that is obviously far less than that on individual humans in the original state of nature. States are not driven by the same necessities owing to their far greater self-sufficiencies. States are drawn into relations primarily out of self-interest, that is expediency, and because they usually exist in close quarters with each other. Their proximity, their frequently bordering and contiguous location, and their contacts and encounters raise the possibility, even the likelihood that sooner or later collisions and clashes will occur between them. On this understanding, the society of states, insofar as one can speak of such a society, is a mainly instrumental sphere and is far less developed than domestic society.

(3) Justice is confined to states whose governments usually have extensive obligations to their citizens (and vice versa) but not to the governments or citizens of other states, or to humankind in general. A weaker (and I think

more realistic) version of this proposition is the claim that the obligations of sovereign governments to their citizens must have priority over their obligations to each other or to humankind: whatever morality may be involved in foreign affairs it must take a back seat to domestic political obligation (see chapter 6).

(4) States are sovereign in the meaning of being constitutionally independent.[19] Each one has its own constitution, which is not part of any other state's constitution. This means that constitutional responsibility is confined within them. It would be foreign interference (and also paternalism) for the government of one state to assume responsibility for the security and well-being of another state and its citizens without the consent of the latter—even if the government of the second state refused to assume responsibility itself. It is up to the citizens of the second state to make their government accountable to them; it is not up to any foreign power to do that for them—even if they were able to do it. Political ethics by this logic is confined to states. To justify benevolent external intervention it is necessary to invoke a morality that overrides sovereign statehood—such as universal human rights. But taken to its logical conclusion this denies the fully adult political agency of independent states and citizens, and therefore the sovereignty foundations of international relations.

(5) Finally, although there is such a thing as international law, it cannot be readily enforced and cannot therefore qualify as "law" properly speaking. According to this conception of world affairs, international law is merely those customs, conventions, usages, and agreements that are convenient to states and conducive to defending or advancing their national self-interests. States observe the law of nations—when they do observe it, which is by no means always the case—because on balance it is in their interests to do so: it smoothes their external relations by making those relations more predictable, more orderly, and more stable than they would otherwise be. It is an arrangement of convenience and comfort: if it were not of some expedient use to them it would not exist. International law is therefore an instrumental sphere of self-interest and expediency: it cannot involve or invoke issues of justice between states.

Power and Legitimacy

By reminding us of the vital importance of power in human affairs these propositions make a fundamental statement. Power, as indicated, is life itself: humans are first of all natural agents with brainpower and muscle power. Humans have a mortal existence bordered by birth and death. They have a natural desire to live and aversion to die. The possibilities and limitations, opportunities and hazards, created by power are a reality or given of human existence. Without power we humans are nothing. To live is to enjoy and exercise our power. To die is to lose everything we have. Without our brains and most of our bodies we cannot exist naturally. Without some further means of artificial power, from traditional agriculture and the alphabet to the modern nation state and high technology, we cannot hope to live above the bare floor of human existence. One could go on at great length in the same vein. Realists overstate their case, however, when they assign to power the exclusive role of arbiter in world affairs.[20] They overstate even when they try not to, as when E.H. Carr says that although "politics cannot be satisfactorily defined exclusively in terms of power, it is safe to say that power is always an essential element of politics . . . Politics are, then, in one sense always power politics."[21] He is closer to reality, I believe, when he claims "it is as fatal in politics to ignore power as it is to ignore morality."[22] This proposition could equally be reversed. Both propositions taken together express an underlying thesis of this book.

The international system is a condition of anarchy in the primary dictionary meaning of the term: "Absence of government; a state of lawlessness due to the absence or inefficiency of the supreme power."[23] It would be not only unrealistic but also mistaken to deny that sovereign states are self-centered and strongly concerned with advancing and defending their interests in foreign relations—and justifiably so insofar as they are responsible for the security and welfare of their citizens. One should add, following Hobbes, that states are far more self-sufficient than individual humans. The most effectively organized and best-managed states are more self-sufficient than any other corporate groups: which is why almost all such groups—business corporations, churches, schools, universities, trade unions, professional associations, and much else—depend upon states for security, law and order, and other basic collective goods. So the motivations and inclinations of states to be sociable and cooperative are less than for most other groups or individuals. States are constitutionally accountable to their citizens but they are only circumstantially and conditionally responsible to each other. States are only responsible to humanity to the extent they choose to be.

Yet states are entangled with each other, and with humanity, to a greater extent than "independence," "self-interest," and "choice" imply: they share common borders and they are almost always involved in elaborate contacts and transactions with each other. One cannot speak of international relations—anymore than of domestic political life—using the instrumental language of power alone without misrepresenting, distorting, and misunderstanding those relations because they involve not merely conflicts of interests, balances of power, and patterns of behavior but also standards and expectations of conduct. In the course of their foreign relations states incur, almost inevitably, mutual debts and obligations. Although they cannot be enforced by an overarching sovereign they nevertheless have some kind of normative standing, and often legality. States owe things to each other and they must act accordingly, which is to say that they are under a bond of some kind to recognize their mutual debts. The states system is an arrangement not only of interests but also of promises: *pacta sunt servanda*: a partly instrumental and partly normative world. It is true that states are only accountable to humanity to the extent they choose to be. But they make that choice, which is usually indicated by their adoption and adherence to international humanitarian law, which is made by states and by nobody else. As argued in chapter 2, the deeply skeptical language of Thrasymachus is inadequate for understanding the entanglements and commitments of sovereign states.[24]

This is reflected in the working vocabulary of international relations, which is significantly and inescapably normative. Consider, for instance, the word "treaty" that is defined as "a contract between two or more states, relating to peace, truce, alliance, commerce, or other international relation; also, the document embodying such contract, in modern usage formally signed by plenipotentiaries appointed by the government of each state. (Now the prevailing sense.)"[25] That English word has been in use since the early fifteenth century. Treaties are international legal expressions of the normative activity of promising and consenting, which presupposes that they are binding, at least to some degree, and must therefore be honored and kept. This, in turn, implies good faith. If international relations were a purely instrumental world of power and self-interest such language would not exist because there would be no need for it—not even as a mask on power. Everyone would understand that the game was exclusively instrumental and so the mask would be transparent. It would not be a mask. The game would not truly be a "game" because games require noninstrumental rules to exist and be played: the on side rule in soccer, the foul ball rule in baseball. International relations would be confined to danger, opportunity, threat, deterrence, collision, collusion, conspiracy, conquest, exploitation, and so forth: the Machiavellian language of power politics. That would not be an international game. It would be mere conflict and struggle.

There are of course occasions when confidence and expectations of fair dealings between states deteriorate or even break down and international relations descend into a condition that approximates Hobbes's state of nature. Great wars, cold wars, major revolutions, religious reformations, great depressions, and other such calamities can and do interrupt international society—sometimes on a wide scale and for lengthy periods. But such occurrences can be denoted conceptually and linguistically precisely because they contrast with different eras and situations—such as peace, stability, sociability, and reciprocity between states. War and peace are very different conditions but they are closely related, and they cannot be completely understood independent of each other. Even during international Dark Ages when mutual obligations between states are interrupted and suspended these inclinations and practices are not entirely eliminated—as events during the Cold War indicate. Not only did diplomatic activities between the protagonists continue during that period but important international arrangements were put in place, which involved normative undertakings: for example, the 1975 Helsinki accords, which registered a "commitment" of the protagonists to uphold "peace, security and justice," to recognize "freedom and political independence," and to respect "human rights."[26] This arrangement had substance and was not merely formal. It cannot be adequately captured using instrumental language alone.

Even war cannot be fully captured by instrumental language because war involves not only threats and acts of human battle and physical destruction but also grievances and claims, condemnations and justifications, between the belligerents. War is an inherently normative activity. Most states do not enter into war without a cause, usually a great cause, as captured by normative expressions: *causa belli, jus ad bellum,* self-defense, necessity, security, survival, and so forth. In short, the third proposition, which confines political obligation to domestic politics, is a misunderstanding and misrepresentation of world affairs in historical reality.

What of the less categorical and more nuanced version of realism, which only claims that international obligations are secondary to the obligations of the state and the citizen? The first responsibility of statesmen is to their citizens and it must be that way in a world of sovereign states. They are responsible for their citizens' security and welfare. This is what national government is fundamentally about. This is what political independence involves and calls for. I cannot foresee civic responsibility making way for some alternative arrangement, such as responsibility to humankind, anytime soon. If it did make way the political world would have changed fundamentally, from a world of independent states to a world community, a *civitas maxima,* perhaps a world of peace as envisaged by Kant. This remains a dream or vision, typically of certain intellectuals and humanitarians, who cannot be reconciled to the imperfect human world in which we are obliged to live. But state responsibility does not exclude international obligations and cannot rule out questions of justice and injustice in relations of states, or even questions of human justice. States can at one and the same time have responsibilities both to their citizens and to other states: not the same responsibilities, but responsibilities nonetheless. They can also take upon themselves some degree of responsibility for human rights and human well-being beyond their borders: some states demonstrate a bona fide humanitarian will in their foreign policies. They can also jointly bear responsibility for the common good of the world at large, at least to some extent in certain spheres, such as the global environment.

States exercise, in the normal conduct of their affairs, plural responsibilities. They face inward and outward at the same time. And their foreign policy can be concerned both with foreign states and with foreign people, either as individuals or as populations. All that involves the possibility and often the reality of normative dilemmas of foreign policy. Justice in world affairs, more than most other spheres, is fraught with such predicaments. Instead of arbitrarily postulating the priority of domestic obligations over international obligations it would be more realistic and accurate to conceive of these different spheres as provoking normative questions, including questions of justice, into which the study of world affairs must necessarily inquire. The fact that domestic responsibility is likely to have priority in any clash with international responsibility or global responsibility does not refute the claim that the latter kinds of responsibility can and do have a place, even a significant place, among the responsibilities of statecraft.

This brings me to the fifth realist proposition concerning international law, which is certainly a convenience to states and if it were not convenient I doubt that it would exist. Why would independent governments freely enter into treaty relations or observe common customs if it were not useful or advantageous to do so? The answer is obvious: they would not. But an entirely instrumental world would exclude the idea of a treaty because treaties—and also conventions, declarations, protocols, alliances, concordats, leagues, and the rest—embody responsibility or accountability. States are usually careful to commit themselves only to treaty obligations they can observe and keep—or they know they will not have to keep. The main point of treaty arrangements is to bind participants and prevent breach of promise or repudiation of consent. Underlying that is the principle of good faith, which is fundamental to the law of nations and to international society generally. Even the legal principle that states cannot be held to their treaty obligations when circumstances fundamentally change (e.g. as a result of war) is a principle of justice: *rebus sic stantibus*. Not to allow for such contingencies would be to ignore or neglect impinging factors that reduce the capacity and freedom to act responsibly and would thus distort the accountability and answerability to which any state could fairly be held. This is the equivalent of the notion of extenuating circumstances in domestic law, which is essential in accurately and fairly determining legal responsibility.

Keeping one's treaty obligations can be justified by general utilitarian reasoning: for example, that it would be harmful to the common interest of all states if the treaty system were to break down. Jeremy Bentham expresses that idea as "the equal utility of states," which he considers to be the basic moral principle of diplomacy and international law.[27] He argues that the system of states is not only an arrangement of order but also "a norm of order," and that statesmen must therefore be promoters and preservers of international norms. Treaty obligations also express a procedural morality that is characteristic of traditional international law. This reasoning is evident in John Rawls's conception of international justice as that which is "fair between nations."[28] Treaties bring sovereign states together and tie them together and one important basis upon which that bonding and binding can be achieved is the expectation of fair dealing. Without such an expectation, it is unlikely that states would enter into treaty relations. According to Rawls, this expectation presupposes impartial and nondiscriminatory procedures between states: legal equality, nonintervention, *pacta sunt servanda*, right of self-defense, *jus ad bellum*, and *jus in bello*. These are among the most important principles of international justice.

In short, although instrumental calculations and actions are realities of world affairs, so also are normative considerations and obligations, including those of justice. How could it be otherwise in human relations? This is not to suggest that justice shall prevail, for there will always be injustice as well: there will always be somebody, somewhere who is prepared to do somebody else down—if given the opportunity. This is an inescapable feature of the human condition. It is probably more evident in international relations than any other sphere of human relations. But it is not confined to international relations. And it is by no means the whole of international history. If it were that way we would have no operative language to express the ideas of justice and injustice in world affairs. But we have such a language and we have had it for a long time. The core normative discourse of the postmedieval state system, the language of international law and diplomacy, is as old as that system because it is part and parcel of it.

Varieties of Justice

Justice—like so much of world affairs—is pluralistic. There is not only one idea of international justice but several. Among the most noteworthy are the following: commutative justice, distributive justice, humanitarian justice, and corrective justice. There are also different levels at which justice may be claimed and pursued: justice for individual human beings as such, justice for citizens in their states, justice for states in their international relations, and justice for the world considered as a whole. These various notions and levels of justice follow different tracks that may intersect and may thus provoke normative disputes and dilemmas.

Justice involves both procedures and outcomes, and we would not do intellectual justice to the subject if one commanded our attention to the neglect of the other. This fundamental distinction is usually explored under the headings "commutative justice" and "distributive justice," which are the two main branches of the theory of justice.[29] The first is expressed by such terms as "fair play," "fair chances," "equal opportunities," "equal consideration," "due regard," "due process," and so forth. This is the justice built into the noninstrumental rules of games, legal systems, constitutions, and classical international law. It is the central idea of the liberal theory of justice. Commutative justice is conveyed by the expression "level playing field": provided they are impartial and generally applicable the rules are constitutive of justice; if they are observed and followed by all the players there is no legitimate ground for complaint about the outcome of the game. In baseball it is "three strikes and you are out" for every batter without exception. There are no privileges or exemptions.

Commutative justice is preeminently the justice of a world of free and capable players whose separate or sectional interests and activities may conflict and collide and who therefore require some fair rules in order to enter and play the international game. The rules of the game are constitutive of justice. In states, commutative justice is embodied in constitutional frameworks, in parliamentary procedures, in legal procedures of courts of law, in electoral laws and procedures, and the like. These are typical institutional frameworks of commutative justice in countries that operate in accordance with the rule of law. In international relations, commutative justice is embodied in the practice of mutual recognition, in the immunity of resident embassies and diplomatic staff, in the principle of good faith, in the most-favored-nation principle of international trade, in the rules and procedures of international organizations, such as those of the UN Security Council. These are typical institutional frameworks of the international rule of law.

The second main branch of justice concerns results or outcomes: distributive justice. This is the justice that is sought after by apportioning goods according to criteria such as need, merit, sacrifice, the common good, and so forth. It is the central idea of utilitarian ethics: the just distribution of scarce resources: a necessary element of social justice and economic justice. Distributive justice can be considered from the perspective of procedure, but the determining consideration is the consequence of applying the procedure: the rules are instrumental to justice and not constitutive of it. If the outcome is one-sided the procedure is morally questionable. Distributive justice can be pursued within states: for example, taxation policies aimed at income redistribution to assist the least well off or health and welfare schemes that seek to sustain minimum income floors or social safety nets or universal medical care. It can also be pursued in relations and transactions between states. It is revealed in demands for a redistribution of global wealth to reduce gross international economic disparities and to assist poor countries to develop their economies: for example, international development assistance, special banking arrangements for less developed countries, and so forth. Nowadays, international organizations such as the international monetary fund (IMF) and the World Bank speak the language of distributive justice as well as that of economic productivity—even if the resources they distribute to poor countries on that basis are limited. In the same vein, certain rich countries have cancelled some of the debts owed to them by certain poor countries on the moral grounds that their indebtedness is caused by circumstances beyond their control, and thus constitutes an unfair burden.

International distributive justice is also revealed in purposive and collaborative international arrangements, such as military alliances. Contributions to the military power of the North Atlantic Treaty Organization (NATO) are based on the individual capacities of the member countries of the alliance. The contributions are and must be unequal because their military and economic capacities are not equal: the United States and Denmark are profoundly unequal in this regard. The benefits are and must be equal, however, because the United States, Denmark, and every other member state of NATO must be assumed to have an equal will to join together, stand together and make equal sacrifices in a common cause in defense of each other.[30] It is their unity of purpose, effort, and sacrifice that justifies the equal benefits they receive from their alliance.

Distributive justice can also be conceived at the global level: what Hedley Bull refers to as "the common good of the world."[31] This is the shared or collective well-being of the world taken as a whole. Global distributive justice is perhaps most clearly evident in environmental concerns: the hole in the ozone layer is a threat to everybody on earth. But it is also evident in economic and security concerns: the notion that the world economy and world peace are collective goods that exist for the benefit of everyone on the planet and therefore ought to be arranged and managed as a joint enterprise for common benefit on a worldwide basis. This notion is still largely visionary and it clearly stretches the collective will and capabilities and perhaps also the imagination and credulity of most people. But as the world becomes discernibly more integrated, more socially unified, the perception and plausibility of the notion can be expected to increase.

Two other categories or sub-categories of justice in world affairs deserve mention: human justice and corrective or compensatory justice. The first is justice for human beings as such. This is the justice involved in human rights. These can be negative civil liberties against the sovereign rights of governments: such as the right not to be unlawfully imprisoned, tortured, or killed by the authorities or agents of a state. *Habeus corpus* in English and American law, which is the right not to be imprisoned without trial, is the model of a negative right. These are among the foremost "natural rights" of John Locke and Thomas Jefferson. They constitute an important sub-category of commutative justice. To complicate matters, human rights nowadays can also signify claims to positive economic and social assistance or what have been termed subsistence rights: adequate food, clothing, shelter, and so forth.[32] These positive human rights constitute a sub-categories of distributive justice. Since negative human rights invoke commutative justice whereas positive human rights point to distributive justice, they are likely to come into conflict at some point. The fundamentally different values expressed by these contrasting moral ideas define a great philosophical and ideological divide between those of a more liberal and individualist persuasion and those of a more equalitarian and collectivist outlook.

Corrective justice is a version of legal justice that involves a claim for compensation for something lost owing to wrongdoing or damages caused by somebody else. In international relations such claims can arise between contingent states, where the negligent or wrongful actions of one state's officials or citizens visit damages on a neighboring state, as in the damming or diverting of international rivers or the producing of air-borne or water-borne pollution, such as acid rain. A significant body of international environmental law involves corrective justice.[33] It is also evident in the notion that compensation is owing to third party states that suffer undeserved damages as a result of warfare between other states: for example, the decision by the UN Security Council to compensate Jordan for adverse effects of international economic sanctions in the UN authorized war (1990–91) to drive Iraqi forces out of occupied Kuwait.[34]

It should be evident that claims to justice based on these different concepts may come into conflict. This is most obvious as regards sovereign rights of states, on the one hand, and negative human rights, on the other hand.

Some conflicts present knotted moral or legal dilemmas: such as that in the United States over the Patriot Act which touches, at certain points, on civil liberties in the pursuit of public protection in the fight against terrorism.[35] This is a domestic instance. Similar conflicts and dilemmas also occur at the international level. Hedley Bull points out that "just as the common good of the state may require limitation of the liberty of action of an individual, so may the common good of the world as a whole."[36] Claims of states to sovereignty and nonintervention may collide with the common interest of international society. This is evident in the collective security rules and requirements of the UN Security Council. Sometimes the common good of the world as a whole may have to be purchased at the expense of human rights. The difficulty involved is evident in the tension between the International Criminal Court (ICC) set up to enforce humanitarian norms of individual responsibility, and the United States, which is willing to defend international peace and security but not at the risk of subjecting their leaders and soldiers to the ICC. This unacceptable risk has been a justification of the United States in refusing to be a signatory to the treaty that establishes the Court.[37]

International justice is conditioned by the fact that we live in a normatively plural world. There is not one overarching idea of justice in world affairs; there are several intersecting ideas. There is no clear hierarchy of principles or measures of justice in world affairs either. It is not possible to rank criteria of justice to determine which one shall trump another when they come into conflict. The most that one can reasonably expect is an approach in which different or opposing claims to justice are balanced and weighed in as detached and even-handed a fashion as possible. In English civil law the idea is expressed as a "balancing of probabilities" to assign responsibility and award damages by judges and courts. In world affairs this approach relies upon the virtues of statesmen: their discernment, insight, judgment, even-handedness, good will, and so on. That, or something like that, is at the heart of international justice.

There are no Olympian heights from which to contemplate international justice. Academic philosophers may work out an abstract theory from their ivory towers (see chapter 9).[38] But the international world does not and cannot operate like the academic world. The academic quest for a philosophically coherent theory of justice has the counterproductive effect of segregating and insulating international thought from the complicated and messy international affairs we are trying to understand. To search for an overriding principle of justice is not an empirical way to think about justice in world affairs. Such a way is only open to us if we frankly recognize the

156 • Classical and Modern Thought on International Relations

pluralism of international justice and the difficult circumstances of international relations. Aristotle points the way by conceiving of justice as a civilizing activity of striving to balance one party's legitimate interests against another's without prejudice in search of the mean before rendering judgment.[39] Following that empirical reasoning, dialogical justice in world affairs is the *rapprochement* that can be reached between worthy but conflicting claims for justice none of which can be fully satisfied without creating injustice.

CHAPTER 9

Lifting the Veil of Ignorance: John Rawls's Society of Peoples

> Politics cannot be learned once for all, from a text-book, or the instructions of a master. What we require to be taught . . . is to be our own teachers. It is a subject on which we have no masters to follow; each must explore for himself, and exercise an independent judgment.
>
> John Stuart Mill

John Rawls is widely regarded as one of the leading political philosophers of the twentieth century. His major works on justice and political liberalism have been translated into many languages and they are read around the world and not only the United States.[1] He revitalized the social and political thought of Kant and gave it his own distinctive twist. His *The Law of Peoples* moves a considerable distance beyond his earlier work, which deals almost entirely with domestic justice and largely ignores international justice.[2] I do not intend to review every aspect of this book.[3] I shall focus on his specific notion of a "Society of Peoples" as viewed from the perspective of classical international society thinkers.[4]

The "Veil of Ignorance"

Rawls's neo-Kantianism is captured by the expressions the "Original Position" behind a "veil of ignorance."[5] This is an imagined or hypothetical condition that excludes situational and self-regarding knowledge from social contracts. Rawls's contractors are deprived of knowledge of themselves, of their personal characteristics and habits, hopes and fears, health and happiness; they have no knowledge of their family, friends, occupation, religion, nationality, or any other information particular to their situation. This is necessary because ordinary people evidently would never be inclined to set up "just" political or social institutions if they were allowed to construct them from their parochial standpoint. Eliminating self-and-situational knowledge is supposed to overcome partiality in fundamental political decisions. This hypothetical condition, in which people are blindfolded like the pure marble lady of justice, is the pivotal idea of Rawls's political thought.[6]

Rawls postulates a "Second Original Position" in the context of world society. His "Law of Peoples" consists of "just" principles and norms of international law that are followed by "peoples" "in their mutual relations."[7] These "liberal peoples" and "decent peoples" compose his "Society of Peoples." He seems to conceive of his "Law" as ultimately extending to all the "peoples" of the world: "the representatives of liberal peoples [would] make an agreement with other liberal peoples . . . and later with nonliberal though decent peoples."[8] He evidently believes they would contract into it if presented with a true opportunity to do so, which the "Second Original Position" is supposed to provide. This is because they would then be "subject to a veil of ignorance" and would "not know" any facts about their "territory," "population," or "natural resources," or "other such information" that would distort their judgment. The point is thus to liberate human reason, in eighteenth-century Enlightenment fashion, from experience, circumstances, and prejudice.[9] These agreements would thus be "fair."[10] He asserts the moral superiority of "liberal societies," which he equates with a "just society," and he expects that his international liberalism as expressed by the "Law of Peoples" can accommodate the diversity of human societies around the world.

Rawls makes intermittent reference to historical evidence and it seems clear that he wishes to demonstrate that his theory is in some ways empirical. He "draws on" various works, a few of which are historical accounts. But most of his sources are abstract theories or models. There is little indication of sustained independent study of international affairs on his part. There is not much allowance for human imperfection or the widely noted limits of international ethics. There is scarcely a hint of the knotted moral dilemmas, the difficult and even desperate choices that punctuate the subject historically: what Herbert Butterfield refers to as "the tragic element in modern international conflict."[11] Although Rawls is fully aware of the diverse cultures and societies of the world he seems to think that would present no serious obstacle to an international theory of justice based on a "Second

Original Position." This huge diversity of collective selves and situations would, presumably, be brought into just intersocietal relations by the international "veil of ignorance."

John Rawls conceives of the political philosopher's role as that of supplying a plan for transforming world affairs from an unfair system of states into a just "Society of Peoples." His philosophy is the epitome of "rationalism" in Michael Oakeshott's meaning. He believes that "the proper organization of a society and the conduct of its affairs" should be "based upon abstract principles."[12] It is the business of the political philosopher to come up with guidelines for bringing about a more perfect political world. He explicitly writes of his "Society of Peoples" as a "realistic utopia." His theory is visionary and full of hope. That it is "realistic," that is, by taking adequately into account the facts of the world as we know them, is open to question. International relations is a sphere of human relations that is profoundly affected by situational and self-regarding knowledge, and particularly collective or national self-interest, rooted in diverse cultures and civilizations. To postulate "a veil of ignorance" in the study of international ethics is to soar so high as to risk losing sight of the normative limits and moral predicaments of the subject.[13] "Some may find these sentiments too noble to bear," as Thomas Nagel puts it.[14] This skeptical and sober view is also characteristic of the classical international society thinkers.[15] This chapter, then, is a reading and critique of Rawls's international thought from the perspective of traditional international ethics. His towering liberalism is also contrasted with J.S. Mill's more earth bound views of the subject.

"Peoples" versus States

Rawls develops his theory of "peoples" by arguing against the (mainly American) neorealist theory of "states," which he refers to as "the realist theory."[16] "I [shall] reply to the realist theory [which holds] that international relations have not changed since Thucydides' day and that they continue to be an ongoing struggle for wealth and power."[17] It is curious—considering the liberal and specifically Kantian ancestry of his thinking—that Rawls bypasses classical realism out of preference for a late-twentieth-century social science conception: so-called neorealism. It is a pity that Rawls did not have Hobbes as his paradigm realist, for it would have engaged him in responding to Hobbes's foundation claim that international covenants are against reason because political communities are not analogous to individual men or women. Rawls's "Second Original Position" would have had to be tested against Hobbes's international "state of nature" in which social contracts between states would make no sense because "there does not follow from it that misery, which accompanies the liberty of particular men."[18] Yet there is an advantage in employing the neorealist notion of "states": they stand in much sharper contrast to Rawls's "peoples" and they consequently reinforce his argument that only "peoples" are "reasonable." Classical realist notions of states blur that distinction.

According to Rawls, the "moral nature" and "moral motives" of "peoples" makes them normatively superior to "states." "Peoples" are internationally obligated and regulated. They are "reasonable." They relate to each other in accordance with the principle of "reciprocity." They are favorably disposed to "justice."[19] "What distinguishes peoples from states—and this is crucial—is that just peoples are fully prepared to grant . . . proper respect and recognition to other peoples as equals."[20] "States" are merely "rational" and "prudent"—in the purely instrumental meaning of those terms. They are exclusively preoccupied with their own narrow interests. They are sovereign. "Peoples" lack "traditional sovereignty." The government of a "people" cannot claim "internal sovereignty or (political) autonomy" or any "right to do as it wills with people within its own borders."[21] Such a government possesses a restricted right to wage war and a regulated right of nonintervention. Rawls's "peoples" are tolerant of each other—unlike his "states." "Liberal peoples" are particularly tolerant in that regard. Reasonableness and toleration are two of the keys to Rawls's "Society of Peoples."

> The term "peoples," then, is meant to emphasize . . . peoples as distinct from states . . . their moral character and the reasonably just, or decent, nature of their regimes . . . peoples' rights and duties in regard to their so-called sovereignty derive from the Law of Peoples . . . They are not moved solely by their prudent or rational pursuit of interests, the so-called reasons of state.[22]

Rawls thus believes that, owing to their moral superiority, "peoples" ought to displace "states" as the primary political units of international relations. This calls for two observations. First, he seems unaware that the neorealist conception of "states" is an abstract and ahistorical model—a caricature—that conforms poorly to the evolving role of existing states. Historically states have not possessed his "traditional sovereignty," the unfettered right to do absolutely as they please. There have always been some limits. Over the past century, the limits on state sovereignty have been tightened. The right of war, for example, is noticeably circumscribed from what it once was. The right of conquest and colonization is a thing of the past.[23] The right of nonintervention exists, but it is not absolute: it is limited by the right of self-defense and by the duty of respecting and upholding international peace and security.[24] Existing states recognize and generally respect each other "as equals," which is a fundamental norm of the UN Charter and of international law generally. By using a notion of the state borrowed from neorealist theory, rather than that of classical international thought, Rawls's discussion of "states" versus "peoples" is empirically wide of the mark from the start.

Second, turning to the notion of "peoples," Rawls's text nowhere identifies discernible groups of human beings, either those of the past or those of the present, whom he considers to qualify as "peoples." Looking for existential peoples in history in order to determine if they are a plausible category for political and moral reflection is not his purpose. Instead, he constructs his "peoples" in theory: they exist solely by philosophical meditation. He expends considerable effort stipulating how his conceptualized "peoples" see themselves, what they strive for, what they are prepared to grant to other "peoples," and so forth. "We view peoples as conceiving of themselves as free and equal peoples in the Society of Peoples (according to the political conception of that society)."[25] He enumerates the rights they can claim. Yet, *what* "peoples" are and *who* are "peoples" remain unspecified. This fundamentally important sociological and historical reality is almost completely absent from his text. His "peoples" spring fully formed from his theory of international justice.

The closest Rawls gets to existential peoples in history is a footnote in which he quotes J.S. Mill's famous definition of "nationality" in *Considerations on Representative Government.* "A portion of mankind may be said to constitute a Nationality, if they are united among themselves by common sympathies, which do not exist between them and any others— which make them cooperate with each other more willingly than with other people, desire to be under the same government, and desire that it should be government by themselves, or a portion of themselves, exclusively."[26] But in marked contrast to Rawls's a priori approach, Mill's definition is influenced by nineteenth-century developments, particularly the emergence of small nations and nationalities in Europe, which were beginning to lay claim to self-government and sovereignty. Mill's "nationalities" have names: Belgians, Greeks, Hungarians, and so forth. They are involved in events: the Greek rebellion against Turkey in 1830, the Belgian rebellion against the Dutch in 1831–32. They have a historical existence. They have national characters. Rawls's "peoples" have neither names, nor histories nor identities; they only have a standing and a role in a philosophical system.

Rawls's only recognizable "peoples" are, in actuality, certain existing nation-states upon which he evidently looks with some favor. He is particularly concerned to spell out the philosophy of "liberal peoples," and there is little doubt but that he has the American people in mind in doing so. They come nearest to his archetype of a "liberal people." Rawls's "liberal peoples" are an abstraction of Americans at their best. Rawls's "Society of Peoples" is an American world in vision and hope: a world of "peoples" who are, hopefully, on their way to becoming rather like the American people. This is Rawls's progressive liberal world.

It is perhaps understandable that Rawls would shy away from the tricky business of identifying discernible groups of humans who shall count as "peoples." The notion of "the people" in international history and international law is a confusing field of inquiry scattered with traps, snares, and pitfalls. In this connection, Ivor Jennings's often quoted remark about self-determination is worth quoting one more time. It seems entirely reasonable, as President Woodrow Wilson proclaimed, to let "the people" decide their political fate. But "the people cannot decide until someone decides who are the people."[27] Making such a decision is anything but straightforward. The star-crossed effort to do that in Central and Eastern Europe after World War I is only the most memorable example of the difficulty.

In the era of decolonization, the term "people" was applied to populations defined by the borders of preexisting colonial territories. This is a version of the doctrine of *uti possidetus juris*: "as you possess, so you may continue to possess." The Nigerians were a people but the Ibos (one of many indigenous ethnolinguistic groups living within the inherited colonial territory of Nigeria) were not. The whole population of colonies and other dependencies, and only those territory-defined populations, were entitled to self-government according to 1960 UN General Assembly Resolution 1514. From about that time the United Nations became increasingly unwilling to consecrate partitions of territories or secessions along ethnonational lines owing to overriding considerations of existing state interests and the general and often urgent concern to preserve international order. In 1971, Rupert Emerson observed not without good reasons: "there are no rational and objective criteria by which a 'people' in the large and in the abstract can be identified."[28] Similarly, in the Helsinki Declaration of 1977 peoples are the populations of existing sovereign states. In 1983, the Legal Adviser to the British Foreign and Commonwealth Office observed "there is no internationally accepted definition of the term 'peoples'."[29]

When peoples acquire definite meaning in international relations and law they turn out to be the populations of bordered territories that are recognized as sovereign states or—in the past—as colonies or other dependencies of sovereign empires. Alternatively, peoples are recognized as national minorities, most of which typically have a singular desire to become sovereign states, the sooner the better.[30] The author of an important study of self-determination of peoples in international law argues that "no right of secession has been granted to nations, ethnic groups or minorities." Further, "no right has yet been conferred by general international norms on the whole population of sovereign States freely to decide by whom they should be ruled: 'consent of the governed' . . . has been perceived as too dangerous for the present fabric of world community."[31] This taut international bridle may be owing to the fact that existential, historical peoples, that is, ethnonationalities, have often been a headache, sometimes far worse, in the never-ending quest for stability in world affairs. The history of nationalism has been in significant part a story of intolerance, of confrontation, of conflict and war.[32]

It is widely acknowledged that any contemplated international practice that would recognize peoples distinct from existing states would have the effect, intended or not, of disrupting international order by threatening the territorial integrity of those very same states. This became apparent as soon as politicians and diplomats began to contemplate the recognition of the subject peoples of Central and Eastern Europe at the end of World War I. "I am proposing government by the consent of the governed." This is what President Woodrow Wilson declared in an address to the U.S. Senate in 1917. Wilson thought peoples were moderate and enlightened. There was deep skepticism on this point even in his administration, and at the highest level. His Secretary of State, Robert Lansing, wrote in 1919 that the self-determination of peoples was "simply loaded with dynamite" and that international order would be placed at risk if it were pursued as a matter of American policy. This of course happened.

Rawls nowhere addresses this stormy and dangerous reality and the difficulties it presents to his political philosophy of "peoples." Instead, like Wilson, he postulates opposite characteristics of a utopian kind. Rawls's "peoples" are "reasonable" and "tolerant"—models of international civility. No doubt, many nations are relatively civil, and it probably makes sense to distinguish between civic nationalities and ethnic nationalities, as historians and sociologists frequently have done.[33] There is a positive and constructive side to the rise of peoples in world affairs. Much of that has to do with the value of being the citizen of a nation-state as compared to being the subject of a sovereign government: the sovereignty of the people versus that of a ruler, dynasty, or empire. Some "liberal peoples," including the British and the Americans, have been comparatively tolerant historically—if we overlook religious conflict in English history and racial conflict in American history.

But there is also a negative and disruptive side that is absent from Rawls's argument. The rise of nations and peoples in international history is a story in no small part of nationalism, of revolution, of imperialism, of war: the English Civil War, the French Revolution and the Napoleonic Wars, the American Civil War, the Bismarkian Wars of German unification, the overseas wars of British and French imperialism, the wars of national liberation, and the rest. Some nations or peoples on the march are rather like religions on crusade: the French nation marching with Napoleon. This similarity, often noticed by historical commentators, seems lost upon John Rawls, who, ironically, is concerned to limit the intolerant and uncompromising claims of religion in public life.[34] To write of peoples as if they are *by definition* more civilized and less belligerent than states—as John Rawls writes of them—is to neglect the historical record of actual peoples. It is to deal in theoretical abstractions. History has hardly any place in his political philosophy.

There is very little in historical or contemporary practice that can warrant treating peoples, *as such*, as a foundation of international politics. There are no indications, at least none of which I am aware, that existential, historical peoples are likely to supplant existing states in international practice in the foreseeable future. Nor are Rawlsian "peoples" becoming a parallel system based on a "Law of Peoples" distinct from that of existing states based on international law. Nor is international society moving, or even inching, toward a "Society of Peoples." This stubborn evidence, and much else like it, may indicate something of the misplaced utopianism of Rawls's thought on the subject.

The "Law of Peoples" versus International Law

A "Society" of political collectivities that warrant the label "Peoples" requires that they be subject to a corresponding law, a "Law of Peoples." Rawls comments: "the main point" is that there are "basic principles of political justice" that "free," "independent" and "well-ordered peoples" would be prepared to recognize as "governing their conduct." These principles compose the "charter" of the "Law of Peoples."[35] They are basic norms for judging international conduct and for consecrating international organizations, such as his "Confederation of Peoples (not states)"—inspired by Kant's "Federation of Free States"—which is supposed to have "a role similar to that of the United Nations."[36] The principles that Rawls ascribes to his "Law of Peoples" are summarized as follows:

(1) Peoples are free and independent, and their freedom and independence are to be respected by other peoples; (2) Peoples are to observe treaties and

undertakings; (3) Peoples are equal and are parties to the agreements that bind them; (4) Peoples are to observe a duty of non-intervention; (5) Peoples have the right of self-defense but no right to instigate war for reasons other than self-defense; (6) Peoples are to honor human rights; (7) Peoples are to observe certain specified restrictions in the conduct of war; (8) Peoples have a duty to assist other peoples living under unfavorable conditions that prevent their having a just and decent political and social regime.[37]

Given the care and emphasis that Rawls invests in distinguishing "peoples" from "states," it is surprising how closely the foregoing principles resemble those of the UN Charter and other bodies of international law in most fundamental respects. Rawls's "Law of Peoples" appears to be abstracted from established concepts of international law that apply to sovereign states.[38] Here he abandons neorealist "states" and presupposes existing states instead. Existing states are "independent" and their independence is to be respected by all other sovereign states; existing states are bound "to observe treaties"; existing states are "equal" under international law; existing states have a "duty of non-intervention"; existing states have a "right of self-defense"; existing states have contracted to respect human rights; existing states have subjected themselves to "restrictions in the conduct of war." In short, existing states have many characteristics of Rawls's "peoples" and few characteristics of Rawls's "states." This ambiguity is never clarified.

The fact that Rawls "Law of Peoples" is virtually identical to existing international law at most points could be interpreted as indicating that "peoples" are very similar to existing states and that a "Society of Peoples" already exists in the form of a society of states. Rawls could thus be seen to advocate a normative approach to international relations that is difficult to distinguish from the classical international society approach.[39] I believe this is a misinterpretation of Rawls's argument, which is far more radical than this suggests.

Rawls's "Law" is a philosophical idea and not merely a reiteration of international law: it springs from his ethical theory. A conceivable future world of Rawlsian "peoples" who are subject to the "Law of Peoples" is portrayed as a decided improvement upon existing international arrangements and practices based on sovereign states. Rawls's "peoples" turn out to be significantly different than existing states. His "Law" consists of "principles of political justice." His "peoples" are charged with the daunting responsibility of building a more "just" world.[40]

Rawls illuminates his idea of toleration among peoples by a few remarks on the American Civil War. The "impasse" between North and South could not be bridged because the parties involved in the dispute refused "to accept the idea of the politically reasonable," and that led in the end to the Civil War. "Political liberalism begins with terms of the politically reasonable and builds up its case from there . . . by preparing the way for peoples to develop a basic structure that supports a reasonably just or decent regime and makes possible a reasonable Law of Peoples."[41] It is interesting that Rawls's example is a civil war, not an international war, and the American Civil War at that. His thought runs in domestic grooves. He sees "political liberalism" as providing a reasonable basis for resolving fundamental disputes peacefully, including those between "peoples" that pose a threat of war. He seems to believe—somewhat reminiscent of Kant—that what is reasonable to citizens of domestic liberal societies would also be reasonable to "peoples" of the "Society of Peoples."[42]

The ethical theory behind existing, historical international law is mainly conservative. At the core of the UN Charter is a fundamental responsibility of existing states to defend international peace and security. This responsibility falls most heavily on the great powers, that is, the permanent members of the Security Council. The notion of "great powers" with special UN Charter responsibilities is an important qualification of the principle of international equality in existing international law. The veto granted exclusively to the permanent members deprives all other UN member states of the protection of the traditional immunity rule rooted in their sovereignty. Martin Wight thus saw the Security Council as a Hobbesian institution.[43] Rawls reflects on "just peoples" and "decent peoples," among others, but never on great peoples and much less great powers. The international inequality entailed by great powers would be repugnant to his "principles of political justice." Rawls's egalitarianism makes it impossible for him to operate with that important realist qualification. One is provoked to ask how his "Society of Peoples" could exist and survive without it.

His text addresses the "problem of war" but bypasses the responsibilities of the great powers, particularly the responsibility to defend international peace and security. Who shall keep the peace of the world in Rawls's "Society of Peoples"? His "Law of Peoples" makes no mention of that heavy responsibility. There is "a right to help to defend allies" but this is not an international obligation and much less is it a universal duty.[44] Rawls appears not to be concerned about the issue of international peace and security, which arguably is the most important international issue one can contemplate. On the contrary, he goes so far as to argue that in his "Society of well-ordered Peoples" there will be "no reason to go to war."[45] Rawls's visionary "Society of Peoples" is undisturbed by the worrying possibility of general war or even major warfare. His "Confederation of Peoples" seems to pacify the world more or less automatically—presumably because "peoples" are theorized as "reasonable" and "tolerant." Rawls accepts as "correct" Kant's hypothesis of a *foedus pacificum* according to which "armed conflict between democratic peoples will tend to disappear as they approach that ideal."[46]

This reads like an expression of hope that does not satisfactorily address the crucial question: how are we to get from our existing, imperfect international law of sovereign states to Rawls's idealized "Law of Peoples"? How reasonable, that is, sensible, is it to contemplate and recommend such a transformation of world politics? How Rawls would come to terms with the problem of international peace and security during a transitional period between present and future in the absence of great powers with special charter privileges and responsibilities for that purpose is not addressed. I speculate that this stems from Rawls's disinclination to see the problem of war and peace in its full international complexity and difficulty, as for example Hobbes sees it: his text contains no reference to Thomas Hobbes or his famous axiom: *The safety of the people is the supreme law.*[47] This disinclination may derive from Rawls's starting point, which is domestic political theory: "This beginning point means that the Law of Peoples is an extension of a liberal conception of justice for a *domestic regime* to a *Society of Peoples.*"[48] Unlike Hobbes (and most other political theorists of the modern state), Rawls sees no difficulty in extending the domestic idea of society or regime to the international sphere. In this regard his thinking is very different from that of most classical international society thinkers, who are inclined to emphasize the hazards and pitfalls involved in the "domestic analogy": that is, applying the ethics of domestic society to international society.

Rawls's "right of war" is "limited to self-defense" and "to protect human rights." The right of "self-defense" is well established by international law and requires no further comment. The doctrine of humanitarian war is something else. It is evident in contemporary international society—probably more evident than it has ever been—but it is also controversial.[49] The right of war "to protect human rights" would appear to conflict with the "duty of non-intervention." There is much evidence from international relations, past and present, that this is so. The possibility of fundamental conflict between these norms is not resolved or even addressed in Rawls's text. That, presumably, is because Rawls's values are not the potentially conflicting values of a pluralist world that actually exists. Rather, they are postulated as compatible values of an imagined, anticipated and hoped for solidarist world that does not exist, where every value has its appointed place in a normative hierarchy defined by philosophy, and where conflicts over basic values are ruled out theoretically.

John Rawls believes that the doctrine of public reason can be extended to "the political Society of well-ordered Peoples" under the "Law of Peoples."[50] That would, in effect, domesticate the "Society of Peoples." As such, it expresses a "thick" morality, to borrow Michael Walzer's term.[51] Thomas Nagel points out that Rawls's conception of a just society is one of "exceptional solidarity."[52] Applied to a well-founded and long-standing domestic society, such as the United States, Rawls's doctrine of public reason may be conceivable at some point in the not-too-distant future. Applied to international society, or the "Society of Peoples," it has earmarks of utopianism.

Rawls's argument is cosmopolitan in the Kantian sense. Rawls's "peoples," like Kant's "republics," are composed of individual human beings from the first stage of the social contract to form "peoples," to the second stage of a contract between "peoples," to the final stage of political justice for all the people of the world: what Kant refers to as cosmopolitan right.[53] Rawls's neo-Kantianism envisages progressive international change in which foreign policies and international actions of "peoples" are to be judged by their contribution to the creation of a just world for all people. This imagined future "Society of Peoples" takes the world far beyond the present imperfect society of states. But unlike Kant, whose international thought was restrained and pessimistic in its expectation as to when liberal international justice could be achieved, Rawls seems to expect it in the not-too-distant future even if it may not be just around the next corner.

The Dominion of "Well-Ordered Peoples"

Rawls's "Law of Peoples" is conceived to be "universal in reach."[54] The "Society of Peoples" makes provision for diverse "peoples" of the world and specifically for "five types of domestic societies" and not merely for "liberal societies."[55] This might seem to contradict my criticism that Rawls's theory ignores existential, historical peoples. However, his typology is not empirical; it is conceptual. It involves only "peoples" and "domestic societies" that he has preconceived. It ranks them according to political merit defined by his theory of liberal justice. Rawls wants to subject all his "peoples" and "domestic societies" to one universal standard of conduct laid down by his liberal theory. His notions of "just peoples" and of "decent peoples" imply three defective types of "domestic societies" that do not qualify for full membership in the Rawlsian world: "outlaw states," "societies burdened by unfavorable conditions," and "benevolent absolutisms." It is worth noting that none of these societies is characterized as a "people," which also hints at their defectiveness. I shall only discuss his "outlaw states."

Rawls spells out his concepts of "just peoples" and "decent peoples." "Just peoples," that is, liberal democracies, fulfill his conception of "political justice": they not only provide for full liberal democracy internally but they also "are fully prepared to grant . . . proper respect and recognition to other peoples as equals."[56] "Decent peoples" are decent because they do not "deny human rights," because they do not "deny their members the right to be consulted," and because they "allow a right of dissent."[57] They seem to be "liberal societies" in the making. Perhaps the American people were "decent" before they became "liberal" and "just." Both "just peoples" and "decent peoples" qualify as "reasonable." It remains only for "decent" peoples to progress into liberal democracies.

Rawls's international thought is thus progressive. He visualizes and looks forward to "the extension of the Law of Peoples" to "domestic societies" that are not yet "liberal" or "decent." These present problems of inclusion in his world of justice. It is clear, however, that Rawls's "Society of Peoples," and its "liberal" and "decent" "peoples," cannot justifiably ignore the existence of such "societies." They cannot merely stand by and coexist with them. They cannot be pluralists in the traditional international society meaning of that term. They are bound by the universal duty to protect human rights, and that directs their attention to such "societies." "Liberal" and "decent" "peoples" must be devoted to the "long-run aim . . . to bring all societies eventually to honor the Law of Peoples and to become full members in good standing of the society of well-ordered peoples."[58] The entire world must be converted to liberalism. Rawls's three defective types of "domestic societies" presumably would not qualify for full membership in the "Society of Peoples" until they are converted to its principles. Where will they be lodged in the meantime? And how will this conversion be achieved? Rawls, the optimist, seems to believe that most "domestic societies"—once they have been enlightened behind the veil of ignorance to grasp the principles of liberal justice—will voluntarily adopt the superior ways of "just" peoples and "decent" peoples. The populations of such defective societies seem rather like pagans who convert freely and joyously to Christianity once they have heard its good news from the missionaries.[59]

"Outlaw states" pose a special problem of resistance and recalcitrance, however. Rawls asks "whether it is ever legitimate to interfere with 'outlaw states' simply because they violate human rights, even though they are not dangerous and aggressive toward other states." He answers: "Certainly there is a *prima facie* case for intervention of some kind."[60] He also asks: "Is there ever a time when forceful intervention might be called for?" He answers: "If the offenses against human rights are egregious and the society does not respond to the imposition of sanctions, such intervention in the defense of human rights would be acceptable and would be called for."[61] In that respect, his theory is interventionist rather than noninterventionist. But he clearly hopes that will not be necessary and he believes that if peoples "are exposed to liberal civilization . . . in a positive way . . . violations of human rights may diminish . . . [and] the circle of mutually caring peoples may expand over time."[62]

Rawls's international thought raises the awkward question of how to deal with societies that are not yet fit for membership of the "Society of Peoples." He does not discuss, directly, the issue of fitness but he does rehearse some problems and possibilities of "foreign policy" that might be encountered in the endeavor "to bring all societies to this goal."[63] In Rawls's "Society of Peoples" no "domestic societies" can be ignored and left alone: none can opt out. In his solidarist liberal world there can be no live and let live, no coexistence with "outlaw states." All "domestic societies" must be included and involved. But how? Here Rawls the philosopher finds himself getting into pragmatic questions of foreign policy. He justifies the use of "pressure" by "well-ordered peoples" on "outlaw regimes to change their ways." However, he notes "this pressure is unlikely to be effective" and "may need to be backed up by the firm denial of economic and other assistance, or the refusal to admit outlaw regimes as members in good standing in mutually beneficial cooperative practices." He also says conversion of (what would be) resistant and recalcitrant societies "calls for political wisdom," that "success depends in part on luck," and that "these are not matters to which political philosophy has much to add."[64] This is one of the few expressions of skepticism in his text.

The normative issue of inclusion with which Rawls, the liberal internationalist, is struggling is reminiscent of a real historical struggle between European peoples and non-European peoples during the age of Western imperialism: what to do about peoples who either will not or cannot reciprocate European cum Western standards of morality and law? The problem of reciprocity is an old one in the practice and theory of international society. For many centuries European rulers spoke of "the unreciprocating will of the unspeakable Turk."[65] The solution to the problem was the "Standard of Civilization" according to which barbarian peoples could legitimately and lawfully be subjected to political trusteeship by civilized peoples until they become civilized, that is, Westernized.[66] John Stuart Mill justified a qualified and circumscribed paternalism for "barbarians" in the mid-nineteenth century.[67] He advocated a "delegated" administration that held only a "negative" power over a "distant" dependency. He explicitly warned against "measures of proselytism . . . to force English ideas down the throats" of dependent peoples of different cultures.[68] Admission to international society did not require religious or ideological conversion. Mill was a pluralist at heart.

Would Rawls's "Law of Peoples," in the face of a refusal to reciprocate by resistant and recalcitrant "domestic societies," require that they should become international wards under the tutelage of "liberal peoples" and "decent peoples" until they are reformed?[69] Would that tutelage call for the justifiable use of armed force in the face of defiance and resistance? Would that tutelage require ideological conversion to liberalism and democracy? Those are the most troubling normative questions presented by Rawls's "Law of Peoples." They are questions that he does not entirely face up to.

These questions are more demanding with regards to Rawls's liberal international theory than to Mill's. John Stuart Mill was, after all, a mid-Victorian thinker and a Political Secretary for the British East India Company. The age of European Empire was reaching its zenith when he was framing his political philosophy. There was, as yet, no prospect of a universal society of states that would embrace both Europeans and non-Europeans as equals. "Barbarians" were a perceived obstacle to Western expansion and colonization: in that regard nothing had changed in European thought since the time of the ancient Greeks and Romans who established the distinction between civilization and barbarism. Paternalism proved to be a fitting justification for a mid-Victorian. So it is perhaps understandable that Mill's liberalism had definite limits when it came to the inclusion of non-Western peoples in a universal international society. Mill's liberalism requires conformity with the nineteenth-century international law of reciprocity. But it does not call for conversion to Western ideology in domestic affairs. It remains fully tolerant of human diversity.

John Rawls was a late twentieth-century American liberal-egalitarian academic who lived in a world that had been liberated from Western imperialism during his lifetime. This recently liberated world (Asia, Africa, the Middle-East, etc.) was accommodated by an opening and widening international society based on equal state sovereignty, territorial integrity, and nonintervention. These pluralist principles are fundamentally anticolonial and anti-paternalist. Decolonization and independence thus involved, at the heart of the episode, conformity with international law. But it did not require any fundamental domestic transformation beyond ensuring that the new states were integrated into international society and subscribed to its basic norms.

Given this recent history, it is interesting that Rawls international liberalism contains an intimation of trusteeship—although at one point, as a good Kantian, he explicitly warns against acting "paternalistically" in connection with providing assistance to "burdened societies."[70] But this disclaimer rings a bit hollow in the light of his overall argument. His "Law of Peoples" has an intrusive cosmopolitan quality: it is deemed to be fitting for every "society" and not merely for those "societies" who accept it and recommend it for others. It is not merely an international law but is also a domestic law. There is a universal duty to bring it into existence everywhere. There is a solidarist vision of one world based on the "Law of Peoples." There is little evident contemplation of international pluralism, the doctrine of live-and-let-live regardless of domestic customs, practices, and institutions. The requirement of ensuring that all societies should enjoy the advantages and assurances of the "Society of Peoples" and its "Law," and that none should be denied or excluded, would seem to invite some form of intervention and trusteeship until all "domestic societies" can be brought into Rawls's liberal world on a basis of equality.

In short, there is a lingering problem of universal consent in Rawls's *The Law of Peoples*. His international theory seems to imply that "peoples" who do not see the value of it and do not buy into it shall be made subjects of it nonetheless. This, presumably, is because it is "right and just" for them too. If that interpretation is correct, it is a controversial moral stance for a modern liberal who cannot subscribe to the doctrine of natural law and who emphasizes that, unlike natural law, "the Law of Peoples falls within the domain of the political."[71] In other words, there is a discernible tension between the positive law doctrine of a "Second Original Position," which presupposes universal consent and cooperation, and the possibility of having to justify the use of coercion or force to overcome nonreciprocity, recalcitrance, and resistance to the demands of justice on the part of "outlaw states."

To resolve this problem would seem to require, either that the "Law of Peoples" is less than universal and "domestic societies" can opt out, or that resistance by them can be met with externally imposed and enforced political education: that is, armed intervention for international liberalism. The first option would render the international society more fractured and divided than it currently is under existing international law. Rawls clearly conceives of his "Law of Peoples" as universal to humankind. This implies that it should be enforced across the world and not only in the "liberal" and "decent" parts of the world, that is, the West and its neighborhood. Rawls nowhere confronts such normative dilemmas and possibilities.

Political Liberalism versus Cujus Regio, Ejus Religio

John Rawls is concerned about religion in relation to justice not only in domestic society but also in his "Society of Peoples." He notes that Catholics and Protestants historically fought wars over religion and brought them to an end only by agreeing to a modus vivendi, which "meant that should either party fully gain its way it would impose its own religious doctrine as the sole admissible faith [in a county]." He is alluding to the doctrine of cujus regio, ejus religio (as sovereign, so religion). Rawls also notes a further development, in which domestic constitutions are arranged and "honored as a pact to maintain civil peace."[72] Here he is referring to religious toleration and religious liberty under constitutional law—such as the U.S. Constitution and Bill of Rights. He is critical of both arrangements for not providing "stability for the right reasons," that is, reasons that would anchor religion in "a democratic society's political (moral) ideals and values."[73] In short, those arrangements are flawed because they do not subordinate religious faith to liberal justice and its principles. They serve merely "to quiet divisiveness and encourage social stability."[74] They are merely utilitarian.

Rawls places the ideology of political liberalism clearly above religion of all sorts. He recognizes the potential of religion to destabilize the political order. He also recognizes the value of religious liberties. But he clearly sees a necessity to subordinate them to public reason, and to enjoy them for the right reasons, that is, reasons that any "reasonable" person, regardless of their religion, could affirm and accept. He seeks a doctrine of religious toleration that validates and strengthens liberal-democratic constitutions for their own sake and not merely for the sake of "social stability." He calls for a separation of church and state that protects religion from the state but, more importantly, that protects the state from religion: "it protects citizens from their churches and citizens from one another."[75] "Political liberalism does not dismiss spiritual questions as unimportant, but to the contrary, because of their importance, it leaves them for each citizen to decide for himself or herself."[76] Such religious protection and freedom would thus be universally valid. Religious beliefs, along with all other social beliefs, would rest on "the most reasonable and deepest basis of social unity available to us."[77] This basis would of course be liberal, secular, and divorced from religion. Liberalism would be supreme and religion subordinate to it.

In rejecting the doctrine of cujus regio, ejus religio for providing stability for the wrong reasons, Rawls is disowning the oldest principle of peace in the history of postmedieval international society. This principle was initially constructed out of the ruins left by the religious wars of sixteenth-century Germany, between Catholics and Lutherans. It revealed the extent of the violence and destruction of which Christians were capable when fighting among themselves, and brought home the importance of coexistence, of live-and-let-live, on questions of religion. Probably the most significant historical occasion in the framing of that principle was the Peace of Augsburg (1555), which responded to those religious wars. Catholics and Lutherans bound themselves to respect each other's religious beliefs, liturgy, and ceremonies *in each other's country* and to renounce the right of armed intervention to defend the one true Christian faith, namely their own.[78] Catholics and Lutherans could still believe they possessed the only true Christianity, and they could refuse to tolerate any other Christian sect in their country. But they could no longer justifiably and legally wage war to establish it in other countries.

This principle of coexistence has been handed down or relearned anew, by succeeding generations, over the past 450 years. The principle's remote but immediately recognizable offspring is Article 2 of the UN Charter, which affirms the doctrine of equal sovereignty, territorial integrity, and nonintervention. Arguably the historical staying power of this principle is its limited aim, namely to avert warfare between states over questions of religion—and more recently over questions of ideology. One virtue of the principle is its recognition that outside interference with the culture and civilization of foreign countries is provocative of a sharp sense of wrongdoing, because it is meddling with peoples' most deeply held values and beliefs. It has the further virtue of being a minimalist rule of live-and-let-live that is easy to recognize, understand, and follow. It does not require that one must accept the values and beliefs of those one coexists with. It merely requires that one coexists with them regardless. It expresses a "thin" morality, to borrow Michael Walzer's companion term.[79] It can therefore be extended with greater chance of acceptance across a wider area of the planet, arguably much wider than could Rawl's far more demanding and intrusive liberal principle of politically reasonable toleration.

As indicated, Rawls's idea of toleration requires that religion—all religions and every religion—must be subordinate to political liberalism and liberal justice. It is not so difficult to grasp that idea in the context of a historical liberal society, such as the United States, where religious pluralism (initially among Christian sects) has been well founded and validated constitutionally for several centuries, where an idea of individual liberty is well entrenched, and finally, where public reason is at least one of the recognizable features of political discourse. It is even plausible for Western liberal society at large. It is more difficult to grasp that idea, indeed it is almost impossible to imagine in the wider postimperial international society, where pluralism registers a diversity of cultures and civilizations, where the notion of individualism may or may not be present but most likely is not, and where morality is more likely to be based on the group including the religious community, than on the individual.[80] For such a pluralistic world as that, Rawls restrictive liberal idea of toleration looks more like political intolerance and interference with the life ways and belief systems of devotionally non-liberal societies.

Following on from my remarks in the previous section, one is left wondering again how Rawls's "politically reasonable toleration" could be established across a world of such diversity without a firm underlying basis of consent to this arrangement on the part of all, and without an overarching authority to enforce its "Law"? Nowhere in his text does Rawls face the full force of these difficulties and obstacles. It is for compelling reasons such as these that classical thinkers are disposed to investigate and theorize historically evident ideas of international society most of which are in sharp contrast with those of domestic society and are consequently far removed from John Rawls's notions of political liberalism. *Cujus regio, ejus religio* is one of the most important of such ideas.

Lifting the "Veil of Ignorance"

John Rawls's principles of liberal justice are inoculated from the facts and circumstances of our known or experienced political world: empiricism. In that regard, his theory is a departure from Kant's liberal theory, which takes into account what he calls "nature": that is, the evident differences of human beings, such as religious differences.[81] It is also and even more a departure from J.S. Mill's liberal theory that is highly attuned to the facts of human diversity around the world. By resorting to an "Original Position" behind a "veil of ignorance" Rawls introduces an intellectual device to get around this fact of difference instead of facing it. Granted his political theory has plausibility as applied to "well-ordered" domestic societies, such as the United States. This is because it is abstracted from American political history and constitutional theory. It is the perfection or idealization of this society in the mirror of political philosophy. It has less plausibility, arguably far less, when applied to the international world. Yet it is intended for understanding and reforming that world. It exhibits several flaws and failings in that regard.

First, it excludes human beings as they exist and as they may be expected to continue to exist, warts and all, in their earthly circumstances. As indicated, Rawls's social contractors are sequestered from the existential world they live in and experience, unlike those of the classical social contract philosophers. Hobbes's people make a social contract in acute awareness of themselves and their circumstances. For Hobbes, as Oakeshott puts it, "man is a creature civilized by fear of death."[82] Rawls avoids that exercise entirely. Instead, he installs human ciphers devoid of identities and relations who are, in effect, consenting to liberalism in the dark. He does exactly the same with his internationally contracting "peoples." By conceiving of international justice via the "veil of ignorance" he is also asking his readers to suspend their empirical knowledge of world affairs and its possibilities and limits. Rawls has been portrayed, in that connection, as "the most unworldly of social and political philosophers," and as having "a religious temperament."[83] This is nowhere more evident than in his political philosophy of international relations.

Second, Rawls's theory of international justice leaves largely unexamined what arguably is the most important recurring question of world affairs: namely that of order.[84] He writes of a "society of well-ordered peoples" but he does not spell out his notion of order.[85] "Well-ordered" seems to be a given condition to be taken for granted rather than a valuable and desirable condition to be arranged by intelligent political effort, such as Hobbes theorizes. Rawls makes ample place for political *reason* in his theory; but there is no place for political *will*. What is it that would drive anyone to establish or join his "Society of Peoples"? Is it Hobbesian fear of chaos and insecurity? Evidently not. Is it humanitarian hope? Perhaps. But hope alone is hardly a solid foundation for a permanent and successful institution of world affairs as implied by Rawls's "Society of Peoples." Is it the pursuit or defense of one's interests? Yes—but only if they are "reasonable interests guided by and congruent with a fair equality and a due respect for all peoples."[86] This, however, is the surrender of will to reason: the qualification destroys the proposition and we are back where we started.

Where is the political will to set up and sustain a "Society of Peoples"? By postulating the "veil of ignorance" this empirical question does not enter into Rawls's international thought. But that question cannot be ignored. The fatal flaw of the "veil of ignorance" emerges at this point. It has no historical or empirical substance. It is entirely notional and, one is tempted to say, fictional. It is utterly removed from the real world of experience and history. That is its grave defect as a concept for coming to terms with international ethics. This recalls a famous skeptical remark of Francis Bacon made in the early seventeenth century: "As for the philosophers, they make imaginary laws for imaginary commonwealths, and their discourses are as the stars, which give little light because they are so high."[87]

Third, and closely related to the previous point, Rawls's theory of international justice shies away from the recalcitrant and non-obliging pluralism of world affairs. He conceives of a "reasonable pluralism" that can be "reconciled" and even "united" with his global principles of liberal justice.[88] He distinguishes that loftier pluralism from "the fact of pluralism as such."[89] This also begs a huge question: how plausible is his belief (and evident conviction) that some agreed basis of global "liberal justice" is realizable in face of the manifest and inescapable diversity of the human societies of the world, many resting on *weltanschauungen* as correct and compelling to them as liberalism may be to us? Rawls's "reasonable pluralism" is not the pluralism one finds in classical international thought. This is the plurality of co-existing sovereign states and nations with distinctive domestic societies, histories, religions, customs, and so forth: "the fact of pluralism as such." This is the pluralism one finds in J.S. Mill's liberalism. This latter pluralism is evident even in Kant's argument on "the idea of international right," namely, that "nature wisely separates the nations" by linguistic and religious differences that promote a "peace" that is "created and guaranteed by an equilibrium of forces and a most vigorous rivalry."[90] Rawls here is moving beyond Kant and at a fast speed.

John Rawls is a liberal internationalist of a deeply solidarist denomination. His "Society of Peoples" is not a horizontal arrangement of multiple states that are subject to a thin but universal international law that allows for a diversity of domestic constitutions around the world: an international society as conventionally understood. Rather, it is a cosmopolitan arrangement, resting on a thick notion of a community of humankind. In *The Law of Peoples* Rawls goes far beyond his argument in *A Theory of Justice*. In that earlier work, international justice is served by the "basic principles of the law of nations," including the "equality of nations," "self-determination," "the right of a people to settle its own affairs without the intervention of foreign powers," the "right of self-defense," the principle "that treaties are to be kept," the "laws of war," and so on.[91] The earlier Rawls is content to regard all nations as, prima facie, the same in ethical terms if they subject themselves to "the law of nations." Their domestic constitution is a matter for them-selves. Because the law of nations evolved historically and pragmatically in response to the facts and circumstances of world affairs, it never required a prior international "veil of ignorance" to be established. Consequently, the earlier Rawls had no need of any "Second Original Position." His thinking at that stage was consistent with the thought of classical international society thinkers with whom he could then easily be associated.

The core of these criticisms of Rawls's later international theory is its lack of a sense of political reality, its disconnection from the historical facts of world affairs as we know them, and its inattention to the limits of ethics in that world.[92] There is a great deal of emphasis on what is best but little emphasis, if indeed any, on what is best under the circumstances. The situational context in which real human beings live is considered not only irrelevant but also obstructive to international justice. There is a recurrent and determined "pursuit of the ideal," to borrow a phrase from Isaiah Berlin.[93] History is progressive if properly arranged and managed. Human beings are perfectible in history. Rawls account of international justice exhibits, in striking fashion, what Michael Oakeshott terms the Pelagian or other worldly "politics of faith," which he contrasts to the worldly "politics of skepticism."[94] Rawls's later liberalism consistently takes the high and straight road. *The Law of Peoples* discloses a thinker who earnestly believes that political philosophy can change the world for the better, and that political philosophers should attempt to do exactly that.

There is another, more detached and skeptical branch of liberalism that notices and emphasizes limits in establishing and enforcing justice—or any other value—in political affairs. It allows for human imperfection. It acknowledges circumstances and other confines of human conduct. It is open to prudential and consequentialist justification of policies and actions. It knows that international circumstances that exist at any given time or place largely decide the extent to which a principle should be followed. It knows that "ideals and principles" can conflict and that we must sometimes choose between them: the pluralism of values. It makes allowance for tragedy in both war and peace. It notices and tries to come to terms with human limitations in world affairs, both instrumental and ethical. It recognizes, with J.S. Mill, that political knowledge cannot be definitively learned from a textbook or the instructions of a teacher but can only be acquired by open-minded reflection on the political world in its complexity. In short, this other liberalism accepts that political philosophy must necessarily follow a low and winding path without any entirely clear destination in view. Even Kant acknowledged limits of human perfectibility: "No more rigorous moralist than Immanuel Kant has ever lived, but even he said, in a moment of illumination, 'Out of the crooked timber of humanity no straight thing was ever made'."[95]

Isaiah Berlin, who knew John Rawls, was a leading late twentieth-century exponent of this other, more skeptical liberalism. The following quotation from one of his essays on pluralism sums up, far better than I ever could, my criticism of John Rawls's "Society of Peoples." One is left to wonder if in writing this passage Isaiah Berlin had John Rawls's political philosophy in mind.[96]

> Collisions of values are of the essence of what they are and what we are. If we are told that these contradictions will be solved in some perfect world in which all good things can be harmonized in principle, then we must answer, to those who say this, that the meanings they attach to the

names which for us denote the conflicting values are not ours. We must say that the world in which what we see as incompatible values are not in conflict is a world beyond our ken; that principles which are harmonized in this other world are not the principles with which, in our daily lives, we are acquainted; if they are transformed, it is into conceptions not known to us on earth. But it is on earth that we live, and it is here that we must believe and act.[97]

Postscript

I feel obliged to end with a caveat, not only for the argument of this final chapter but also for the book as a whole. While the liberalism of this study is fundamentally different from the liberalism of John Rawls, it could not have been stated without the powerful stimulus supplied by *The Law of Peoples*. We who incline to skepticism, to acceptance of human imperfection, to discerning and respecting the limits of human reason and the power of human will in the activity of politics—we need a "veil of ignorance" to see historical international society with greater clarity. John Rawls's *The Law of Peoples* challenges us to think harder, indeed much harder, to articulate and hopefully vindicate our empirical conception of world affairs. Likewise, most of my commentaries and criticisms in previous chapters would have been impossible to frame without other outstanding works, classical and modern, that provoked and challenged the overall argument made in this book. To say this is to return to a statement made at the beginning: namely that any study of international thought must pay attention to leading thinkers, past and present, whose accumulated writings constitute the most important body of knowledge on the subject. Their thought is our legacy.

Notes

Preface

1. I. Berlin, *The Crooked Timber of Humanity* (New York: Vintage Books, 1992), pp. 1–2.

Chapter 1   International Thought

1. See M. Oakeshott, *On Human Conduct* (Oxford: Clarendon Press, 1975), pp. 112–17.
2. Oakeshott, *On Human Conduct*, pp. 124–27.
3. *Oxford English Dictionary On-Line* <http://www.oed.com/>.
4. *Oxford English Dictionary On-Line* <http://www.oed.com/>.
5. T. Hobbes, *Leviathan*, ed. M. Oakeshott (Oxford: Blackwell, 1946), ch. XIV.
6. Hobbes, *Leviathan*, p. 104.
7. C. Perry, "The Relation between Ethics and Political Science," *International Journal of Ethics*, vol. 47 (January 1937), pp. 163–79.
8. M. Keen, *Medieval Europe* (London: Penguin Books, 1991), p. 100.
9. M. Oakeshott, *The Voice of Liberal Learning* (Indianapolis, IN: Liberty Fund, 2001), p. 179.
10. A. Toynbee, *The World and the West* (New York: Oxford University Press, 1953), pp. 8–10.
11. H. Reiss (ed.), *Kant: Political Writings*, 2nd enl. ed. (Cambridge: Cambridge University Press, 1991), p. 18.
12. Fray Bartolome de Las Casas and Francisco de Vitoria. See the brief, penetrating discussion in J.H. Parry, *Europe and a Wider World 1415–1715*, 3rd ed. (London: Hutchinson, 1966), pp. 59, 168–69. Also see C. Brown, T. Nardin, and N. Rengger (eds.), *International Relations in Political Thought* (Cambridge: Cambridge University Press, 2002), pp. 231–41 and J. McManners, "The Expansion of Christianity," in *The Oxford History of Christianity* (Oxford: Oxford University Press, 1993), pp. 315–19.

13. Barbara Tuchman, *The March of Folly: From Troy to Vietnam* (New York: Ballantine Books, 1985).
14. N. Machiavelli, *The Prince*, tr. and ed. G. Bull (Harmondsworth, UK: Penguin Books, 1961), ch. XXV.
15. H. Butterfield, "The Tragic Element in Modern International Conflict," in *History and Human Relations* (London: Collins, 1951), pp. 9–36.
16. See Hans J. Morgenthau, *Politics among Nations: The Struggle for Power and Peace* (New York: Knopf, 1960).
17. G. Vlastos, *Socrates: Ironist and Moral Philosopher* (Ithaca: Cornell University Press, 1991), pp. 212–13.
18. T. Hobbes, *Man and Citizen (De Homine and De Cive)*, ed. B. Gert (Indianapolis, IN: Hacket, 1991), p. 258.
19. "Pericles' Funeral Oration," Thucydides, *History of the Peloponnesian War*, tr. and ed. Rex Warner (Harmondsworth: Penguin Books, 1972), pp. 143–50.
20. H. Bull, *The Anarchical Society*, 2nd ed. (London: Macmillan, 1995), part III.
21. H. Grotius, *De Jure Belli ac Pacis Libri Tres*, tr. Francis Kelsay (Oxford: Oxford University Press, 1925); H. Reiss (ed.), *Kant's Political Writings*, 2nd enl. ed. (Cambridge: Cambridge University Press, 1991); and Hobbes, *Man and Citizen*.
22. Bull, *The Anarchical Society*, Preface.
23. H. Arendt, *The Human Condition* (Chicago: University of Chicago Press, 1958).
24. H. Arendt, *The Origins of Totalitarianism* (New York, Harcourt Brace, 1951).
25. T. Nardin and D. Mapel (eds.), *Traditions of International Ethics* (Cambridge: Cambridge University Press, 1992).
26. See M. Oakeshott, *Rationalism in Politics and Other Essays*, new and exp. ed. (Indianapolis, IN: Liberty Press, 1991), pp. 19–21.
27. Quoted by M. Wight, *International Theory: The Three Traditions*, ed. G. Wight and B. Porter (Leicester: Leicester University Press, 1991), p. 5.
28. Wight, *International Theory*, p. 6.
29. H. Bull, "International Theory: The Case for a Classical Approach," in K. Knorr and J.N. Rosenau (eds.), *Contending Approaches to International Politics* (Princeton, NJ: Princeton University Press, 1969).

Chapter 2   Conversing with Thrasymachus: Voices of Realism

1. M. Oakeshott, "The Political Vocabulary of the Modern European State," *Political Studies*, vol. 23 (1975).
2. A. Watson, *Diplomacy: The Dialogue of States* (London: Allen & Unwin, 1982).
3. G. Grube (tr.), *Plato-Republic*, rev. C. Reeve (Indianapolis, IN and Cambridge: Hackett Publishing, 1992), Book I, pp. 1–31.
4. *Oxford English Dictionary On-line Edition* <http://dictionary.oed.com>.
5. Thucydides, *History of the Peloponnesian War*, rev. ed. tr. Rex Warner (New York: Penguin Books, 1972), pp. 400–08.
6. Thucydides, *Peloponnesian War*, p. 405.

7. Thucydides, *Peloponnesian War*, p. 407.
8. N. Machiavelli, *The Prince*, tr. George Bull (London: Penguin Books, 1975).
9. President Woodrow Wilson, "Fourteen Points," point I. Reprinted in L. Snyder (ed.), *Historic Documents of World War I* (New York: Van Nostrand Company, 1958), p. 164.
10. G. Mattingly, "Machiavelli," in J.H. Plumb (ed.), *The Italian Renaissance* (Boston: Houghton Mifflin, 1987), p. 191.
11. See the penetrating discussion of *virtù* in M. Fleisher, "A Passion for Politics: The Vital Core of the World of Machiavelli," in Fleisher (ed.), *Machiavelli and the Nature of Political Thought* (London: Croom Helm, 1973), pp. 114–47.
12. N. Machiavelli, *The Discourses* (Harmondsworth: Penguin Books, 1970).
13. See E.F. Guarini, "Machiavelli and the crisis of the Italian republics," in G. Bock, Q. Skinner, and M. Viroli (eds.), *Machiavelli and Republicanism* (Cambridge: Cambridge University Press, 1990), p. 33.
14. W. Shakespeare, *Hamlet*, Act III.
15. T. Hobbes, *Leviathan*, ed. Michael Oakeshott (Oxford: Blackwell, 1946), ch. 13.
16. Hobbes, *Leviathan*, p. 82.
17. Hobbes, *Leviathan*, ch. 18, p. 112 (original emphasis).
18. Hobbes, *Leviathan*, ch. 13.
19. Thomas Hobbes, *Man and Citizen (De Homine and De Cive)*, ed. B. Gert (Indianapolis, IN: Hacket, 1991), 258 (original emphasis).
20. Hobbes, *Man and Citizen*.
21. Hobbes, *Leviathan*, p. 83.
22. Hobbes, *Leviathan*, p. 232
23. The two most prominent realist thinkers of that era were E.H. Carr, *The Twenty Years' Crisis, 1919–1939* (New York: Harper Torchbooks, 1964) and Hans J. Morgenthau, *Politics Among Nations: The Struggle for Power and Peace* (New York: Knopf, 1960).
24. Thomas C. Schelling, *The Strategy of Conflict* (Cambridge, MA and London: Harvard University Press, 1980).
25. See J. von Neumann and O. Morgenstern, *Theory of Games and Economic Behavior* (Princeton, NJ: Princeton University Press, 1944). This is the seminal work of game theory which expounds two-person zero sum games as well as cooperative and coalition games. The logic is instrumental and utilitarian, like modern economic analysis, with no consideration of ethics.
26. See J.R. Lucas, *Responsibility* (Oxford: Clarendon Press, 1995). Also see M. Weber on the ethic of responsibility in "Politics as a Vocation," in H.H. Gerth and C. Wright Mills (eds.), *From Max Weber: Essays in Sociology* (New York: Oxford, 1958), pp. 120–28.
27. Schelling, *The Strategy of Conflict*, p. 20.
28. Schelling, *The Strategy of Conflict*, pp. 207–08.
29. Schelling, *The Strategy of Conflict*, pp. 123–31. An earlier version of this analysis is presented in R. Jackson, *The Global Covenant: Human Conduct in a World of States* (Oxford: Oxford University Press, 1990), pp. 64–67.

30. J. Rawls, *The Law of Peoples* (Cambridge, MA: Harvard University Press, 1999), pp. 46–48.
31. K. Waltz, *Theory of International Politics* (New York: McGraw-Hill, 1979), p. 73.
32. Waltz, *Theory of International Politics*, ch. 9.
33. *Oxford English Dictionary On-line* <http://www.oed.com/>.
34. Carr, *The Twenty Years' Crisis*, pp. 153–54.
35. Carr, *The Twenty Years' Crisis*, p. 160.
36. Carr, *The Twenty Years' Crisis*, p. 168.
37. Hans J. Morgenthau, *Politics Among Nations: The Struggle for Power and Peace* (New York: Knopf, 1960).

Chapter 3 Martin Wight, Realism, and the Good Life

1. Martin Wight, "Why is there No International Theory?" in H. Butterfield and M. Wight (eds.), *Diplomatic Investigations* (London: Allen & Unwin, 1966), p. 33. Wight is referring to classical political thought and so am I.
2. For criticisms of Wight along not dissimilar lines, see Roy Jones, "The English School of International Relations: A Case for Closure," *Review of International Studies*, vol. 7 (January 1981), pp. 1–10 and N.J. Rengger, "Serpents and Doves in Classical International Theory," *Millennium: Journal of International Studies*, vol. 17, no. 2 (Summer 1988), pp. 215–18.
3. See, e.g., Wight's various essays in *Systems of States*, ed. H. Bull (Leicester: Leicester University Press, 1977).
4. Anarchism or a completely stateless condition is a very rare topic of political theory. See. H. Read, *The Philosophy of Anarchism* (London: Freedom Press, 1940).
5. Wight, "Why is there No International Theory?" p. 18.
6. "Why is there No International Theory?" pp. 20, 33.
7. "Why is there No International Theory?" p. 22.
8. "Why is there No International Theory?" p. 19.
9. "Why is there No International Theory?" pp. 19, 26.
10. These are the ironical words of Michael Donelan. He is critical of the traditional separation of international theory and political theory on the Kantian grounds "there is now a primordial community of mankind." See Michael Donelan (ed.), *The Reason of States* (London: Allen & Unwin, 1978), p. 77.
11. Thomas Hobbes, *Leviathan*, ed. Michael Oakeshott (Oxford: Blackwell, 1946), p. 82.
12. Wight, "Why is there No International Theory?," pp. 31–32.
13. Hobbes, *Leviathan*, p. 83.
14. Arnold Wolfers, *Discord and Collaboration* (London: Johns Hopkins University Press, 1965), p. 238.
15. Hobbes, *Leviathan*, p. 84.
16. Wight, "Why is there No International Theory?," p. 33.
17. See Hedley Bull, "Martin Wight and the Theory of International Relations: The Second Martin Wight Memorial Lecture," *British Journal of International Studies*, vol. 2 (1976), pp. 101–16. Wight's meanings of these terms are used throughout this essay.

18. Cardinal Richelieu, as quoted by H. Butterfield. "Raison d'État: the Relations Between Morality and Government" (The First Martin Wight Memorial Lecture. University of Sussex, 1975).
19. J. Bodin, *Six Books of the Commonwealth*, tr. M.J. Tooley (Oxford: Blackwell, 1955), book One, pp. 1–6.
20. Gerhard Ritter, *Frederick the Great*, tr. Peter Paret (Berkeley, CA: University of California Press, 1968), p. 70.
21. J.H. Herz, "Rise and Demise of the Territorial State," *World Politics*, vol. 9 (1957), pp. 473–93.
22. See the excellent discussion of Bentham's international theory in Nancy L. Rosenblum, *Bentham's Theory of the Modern State* (Cambridge, MA: Harvard University Press, 1978). These quotations are from ch. 5.
23. Rosenblum, *Bentham's Theory of the Modern State*, ch. 5.
24. R.J. Vincent, *Human Rights and International Relations* (Cambridge: Cambridge University Press, 1986), pp. 123–25.
25. Wight, "Why is there No International Theory?," p. 24.
26. M. Wight, "An Anatomy of International Thought," *Review of International Studies*, vol. 13 (1987), pp. 225–26.
27. Wight, "An Anatomy of International Thought," p. 226.
28. Immanuel Kant, "Idea for a Universal History with a Cosmopolitan Purpose" and "Perpetual Peace: A Philosophical Sketch," both reprinted in Hans Reiss (ed.), *Kant's Political Writings* (Cambridge: Cambridge University Press, 1970), pp. 47, 104.
29. Wight, "An Anatomy of International Thought," p. 226. See also Kant, "Perpetual Peace," p. 105.
30. Kant, "Perpetual Peace," p. 105.
31. Kant, "Idea for a Universal History with a Cosmopolitan Purpose," p. 47.
32. Bull, "Martin Wight and the Theory of International Relations," pp. 104–05.
33. Wight, "Why is there No International Theory?," pp. 24–26.
34. Wight, "An Anatomy of International Thought," p. 227.
35. I refer to Hegel's well-known remark that "the owl of Minerva spreads its wings only with the falling of the dusk," in T.M. Knox (tr. and ed.), *Hegel's Philosophy of Right* (Oxford: Oxford University Press, 1952), p. 13.
36. See Wight's various essays in *Systems of States*.

Chapter 4   Martin Wight's Theology of Diplomacy

1. Martin Wight was a founding member of "The British Committee on the Theory of International Politics," what later came to be known as the "English School."
2. Martin Wight, "Why is there No International theory?," in H. Butterfield and M. Wight (eds.), *Diplomatic Investigations* (Cambridge, MA: Harvard University Press, 1968), p. 22.
3. H. Nicolson, *The Evolution of Diplomatic Method* (London: Constable, 1954).
4. For further discussion see Nicolson, *The Evolution of Diplomatic Method*, p. 10.

5. Martin Wight, "Western Values in International Relations," in Butterfield and Wight, *Diplomatic Investigations*, p. 127.

6. Martin Wight, *Systems of States,* ed. Hedley Bull (London and Leicester: Leicester University Press, 1977), pp. 53–56, 130–31.

7. The pope and the archbishop of Canterbury, among other religious leaders, still dispatch envoys, e.g., to the Middle East and other such places.

8. C. Hibbert, *The English: A Social History* (London: Paladin, 1988), p. 98.

9. G. Mattingly, *Renaissance Diplomacy* (Boston: Houghton–Mifflin, 1955), p. 23.

10. See *Oxford English Dictionary On-Line* <http://www.oed.com/>.

11. See *Oxford English Dictionary On-Line* <http://www.oed.com/>. Also C.T. Onions (ed.), *The Oxford Dictionary of English Etymology* (Oxford: Clarendon Press, 1976), p. 270.

12. See Michael Oakeshott, *On Human Conduct* (Oxford: Clarendon, 1975) and Robert Jackson, *The Global Covenant: Human Conduct in a World of States* (Oxford: Oxford University Press, 1990).

13. Wight, "Why is there No International Theory?" p. 32.

14. M. Wight, *International Theory: The Three Traditions* (London: RIIA and Leicester University Press, 1991).

15. As indicated later in this essay, Martin Wight's international thought, in this regard, is similar to that of Reinhold Niebuhr and Herbert Butterfield. The following passage by Reinhold Niebuhr could have been written by Martin Wight: "The Biblical conception of man includes three primary terms: (a) he is made in the image of God, (b) he is a creature, and (c) he is a sinner. His basic sin is pride. If this pride is closely analyzed, it is discovered to be man's unwillingness to acknowledge his creatureliness. He is betrayed by his greatness to hide his weakness. He is tempted by his ability to gain his own security to deny his insecurity, and refuses to admit that he has no final security except in God. He is tempted by his knowledge to deny his ignorance. (That is the source of all 'ideological taint' in human knowledge.)" "Christian Faith and Natural Law," reprinted in Paul Sigmund (ed.), *St. Thomas Aquinas on Politics and Ethics* (New York: Norton, 1988), pp. 222–23. Also see R. Niebuhr, *Beyond Tragedy* (New York: Scribners, 1937). For Herbert Butterfield's theological diplomacy see *Christianity, Diplomacy and War* (London: Epworth, 1953) and *Christianity and History* (London: Bell, 1949). Also see Paul Sharp, "The English School, Herbert Butterfield and Diplomacy," in S. Mawby (ed.), *Discussion Papers on Diplomacy*, Netherlands Institute of International Relations, 2002 <http://www. clingendael.nl/cli/publ/diplomacy/pdf/issue83.pdf>.

16. For an example of such misunderstanding see Michael Nicholson, "The Enigma of Martin Wight," *Review of International Studies*, vol. 7 (January 1981), pp. 15–22. Also see the reply by Alan James, "Michael Nicholson on Martin Wight: A Mind Passing in the Night," *Review of International Studies*, vol. 8 (April 1982), pp. 117–24.

17. See the insightful comments on this point in Roger Epp, "The 'Augustinian Moment' in International Politics: Niebuhr, Butterfield, Wight and the

Reclaiming of a Tradition," *International Politics Research Occasional Paper*, vol. 10 (Aberystwyth: Department of International Politics, 1991).

18. H. Bull, "Introduction: Martin Wight and the Study of International Relations," in Martin Wight, *Systems of States* (London and Leicester: Leicester University Press, 1977), pp. 11–12. Bull is referring to Wight's essay "The Church, Russia and the West," *Ecumenical Review*, vol. 1 (Autumn 1948).

19. "Pelagius," *Encyclopaedia Britannica*, vol. 14 (1960), p. 448. Peter Brown, *Augustine of Hippo* (Berkeley and Los Angeles: University of California Press, 1969), p. 325. Also see R.F. Evans, *Pelagius: Inquiries and Reappraisals* (New York: Seabury Press, 1968).

20. Hans J. Morgenthau, *Scientific Man versus Power Politics* (Chicago: University of Chicago Press, 1946). Morgenthau's anti–Pelagianism is discussed by Michael Oakeshott, *Religion, Politics and the Moral Life* (New Haven and London: Yale University Press, 1993), pp. 103–05.

21. Reinhold Niebuhr, "Christian Faith and Natural Law," p. 223.

22. Michael Oakeshott, *The Politics of Faith and the Politics of Scepticism*, ed. by Timothy Fuller (New Haven and London: Yale University Press, 1996), pp. 23–24.

23. The adjective "traditional" has been required in the past century owing to the politicization of some Christian churches around the idea of a political Christ. One is here referring to "the reinterpretation of religious values as political values" rather than merely "the involvement of religion with politics," which has been the relation throughout the long history of Christianity. E. Norman, *Christianity and the World Order*, the BBC Reith Lectures, 1978 (Oxford: Oxford University Press, 1979), p. 4.

24. St. Augustine, *The City of God*, tr. Marcus Dods and reprinted in R.M. Hutchins (ed.), *Great Books of the Western World* (Chicago: Encyclopaedia Britannica, 1952), pp. 129–618.

25. Wight, "Why is there no International theory?" p. 26.

26. Bull, "Introduction: Martin Wight and the Study of International Relations," p. 11.

27. Wight, *International Theory*, p. 268.

28. Harold Nicolson as quoted in Wight, *International Theory*, p. 180.

29. Wight, *International Theory*, p. 180.

30. Wight, *International Theory*, pp. 186–87.

31. Wight, *International Theory*, p. 187.

32. Wight, *International Theory*, p. 187.

33. Wight, *International Theory*, pp. 187–88.

34. Wight, *International Theory*, p. 191. See G.F. Kennan, *Realities of American Foreign Policy* (London: Oxford University Press, 1954), pp. 35–36.

35. Herbert Butterfield, *Christianity, Diplomacy and War* (London: Epworth Press, 1953), p. 75.

36. Edmund Burke, "Letters on a Regicide Peace," in F.W. Raffety (ed.), *The Works of the Honourable Edmund Burke*, vi (Oxford: Oxford University Press, 1928), pp. 156–61.

37. Wight, *International Theory*, p. 180.

38. M. Wight, *De systematibus civitatum*, in *Systems of States*, p. 34.

39. Hedley Bull, "Introduction" to Wight, in *Systems of States*, p. 18.

40. See M. Wight, "Western Values in International Relations," in Butterfield and Wight, *Diplomatic Investigations*, pp. 92–102, and M. Wight, "*De systematibus civitatum*," in Wight, *Systems of States*, pp. 21–45. Elsewhere I have argued that global international society is a society of states and statesmen but not, or at least not yet, a society of humans. See R. Jackson, *The Global Covenant* (Oxford: Oxford University Press, 2000), pp. 23–25.

41. *The Oxford English Dictionary, Compact Edition* (Oxford: Oxford University Press, 1971).

42. Wight, *International Theory*, p. 189.

43. *The Prince*, tr. George Bull (Harmondsworth: Penguin Books, 1962), pp. 49–50.

44. I. Kant, "Perpetual Peace," in H. Reiss (ed.), *Kant: Political Writings*, 2nd ed. (Cambridge: Cambridge University Press, 1991), pp. 93–130.

45. A well-known recent example of this quasi-religious sort of thinking is F. Fukuyama, *The End of History and the Last Man* (New York: Avon Books, 1992).

46. H. Butterfield, *Christianity, Diplomacy and War*, pp. 102–25.

47. M. Wight, "The Balance of Power," in Wight and Butterfield, *Diplomatic Investigations*, p. 172.

48. Wight, *International Theory*, p. 156 (original emphasis).

49. Martin Wight, *Power Politics*, 2nd ed. (London: Penguin Books and Royal Institute of International Affairs, 1986), p. 89.

50. G.F. Hegel, *Philosophy of Right*, tr. T.M. Knox (Oxford: Clarendon Press, 1949).

51. The first barbarism is the Saracens, the second is the Albigensian heresy, and the third is the Turks under the Ottoman Empire. See R.G. Collingwood, *The New Leviathan* (New York: Crowell, 1971), pp. 375–87.

52. Adolf Hitler, *Mein Kampf*, as quoted by Wight, *International Theory*, p. 210.

53. Wight, *International Theory*, p. 195.

54. Wight, *International Theory*, p. 195.

55. Hitler to Ciano, as quoted by Wight, *International Theory*, pp. 90–91.

56. Wight, *International Theory*, p. 200.

57. Wight, *International Theory*, pp. 46–47.

58. Lenin as quoted by Wight, *International Theory*, p. 92.

59. Stalin as quoted by Wight, *International Theory*, p. 23.

60. Wight, *International Theory*, p. 47.

61. As quoted by Wight, *International Theory*, p. 47.

62. See R. Stevenson, "The Evolution of Pacifism," *International Journal of Ethics*, vol. 44 (July 1934), pp. 437–51.

63. See *The Gold Coast Legislative Council* (Oxford: Oxford University Press, 1947), *British Colonial Constitutions 1947* (Oxford: Oxford University Press, 1952).

64. President Sukarno as quoted by Wight, *International Theory*, p. 42.

65. Quoted by Wight, *International Theory*, p. 42.

66. Wight's work in this regard is similar to that of Isaiah Berlin.

67. M. Wight, *British Colonial Constitutions* (Oxford: Oxford University Press, 1952).

68. Alexander Hamilton, *The Federalist* No. 6 reprinted in R.M. Hutchins (ed.), *Great Books of the Western World*, vol. xliii, *American State Papers* (Chicago; Encyclopaedia Britannica, 1952), p. 39.
69. Mattingly, *Renaissance Diplomacy.*
70. Wight, "Western Values in International Relations," p. 130.
71. Wight, "Western Values in International Relations," p. 130.
72. Wight, "Western Values in International Relations," p. 131. Here Wight may be alluding to the discussion of the proverb by Kant in the Appendix to *Perpetual Peace*. See Reiss (ed.), *Kant: Political Writings*, p. 123.
73. See Butterfield, *Christianity, Diplomacy and War* and *Christianity and History.*
74. Wight, "Why is there No International Theory?"
75. Quoted by A. Coll, "Normative Prudence as a Tradition of Statecraft," *Ethics and International Affairs*, vol. 5 (1991), p. 45.
76. "You will have guessed that my prejudices are Rationalist, but I find I have become more Rationalist and less Realist . . . during the course of giving these lectures." Wight, *International Theory*, p. 268.
77. Wight, *International Theory*, p. 243.
78. See Niebuhr, *Beyond Tragedy*. Also see J.D. Barbour, "Niebuhr versus Niebuhr: The Tragic Nature of History," *The Christian Century* (1984), pp. 1096–99.
79. See Butterfield, *Christianity, Diplomacy and War* and *Christianity and History.*
80. For a similar view see Roger Epp, "The 'Augustinian Moment' in International Politics: Niebuhr, Butterfield, Wight and the Reclaiming of a Tradition."

Chapter 5   Changing Faces of Sovereignty

1. A.P. d'Entrèves, *Natural Law* (London: Hutchinson, 1970), p. 67.
2. The expression is Laski's. See H. Laski, *A Grammar of Politics* (London: Allen & Unwin, 1978).
3. J.L. Briefly, *The Law of Nations* (London: Oxford University Press, 1938), p. 40.
4. F.H. Hinsley, *Sovereignty* (New York: Oxford, 1966), p. 26.
5. Hinsley, "The Concept of Sovereignty and the Relations between States," in W.J. Stankiewicz (ed.), *In Defense of Sovereignty*, (New York: Oxford University Press, 1969), 275.
6. See R. Falk, "The Grotian Moment," *International Insights*, vol. 13 (Fall 1997), pp. 3–34 and my reply to that claim in chapter 8.
7. Sir George Clark, *Early Modern Europe* (New York: Oxford, 1960), pp. 27–28.
8. E.H. Kantorowicz, *The King's Two Bodies* (Princeton, NJ: Princeton University Press, 1957).
9. Clark, *Early Modern Europe*, p. 28.
10. M. Keen, *Medieval Europe* (Harmondsworth, UK: Penguin Books, 1991), p. 262.
11. J.H. Elliott, "A Europe of Composite Monarchies," *Past and Present*, no. 137 (November 1992), pp. 48–71.

12. J. Canning, *A History of Medieval Political Thought, 300–1450* (London: Routledge, 1996), p. 84.

13. As quoted by Canning, *Medieval Political Thought*, p. 19.

14. This is a modification of the notion of *universitas* theorized by M. Oakeshott, "The Rule of Law," in his *On History and Other Essays* (Oxford: Blackwell, 1983); also see M. Oakeshott, *On Human Conduct* (Oxford: Clarendon Press, 1975).

15. Wight, *Systems of States*, p. 47

16. Keen, *Medieval Europe*, p. 12.

17. Canning, *Medieval Political Thought*, pp. 181–82.

18. Canning, *Medieval Political Thought*, p. 185. Also see Keen, *Medieval Europe*, p. 314.

19. M. Wight, *Systems of States* (Leicester, Leicester University Press, 1977), p. 151.

20. See J. Vincent, "Realpolitik," in J. Mayall (ed.), *The Community of States* (London: George Allen & Unwin, 1982), pp. 73–85.

21. J. Burckhardt, *The Civilization of the Renaissance in Italy*, vol. 1 (New York: Harper & Row, 1958), pp. 120–42.

22. S. Wolin, *Politics and Vision* (Boston: Little, Brown, 1960), p. 143

23. See Norman Davies, *Europe: A History* (London: Pimlico, 1997), p. 490.

24. M.J. Tooley (tr.), *Bodin: Six Books of the Commonwealth* (Oxford: Blackwell, n.d.).

25. Tooley, *Six Books of the Commonwealth*, book I, ch. 10, p. 49.

26. Wight, *Systems of States*, p. 151. A similar view is taken by Keen, *Medieval Europe*, pp. 314–21.

27. F.H. Hinsley, "The Concept of Sovereignty and the Relations between States," in Stankiewicz, *In Defense of Sovereignty*, p. 285.

28. "Well into at least the seventeenth century, the juristic, theological and overtly political works of medieval scholastics continued to be prime sources for the discussion of political thought . . . The writings of . . . Hugo Grotius (1583–1645), amongst very many others, illustrated this trend." Canning, *Medieval Political Thought*, p. 186.

29. See A. Osiander, *The States System of Europe, 1640–1990* (Oxford: Clarendon Press, 1994), pp. 27–28.

30. Wight, *Systems of States*, p. 152.

31. Osiander, *The States System of Europe*, p. 120.

32. J.N. Figgis, *The Divine Right of Kings* (New York: Harper Torchbooks, 1965).

33. M.N. Shaw, *Title to Territory in Africa* (Oxford, Clarendon Press, 1986), p. 17.

34. W.E. Hall, as quoted by Wight, *Systems of States*, p. 115.

35. James Madison in *The Federalist*, no. 10, reprinted in R.M. Hutchins (ed.), *Great Books of the Western World* (Chicago: Encyclopaedia Britannica, 1952), vol. 43, pp. 49–53.

36. Wight, *Systems of States*, p. 159.

37. Figgis, *The Divine Right of Kings*, p. 63.

38. Jennifer Jackson Preece, "Ethnic Cleansing as an Instrument of Nation-State Creation," *Human Rights Quarterly*, vol. 20 (1998), pp. 817–42.

39. See Jennifer Jackson Preece, *National Minorities and the European Nation-States System* (Oxford: Clarendon Press, 1998).

40. For the origins and development of this practice in the emergence of independent states in the new world see Fred Parkinson, "Latin America," in Robert H. Jackson and Alan James (eds.), *States in a Changing World* (Oxford: Clarendon Press, 1993), pp. 240–61. Also see A. Kacowicz, "The Impact of Norms in the International Society: The Latin American Experience" (Delivered at the Leonard Davis Institute Conference on International Norms, Hebrew University, Jerusalem, Israel, May 26–27, 1997).

41. As Fred Parkinson remarks, "The principle of *uti possidetis juris* was a great help in enabling the region to weather the storm of state succession." Parkinson, "Latin America," p. 241.

42. A. Pellet, "The Opinions of the Badinter Arbitration Committee," *European Journal of International Law*, vol. 3 (1992), pp. 178–85.

43. E. Gellner, *Nations and Nationalism* (Oxford: Blackwell, 1993), p. 74.

44. Jennifer Jackson Preece, "Minority Rights in Europe: From Westphalia to Helsinki." *Review of International Studies*, vol. 23 (January 1997), pp. 75–92.

45. Alexander Hamilton, *The Federalist*, no. 6.

46. That is not to suggest that the Americans turned away from war in their continent. They obviously did not. They fought the British Empire in the north and Spain and the Mexican Republic in the south. But the most important wars for them were their wars of territorial conquest as they moved the frontier westward, and most important of all the American Civil War, which kept the Union together.

47. K.J. Alter, "Who Are the 'Masters of the Treaty'? European Governments and the European Court of Justice," *International Organization*, vol. 52 (Winter 1998), pp. 121–47.

48. N. MacCormick, "Liberalism, Nationalism and the Post-Sovereign State," *Political Studies*, vol. XLIV (1996), p. 555.

49. For an argument that sovereignty is a bargaining resource that is being shared among EU states see Robert O. Keohane, "Hobbes's Dilemma and Institutional Change in World Politics: Sovereignty in International Society," in H-H. Holm and G. Sorensen (eds.), *Whose World Order: Uneven Globalization and the End of the Cold War* (Boulder, Co: Westview, 1995), pp. 165–86.

50. MacCormick, "Liberalism, Nationalism and the Post-Sovereign State," pp. 561–67.

51. Quoted by J.H.H. Weiler, "European Neo-constitutionalism: In Search of Foundations for the European Constitutional Order," *Political Studies*, vol. XLIV (1996), pp. 520–21.

52. Weiler, "European Neo-Constitutionalism," pp. 526–28.

53. MacCormick, "Liberalism, Nationalism and the Post-Sovereign State," p. 555.

54. This argument is presented and rejected by Weiler.

55. Weiler, "European Neo-Constitutionalism," p. 518.

56. U. Preuss, "Two Challenges to European Citizenship," *Political Studies*, vol. XLIV (1996), pp. 543–44.

57. Keohane, "Hobbes's Dilemma," p. 177.

58. Keohane, "Hobbes's Dilemma," p. 177.

59. H. Bull, *The Anarchical Society*, 2nd ed. (London: Macmillan, 1995).
60. James Madison in *The Federalist*, no. 51, reprinted in Hutchins, *Great Books of the Western World*, vol. 43, pp. 162–65.
61. D.M. Frame (tr.), *The Complete Essays of Montaigne* (Stanford: Stanford University Press, 1958), book 3, ch. 13, p. 816. This translation is from P. Burke, *Montaigne* (Oxford: Oxford University Press, 1981), p. 33.
62. See Oakeshott, *On History and Other Essays*, p. 145n.
63. Frame, *The Complete Essays of Montaigne*, book 3, ch. 13, p. 816.

Chapter 6   Knots and Tangles of International Obligation

1. Patriotism might be included in the list, but that would be a mistake. Patriotism is not a civic duty: it is not something that a state can demand and require of its citizens and subjects; it is something that it can only hope to cultivate, encourage, praise, and honor. Patriotism is not a moral duty or legal responsibility; it is a political passion. That is evident in the *Oxford English Dictionary* definition: "One who disinterestedly or self-sacrificingly exerts himself to promote the well-being of his country; 'one whose ruling passion is the love of his country.' " *Oxford English Dictionary Online* <http://dictionary.oed.com/entrance.dtl>.
2. This pluralist feature of human conduct is explored with characteristic brilliance by I. Berlin, *The Crooked Timber of Humanity* (New York: Vintage Books, 1992).
3. See the insightful investigation of the idea in J.R. Lucas, *Responsibility* (Oxford: Clarendon Press, 1995).
4. These are an abridgement of definitions of "obligation" available in the *Oxford English Dictionary Online* <http://dictionary.oed.com/entrance.dtl>.
5. D.D. Raphael, *Problems of Political Philosophy*, 2nd ed. (London: Macmillan, 1990), ch. 7.
6. Aristotle, *The Politics*, rev. ed., tr. T.A. Sinclair (London: Penguin Classics, 1981).
7. This is the core of a famous definition of sovereignty and law by J. Austin, *The Province of Jurisprudence Determined* (Cambridge: Cambridge University Press, 1995).
8. T. Hobbes, *Leviathan* (Oxford: Blackwell, 1946), ch. 13.
9. Monism is defined as "Any theory . . . that assumes a single ultimate principle, being, force, etc. rather than more than one." See *Oxford English Dictionary Online* <http://dictionary.oed.com/entrance.dtl>.
10. This jurisprudential concept of pluralism should be distinguished from political science concepts that emphasize societies consisting of multiple cross-cutting affiliated groups, and from anthropological concepts that emphasize societies consisting of a diversity of ethnic or cultural groups. See D. Nichols, *Three Varieties of Pluralism* (London: Macmillan, 1974).
11. For a general discussion with various points of view see S. Caney, D. George, and P. Jones (eds.), *National Rights, International Obligations* (Oxford: Westview, 1996).

12. "Perpetual Peace: A Philosophical Sketch," in H. Reiss (ed.), *Kant: Political Writings*, 2nd ed. (Cambridge: Cambridge University Press, 1991), pp. 102–05.
13. These are usually listed as the primary sources or bases of international law. See M. Akehurst, *A Modern Introduction to International Law*, 6th ed. (London: Allen & Unwin, 1987), ch. 3.
14. See the critique of this conception by former U.S. senator D.P. Moynihan, *On the Law of Nations* (Cambridge, MA: Harvard University Press, 1990).
15. "Comment on 'Treaties as Binding International Obligation,'" *ASIL Insights*, The American Society of International Law (December 1997) <http://www.asil.org/insights/insight25.htm>. Also see F.L. Kirgis, "Treaties as Binding International Obligation," *ASIL Insights*, The American Society of International Law (May 1997) <http://www.asil.org/insights/insight9.htm>.
16. "Comment on 'Treaties as Binding International Obligation,'" *ASIL Insights* (December 1997) <http://www.asil.org/insights/insight25.htm>.
17. See J.H. Jackson, "Helms-Burton, the U.S. and the WTO," *ASIL Insights* (The American Society of International Law) (March 1997).
18. See D. Hendrickson, *Peace Pact: The Lost World of the American Founding* (Lawrence: University Press of Kansas, 2003).
19. "Nothing in the present Charter shall impair the inherent right of individual or collective self-defence."
20. G. Schwarzenberger and E.D. Brown, *A Manual of International Law* (London: Professional Books, 1976), p. 551.
21. See L. Gross, "The Criminality of Aggressive War," *The American Political Science Review*, vol. 41 (April 1947), pp. 205–25.
22. See R. Tuck, *The Rights of War and Peace* (Oxford: Oxford University Press, 1999), pp. 115–18.
23. Kant, "The Metaphysics of Morals," in Reiss, *Kant: Political Writings*, p. 172.
24. Thomas Hobbes, *Man and Citizen* (*De Homine* and *De Cive*), ed. B. Gert (Indianapolis, IN: Hacket, 1991), 258 (original emphasis).
25. Hobbes, *Man and Citizen*, p. 260.
26. Hobbes, *Man and Citizen*, pp. 176–78.
27. Hobbes, *Leviathan*, pp. 117–18.
28. Kant, "The Metaphysics of Morals," p. 133.
29. Kant, "The Metaphysics of Morals," p. 165 (emphasis added).
30. Kant, "The Metaphysics of Morals," p. 172.
31. See L. Mulholland, *Kant's System of Rights* (New York: Columbia University Press, 1990).
32. Kant, "Perpetual Peace: A Philosophical Sketch," p. 103 (original emphasis).
33. One of the best discussions is still J.L. Brierly, *The Law of Nations*, 2nd ed. (Oxford: Oxford University Press, 1936).
34. International Law Commission <http://www.un.org/law/ilc/texts/decfra.htm>.
35. See K.T. Jackson, "International Jurisdiction," in C. Gray, *The Philosophy of Law: An Encyclopedia* (New York and London: Garland Publishing, 1999), vol. I, pp. 431–33.

36. See E.A. Posner, "Do States have a Moral Obligation to Obey International Law," *Stanford Law Review*, vol. 55 (2003), pp. 1909–10.

37. That must be qualified in countries that hold referendums, such as Switzerland and the United States.

38. Quoted in T. Strong, "History and Choices: The Foundations of the Political Thought of Raymond Aron," *History and Theory*, vol. 11 (1972), p. 186.

39. For an excellent discussion and critique see R. Stromberg, "The Idea of Collective Security," *Journal of the History of Ideas*, vol. 17 (April 1956), pp. 250–63.

40. M. Wight, *Power Politics*, 2nd ed. (Harmondsworth: Penguin Books, 1979), pp. 217–18.

41. Martin Wight, *International Theory: The Three Traditions* (London: Leicester University Press for The Royal Institute of International Affairs, 1991) and Hedley Bull, *The Anarchical Society: A Study of Order in World Politics*, 2nd ed. (London: Macmillan, 1995).

42. M. Donelan, *Elements of International Political Theory* (Oxford: Oxford University Press, 1990).

43. See, e.g. R. Fletcher, *The Conversion of Europe: From Paganism to Christianity, 371–1386 A.D.* (London: HarperCollins, 1997).

44. See "The Claims of the Papacy" and "The Christian World-View and Its Implications for the State" in J. Canning, *A History of Medieval Political Thought* (London and New York: Routledge, 1996), pp. 29–43. Also see the lengthy analysis of *regnum* and *sacerdotium* in J.B. Morrall, *Political Thought in Medieval Times*, 2nd ed. (London: Hutchinson University Library, 1960).

45. Quoted by J. Bowle, *Western Political Thought: From the Origins to Rousseau* (London: Methuen, 1961), p. 374.

46. "Government, as by a father; the claim or attempt to supply the needs or to regulate the life of a nation or community in the same way as a father does those of his children." See *Oxford English Dictionary Online* <http://dictionary.oed.com/entrance.dtl>.

47. See W. Bain, *Between Anarchy and Society: Trusteeship and the Obligations of Power* (Oxford: Oxford University Press, 2003).

48. See I. Hannaford, *Race the History of an Idea in the West* (Washington, D.C.: The Woodrow Wilson Center Press, 1996).

49. D. Hay, *Europe: The Emergence of an Idea* (Edinburgh: Edinburgh University Press, 1968).

50. See Ali Mazrui, *Towards a Pax Africana* (Chicago: University of Chicago Press, 1967).

51. See J. Jackson Preece, "Ethnic Cleansing as an Instrument of Nation-State Creation: Changing State Practices and Evolving Legal Norms," *Human Rights Quarterly*, vol. 20, no. 4 (1998), pp. 817–42.

52. See J. Jackson Preece, *National Minorities and the European Nation-States System* (Oxford: Oxford University Press, 1998).

53. This is evident from the international law definition of the sovereign state: a defined territory, with a permanent population, under one supreme government, that is independent of all other such governments.

54. Bernard Williams, *Ethics and the Limits of Philosophy* (London: Routledge, 1985).

55. I. Berlin, *The Crooked Timber of Humanity* (New York: Vintage Books, 1992), pp. 79–80.

56. See R. Jackson, *The Global Covenant: Human Conduct in a World of States* (Oxford: Oxford University Press, 1990).

Chapter 7   Jurisprudence for a Solidarist World: Richard Falk's Grotian Moment

1. Richard Falk makes the "Grotian moment" argument in various writings. However, I shall confine my references to the succinct statement of the argument in his essay "A New Paradigm for International Legal Studies: Prospects and Proposals," in R. Falk, F. Kratochwil, and S.H. Mendlovitz (eds.), *International Law: A Contemporary Perspective* (Boulder, CO and London: Westview Press, 1985), pp. 651–702.

2. Martin Wight, *International Theory: The Three Traditions* (Leicester: Leicester University Press, 1992); Hedley Bull, *The Anarchical Society*, 2nd ed. (London: Macmillan, 1995).

3. For an incisive account of his thought see Richard Tuck, *The Rights of War and Peace* (Oxford: Oxford University Press, 1999), ch. 3.

4. Richard Tuck, *Hobbes* (Oxford: Oxford University Press, 1989), pp. 20–23.

5. Garrett Mattingly, *Renaissance Diplomacy* (New York: Dover Publications, 1988), p. 245 (original emphasis).

6. Mattingly, *Renaissance Diplomacy*, p. 246.

7. *De Jure Belli ac Pacis Libri Tres*, tr. Francis Kelsey (Oxford: Oxford University Press, 1925).

8. Martin Wight, *Systems of States*, ed. Hedley Bull (Leicester: Leicester University Press, 1977), p. 127.

9. Hedley Bull, "The Importance of Grotius in the Study of International Relations," in H. Bull, B. Kingsbury, and A. Roberts (eds.), *Hugo Grotius and International Relations* (Oxford: Clarendon Press, 1990), p. 65.

10. Other Grotian commentators can be found in Bull, Kingsbury, and Roberts, *Hugo Grotius and International Relations*.

11. Bull, "The Importance of Grotius," pp. 65–66.

12. B.V.A. Roling, "Are Grotius' Ideas Obsolete in an Expanded World," in Bull, Kingsbury, and Roberts, *Hugo Grotius and International Relations*, pp. 281–300.

13. Grotius also distinguished "divine volitional law" or the law of God.

14. Hedley Bull, "Natural Law and International Relations," *British Journal of International Studies*, vol. 5 (1979), p. 171.

15. See L. Gross, "The Peace of Westphalia," *The American Journal of International Law*, vol. 42 (January 1948), pp. 20–41.
16. G. Mattingly, *The Armada* (Boston: Houghton Mifflin, 1959).
17. Falk, "A New Paradigm," p. 663.
18. Bull, *The Anarchical Society*, chs. 6, 11, 12, and 13.
19. Falk, "A New Paradigm," pp. 653–59.
20. Falk, "A New Paradigm," p. 657.
21. Falk, "A New Paradigm," p. 666.
22. Falk, "A New Paradigm," p. 673.
23. Falk, "A New Paradigm," pp. 674–80.
24. Falk, "A New Paradigm," p. 655.
25. Falk, "A New Paradigm," p. 666.
26. See E.L. Jones, *The European Miracle: Environments, Economics and Geopolitics in the History of Europe and Asia* (Cambridge: Cambridge University Press, 1981), esp. chs. 6–7.
27. See Immanuel Wallerstein, *The Modern World-System* (New York: Academic Press, 1974). Also see some of the essays in H. Bull and A. Watson (eds.), *The Expansion of International Society* (Oxford: Clarendon Press, 1984).
28. See Myers S. McDougal and associates, *Studies in World Public Order* (New Haven: Yale University Press, 1960).
29. See R.H. Jackson, *Quasi-States: Sovereignty, International Relations and the Third World* (Cambridge: Cambridge University Press, 1990).
30. Bull, *The Anarchical Society*, ch. 11.
31. J.L. Brierly, *The Law of Nations*, 2nd ed. (Oxford: Oxford University Press, 1938), p. 30.
32. This argument is made at length in Robert Jackson, *The Global Covenant: Human Conduct in a World of States* (Oxford: Oxford University Press, 2000).

Chapter 8 Dialogical Justice in World Affairs

1. T. Hobbes, *Leviathan* (Oxford: Blackwell, 1946), p. 83.
2. J.R. Lucas, *On Justice* (Oxford: Clarendon Press, 1980), p. 16.
3. See Susan M. Lloyd (ed.), "Synopsis of Categories," *Roget's International Thesaurus*, 3rd ed. (New York, 1962), pp. xvii–xx.
4. N. Machiavelli, *The Prince*, tr. G. Bull (Harmondsworth: Penguin Books, 1961).
5. Martin Wight, *International Theory: The Three Traditions* (Leicester and London: Leicester University Press, 1991), p. 106.
6. H. Reiss (ed.), "The Metaphysics of Morals," *Kant: Political Writings*, 2nd enl. ed. (Cambridge: Cambridge University Press, 1991), pp. 131–75.
7. R.G. Collingwood, *The New Leviathan* (New York, 1971), ch. XXXV.
8. John Rawls, "Justice as Fairness," in P. Laslett and W.G. Runciman (eds.), *Philosophy, Politics and Society* (Second Series) (Oxford: Blackwell, 1972), pp. 132–57. Also see *A Theory of Justice* (Cambridge, MA: Harvard University Press, 1971), esp. ch. II.

9. Lucas, *On Justice*, ch. 1.
10. *Nicomachean Ethics*, tr. T. Irwin (Indianapolis, IN: Hackett, 1985), book 5, section 2, pp. 117–19.
11. Rawls, *A Theory of Justice*, p. 3.
12. Hobbes, *Leviathan*, p. 94.
13. G. Grube (tr.), *Plato-Republic*, rev. C. Reeve (Indianapolis, IN and Cambridge: Hackett Publishing, 1992), book I.
14. *Remota justitia quid sunt regna nisi magna latrocinia?* This is the opening sentence in Lucas, *On Justice*, p. 1.
15. *An Enquiry Concerning the Principles of Morals*, ed. C.W. Hendel (New York: Bobbs-Merrill, 1957), p. 39 (emphasis added).
16. I make that argument at length in *The Global Covenant: Human Conduct in a World of States* (Oxford: Oxford University Press, 2000).
17. Hobbes, *Leviathan*, ch. 13.
18. Hobbes, *Leviathan*, p. 83.
19. Alan James, *Sovereign Statehood: The Bases of International Society* (London: Allen & Unwin, 1986).
20. "In the world as it is, the final arbiter of things political is power." Robert G. Gilpin, "The Richness of the Tradition of Political Realism," in Robert O. Keohane (ed.), *Neorealism and Its Critics* (Cambridge, MA: Harvard University Press, 1987), p. 304.
21. E.H. Carr, *The Twenty Years' Crisis, 1919–1939* (New York: Harper Torchbooks, 1964), p. 102.
22. Carr, *The Twenty Years' Crisis*, p. 97.
23. *Oxford English Dictionary On-line* <http://www.oed.com/>.
24. Grube, *Plato-Republic*, Book I.
25. *Oxford English Dictionary On-Line* <http://www.oed.com/>.
26. Helsinki Final Act (August 1975) <http://www.osce.org/docs/english/1990–1999/summits/helfa75e.htm>.
27. See N.L. Rosenblum, *Bentham's Theory of the Modern State* (Cambridge, MA: Harvard University Press, 1978), p. 101 (emphasis added).
28. Rawls, *A Theory of Justice*, pp. 378–79.
29. Hobbes, *Leviathan*, p. 98.
30. North Atlantic Treaty Organization, Article V.
31. H. Bull, *Justice in International Relations* (Waterloo, Ontario: University of Waterloo, 1984), p. 14.
32. See H. Shue, *Basic Rights: Subsistence, Affluence and U.S. Foreign Policy* (Princeton, NJ: Princeton University Press, 1980), pp. 22–29.
33. See R. Jackson, "Can International Society be Green?" in R. Fawn and J. Larkins (eds.), *International Society after the Cold War* (London: Macmillan, 1996), pp. 172–92.
34. UN decisions and actions on compensation of adversely affected states are collected in D. Bethlehem (ed.), *The Kuwait Crisis: Sanctions and Their Consequences*, part I (Cambridge: Grotius Publications, 1991).

35. The United States Patriot Act is available on-line at <http://www.usdoj.gov/oig/special/0307/final.pdf>.
36. Bull, *Justice in International Relations*, p. 14.
37. The International Criminal Court is available on-line at <http://www.un.org/law/icc/>.
38. For example, see J. Rawls, *The Law of Peoples* (Cambridge, MA: Harvard University Press, 1999).
39. *Nicomachean Ethics*, book 5, section 8, pp. 134–35.

Chapter 9   Lifting the Veil of Ignorance: John Rawls's Society of Peoples

1. John Rawls, *A Theory of Justice* (Harvard: Harvard University Press, 1971) and *Political Liberalism* (New York: Columbia University Press, 1993).
2. John Rawls, *The Law of Peoples* (Cambridge, MA: Harvard University Press, 1999).
3. Among the important subjects left out are Rawls's discussions of "burdened societies" and "distributive justice among peoples."
4. I have been influenced by Cornelia Navari, "Rawls and the English School," *International Studies Association Conference Papers* (Chicago, 2001). I have also benefited from the comments of Will Bain and Miki Fabry on an early draft.
5. Rawls, *The Law of Peoples*, pp. 32–34, pp. 39–42. Whenever the reader of Rawls's text encounters a capitalized word that is not the first word in a sentence or a proper noun, which is a frequent occurrence, it is an encounter with one of his stipulated definitions. Rawls's practice of capitalizing his concepts gives his text, perhaps unintentionally, the solemn appearance of a pronouncement or proclamation from on high.
6. John Rawls died in 2002. According to one obituary writer: "Margaret Drabble [the Oxford novelist and philosopher] even used Rawls's concept of the 'veil of ignorance' as the basis for a dinner party game played by exiled intellectuals in her novel *The Witch of Exmoor*." John Rawls, *The Telegraph On-line* <www.telegraph.co.uk>, November 27, 2002.
7. Rawls, *The Law of Peoples*, p. 3.
8. Rawls, *The Law of Peoples*, p. 10.
9. Rawls, *The Law of Peoples*, pp. 32–33. Rawls makes positive reference to Rousseau's *The Social Contract* and it is clear that he wants to liberate people from their chains in his own way. This radical French Enlightenment view should be contrasted to the conservative view of Burke, which is more characteristic of the classical international society thinkers, particularly Martin Wight. See J. Welsh, *Edmund Burke and International Relations* (London: Macmillan and St. Martin's Press, 1995).
10. Rawls, *The Law of Peoples*, p. 10.
11. H. Butterfield, *History and Human Relations* (London: Collins, 1951).

12. M. Oakeshott, *Rationalism in Politics and Other Essays*, new exp. ed. (Indianapolis, IN: Liberty Press, 1991), p. 32.

13. I. Berlin, *The Crooked Timber of Humanity* (New York: Vintage Books, 1992).

14. T. Nagel, "Justice, Justice, Shalt Thou Pursue: The Rigorous Compassion of John Rawls," *The New Republic Online* <www.tnr.com>, August 8, 2002, p. 11.

15. I have in mind principally the work of Herbert Butterfield, Martin Wight, and Hedley Bull. Perhaps the most emblematic expression of it is to be found in M. Wight, "Why Is there No International Theory," in H. Butterfield and M. Wight (eds.), *Diplomatic Investigations: Essays in the Theory of International Politics* (Cambridge, MA: Harvard University Press, 1968), pp. 17–34.

16. To avoid confusion I use inverted commas whenever Rawls's conceptualized "peoples" or "states" are referred to.

17. *The Law of Peoples*, p. 46. As representative of that alternative view, he cites R. Gilpin, *War and Change in World Politics* (Cambridge: Cambridge University Press, 1981) and R. Axelrod, *The Complexity of Cooperation* (Princeton, NJ: Princeton University Press, 1997).

18. Thomas Hobbes, *Leviathan*, ed. Michael Oakeshott (Oxford: Blackwell, 1946), p. 83.

19. Rawls, *The Law of Peoples*, p. 28.

20. Rawls, *The Law of Peoples*, p. 35.

21. Rawls, *The Law of Peoples*, p. 26.

22. Rawls, *The Law of Peoples*, p. 27. The word "solely" raises a question as to whether Rawls allows that governments of "peoples" can, when the occasion demands, for example, during emergencies when their security is being threatened, justify their policies and actions on exclusively prudential grounds. It would seem not.

23. S. Korman, *The Right of Conquest: The Acquisition of Territory by Force in International Law and Practice* (Oxford: Oxford University Press, 1996).

24. U.N. Charter, Article 51 and Chapter VII.

25. Rawls, *The Law of Peoples*, p. 34.

26. J.S. Mill, *Considerations on Representative Government*, ed. J.M. Robson (Toronto: University of Toronto Press, 1977), in *Collected Works*, vol. XIX, p. 546.

27. Sir Ivor Jennings, *The Approach to Self-Government* (Boston: Beacon Press, 1956), pp. 55–56.

28. R. Emerson, *Self-Determination Revisited* (Cambridge: Harvard University Press, 1964), p. 63.

29. Quoted by T. Musgrave, *Self-Determination and National Minorities* (Oxford: Oxford University Press, 1997), p. 148.

30. Jennifer Jackson Preece, *National Minorities and the European Nation-States System* (Oxford: Clarendon Press, 1998).

31. A. Cassese, *Self-Determination of Peoples: A Legal Reappraisal* (Cambridge: Cambridge University Press, 1995), p. 334.

32. See James Mayall, *Nationalism and International Society* (Cambridge: Cambridge University Press, 1990).

33. Hans Kohn, *The Idea of Nationalism*, rev. exp. ed. (New York: Macmillan, 1960).
34. "Religion and Public Reason in Democracy," in *The Law of Peoples*, pp. 149–52.
35. Rawls, *The Law of Peoples*, p. 37.
36. Rawls, *The Law of Peoples*, p. 42. H. Reiss (ed.), *Kant Political Writings*, 2nd enl. ed. (Cambridge: Cambridge University Press, 1991), pp. 102–05.
37. Rawls, *The Law of Peoples*, p. 37
38. In that connection, Rawls makes a reference to J.L. Brierly, *The Law of Nations* (Oxford: Clarendon Press, 1963) and T. Nardin, *Law, Morality and the Relations of States* (Princeton, NJ: Princeton University Press, 1983).
39. See Chris Brown, "The Construction of a 'Realistic Utopia': John Rawls and International Political Theory," *Review of International Studies*, vol. 28 (January 2002), pp. 5–21 and A. Buchanan, "Rawls Law of Peoples," *Ethics*, vol. 110 (July 2000), pp. 697–721.
40. Rawls, *The Law of Peoples*, pp. 44, 51.
41. Rawls, *The Law of Peoples*, p. 123.
42. As indicated, this is sometimes referred to as "the domestic analogy." Rawls's international thought is shot through with domestic reasoning. He gives no indication of the difficulties, e.g. as recognized in a famous study by R. Niebuhr, *Moral Man and Immoral Society* (New York: Charles Scribner's Sons, 1960).
43. M. Wight, *Power Politics*, 2nd ed. (Harmondsworth: Penguin Books, 1979), pp. 217–18.
44. Rawls, *The Law of Peoples*, p. 91n.
45. Rawls, *The Law of Peoples*, p. 19.
46. Rawls, *The Law of Peoples*, p. 54. One should note that Kant wrote of "republics" in this connection, not "democracies." See Reiss, *Kant's Political Writings*, p. 99.
47. T. Hobbes, *Man and Citizen (De Homine and De Cive)*, ed. B. Gert (Indianapolis, IN: Hacket, 1991), p. 258 (original emphasis).
48. Rawls, *The Law of Peoples*, p. 55 (original emphasis).
49. For an excellent review of issues see *Humanitarian Intervention: Legal and Political Aspects* (Copenhagen: Danish Institute of International Affairs, 1999).
50. Rawls, *The Law of Peoples*, p. 123.
51. M. Walzer, *Thick and Thin: Moral Argument at Home and Abroad* (Notre Dame, Indiana: University of Notre Dame Press, 1997).
52. Nagel, "Justice, Justice, Shalt Thou Pursue: The Rigorous Compassion of John Rawls."
53. I. Kant, "The Science of Right," in Reiss, *Kant's Political Writings*, p. 172.
54. Rawls, *The Law of Peoples*, p. 85.
55. Rawls, *The Law of Peoples*, p. 63.
56. Rawls, *The Law of Peoples*, p. 35.
57. Rawls, *The Law of Peoples*, p. 61.
58. Rawls, *The Law of Peoples*, p. 93.
59. R. Fletcher, *The Conversion of Europe* (London: Fontana Press, 1998), ch. 13.

60. Rawls, *The Law of Peoples*, p. 93n.
61. Rawls, *The Law of Peoples*, p. 94n.
62. Rawls, *The Law of Peoples*, p. 94n.
63. Rawls, *The Law of Peoples*, p. 93.
64. Rawls, *The Law of Peoples*, p. 93.
65. Martin Wight, *Systems of States*, ed. Hedley Bull (London: Leicester University Press and London School of Economics and Political Science, 1977), pp. 120–21.
66. G. Gong, *The "Standard of Civilization" in International Society* (Oxford: Clarendon Press, 1984).
67. J.S. Mill, "A Few Words on Non-Intervention," in G. Himmelfarb (ed.), *Essays on Politics and Culture: John Stuart Mill* (New York: Anchor Books, 1963).
68. Mill, "Of the Government of Dependencies by a Free State," section 2, *Considerations on Representative Government*.
69. For an extended historical and contemporary inquiry into international trusteeship see William Bain, *Between Anarchy and Society: Trusteeship and the Obligations of Power* (Oxford: Oxford University Press, 2003).
70. Rawls, *The Law of Peoples*, p. 111. I. Kant, "On the Relationship of Theory to Practice in Political Right," in Reiss, *Kant's Political Writings*, pp. 87–92.
71. Rawls, *The Law of Peoples*, p. 104.
72. Rawls, *The Law of Peoples*, p. 149.
73. Rawls, *The Law of Peoples*, p. 150.
74. Rawls, *The Law of Peoples*, p. 150.
75. Rawls, *The Law of Peoples*, p. 166.
76. Rawls, *The Law of Peoples*, p. 127.
77. Rawls, *The Law of Peoples*, p. 123.
78. M.D. Evans, *Religious Liberty and International Law in Europe* (Cambridge: Cambridge University Press, 1997), pp. 46–47.
79. Walzer, *Thick and Thin*.
80. On group morality or "the morality of communal ties" see M. Oakeshott, "The Moral Life in the Writings of Thomas Hobbes," in Oakeshott (ed.), *Hobbes on Civil Association* (Oxford: Blackwell, 1975), pp. 76ff.
81. "Perpetual Peace," reprinted in Reiss, *Kant: Political Writings*, pp. 113–14.
82. "Introduction to *Leviathan*," reprinted in M. Oakeshott, *Hobbes on Civil Association* (Oxford: Blackwell, 1975), p. 36.
83. Nagel, "Justice, Justice, Shalt Thou Pursue: The Rigorous Compassion of John Rawls."
84. This is the great question of international relations, according to Hedley Bull, *The Anarchical Society*, 2nd ed. (London: Macmillan, 1995), part 1.
85. Rawls, *The Law of Peoples*, pp. 17, 86.
86. Rawls, *The Law of Peoples*, p. 45.
87. "The Advancement of Learning," quoted by J. Gross (ed.), *The Oxford Book of Aphorisms* (New York: Oxford University Press, 1987), p. 235.
88. Rawls, *The Law of Peoples*, p. 124.

89. Rawls, *The Law of Peoples*, p. 31.
90. "Perpetual Peace," reprinted in Reiss, *Kant: Political Writings*, p. 114.
91. Rawls, *A Theory of Justice*, pp. 378–79, 457–58.
92. One might compare Isaiah Berlin's essays "The Sense of Reality" and "Political Judgement" in Berlin, *The Sense of Reality*, ed H. Hardy (London: Pimlico, 1996), pp. 1–39, 40–53.
93. I. Berlin, *The Crooked Timber of Humanity* (New York: Vintage Books, 1992), pp. 1–19.
94. M. Oakeshott, *The Politics of Faith and the Politics of Skepticism*, ed. Timothy Fuller (New Haven and London: Yale University Press, 1996).
95. Berlin, *The Crooked Timber of Humanity*, pp. 18–19.
96. Rawls spent time in Oxford where he met such philosopher luminaries as Isaiah Berlin, H.L.A. Hart, and Stuart Hampshire. According to an English obituary that marked Rawls death, "Berlin was fond of likening him, mischievously, to Christ." Ben Rogers, "John Rawls," *The Guardian-on-line* <http://www.guardian.co.uk>, November 27, 2002.
97. Berlin, *The Crooked Timber of Humanity*, p. 13. On ethical complexity and conflict in international relations see M. Cohen, "Moral Skepticism and International Relations," *Philosophy & Public Affairs*, vol. 13 (Autumn 1984), p. 306.

Index

Printed in the United States
43753LVS00003B/244-303